LOVEBROKEN

About the Author

Finley de Witt was born and raised in West Yorkshire. As a youngster, their picture book *Bad Fluff* was published by Tyrannosaur Books. After graduating, they moved to London and studied bodywork and new approaches to mental health. Their short story 'Barnsley Way' was published in a collection about northern grandmothers. They are a writer and trauma specialist.

LOVEBROKEN

Finley de Witt

T

Troubador Publishing Ltd
Unit E2 Airfield Business Park,
Harrison Road, Market Harborough,
Leicestershire. LE16 7UL
Tel: 0116 2792299
Email: books@troubador.co.uk
Web: www.troubador.co.uk

ISBN 978 1805142 256

British Library Cataloguing in Publication Data.
A catalogue record for this book is available from the British Library.

Printed and bound in Great Britain by 4edge Limited
Typeset in 11pt Minion Pro by Troubador Publishing Ltd, Leicester, UK

T

For Dr Bothy,
though he'll be appalled.

And for my Great Aunt Amelia,
who died in the asylum.
I believe you.

Names and details have been changed to protect the guilty –
not least of all, me.

Author's Note

Memory is a tricky thing and this is a story about madness, doubt and remembering. There are multiple ways of perceiving the past; some of them are beyond words.

Part One

Fudge

In the summer of 1982, as soon as I finished my A Levels, my mother enrolled me at Bradford Technical College to learn shorthand and typing. She did this in spite of the fact that the head of sixth form, the adorable Mr Brown, had called me into his office the week before to suggest I try for Oxford or Cambridge. I'd had a crush on him the whole year and I enjoyed telling my best friend, Ruby, what I'd like to do to him if I could.

'He must like you back, Finley, to say sommat like that,' Ruby said, looking awestruck.

I didn't like to tell her he was gay. I was overcome by Mr Brown's confidence in the excellence of my brain and I couldn't wait to tell my mother. At last she'd realise I wasn't as thick as she'd always supposed.

I hung over the banister when I heard her come in. Her thin brown hair was plastered to her scalp and her nose stabbed the air as she threw off her coat. Being northern, there could only be a three-second gap between Peggy getting in and me having the table set for tea, so I needed to be quick.

'MrBrownsaysIshouldapplyforOxbridge,' I said.

'*You're* not clever enough to do that!' my mother cried, disappearing into the front room.

I was crushed. She could at least have pretended I couldn't do it because I got thrown out of Latin.

I was a terrible secretarial student. It turned out I'd learnt to hold my pen in a very awkward way for a right-handed person and it's impossible to take down shorthand like that. Instead, I concentrated on learning to touch-type, and as soon as I'd progressed from 'Judge the fudge' to 'The quick brown fox jumps over the lazy dog', I packed up my pencils and left.

I got a job at the West Yorkshire Association, just up the road from the house my parents had recently moved us into. This ambitious little outfit was based in a newly built and still largely unoccupied business park. In spite of having only seven staff, the association had aspirations to grandeur that included purchasing buff-coloured headed paper, which, in turn, required me to purchase several bottles of buff-coloured Tippex.

When the company's first computer arrived, it was ceremoniously unpacked by the permanent secretary and I was given her clunky typewriter, whose keys had to be struck with great force to make any impression at all. The association was organising an end-of-summer conference and I was given the job of typing up and photocopying all the invitation letters. Five minutes after I'd stuffed two hundred and fifty buff-coloured envelopes, I was told I'd missed the 'e' out of Barnsley. It was my first disaster out in the real world and I made the mistake of telling my mother.

'Well, of course!' she cried, triumphantly. 'L, E, Y – it's Old English for top meadow. Everyone knows that!'

Having failed to punch in the 'e', I now very much wanted to punch her.

When I wasn't at work making a hash of the typing or wondering what was to become of me once they realised I hadn't got the hang of the switchboard, I walked up Cherry Blossom Lane to watch matinees at the little cinema. The air outside each of the houses on our pleasantly named street was either rich with the smell of curry, or pungent with wafts of dope, and there were handwritten notices in several of the front windows offering erotic foot massage and oral sex for a fiver. When my grandparents came over from Wetherby to visit, my father had to hurry them past these delights at a pace they were barely equipped to handle.

Our new house was a stone-built, detached affair, which my parents had bought suspiciously cheaply, even taking into account the area and the amount of renovation it needed. It was built in the 1850s and the deeds said we mustn't brew beer or make candles on the premises, and that no other house must look onto ours. This meant the terraced houses opposite had to have their back kitchens facing the road so we could feel superior whenever we glimpsed the working classes washing their hair in the sink.

The day after the typing fiasco, I sulked in my bedroom, trying to soothe my painful sense of futility by reading the kinds of literary novel I thought I ought to like. My brother had moved to Wakefield the year before to study economics and had flatly refused to let me visit, and Ruby had gone to Salford to train as a nurse. My sometime-boyfriend, Anish, was also down that way doing something incomprehensible with chemicals. I was depressed and lonely, and nothing in *Anna Karenina* was going to pull me out of it.

I spotted a lad in a red string vest and sweatpants climbing out of the upstairs window of one of the terraces. He sat on his haunches on the flat roof, and when I caught his eye, he waved and signalled at me to come over. I straightened my skirt and nipped out of our gate.

He met me at his kitchen door and told me his name was Baptiste, and that he was dyslexic and autistic and hyperkinetic. I had no idea what he was talking about, but I let him take me into his kitchen and sit me on his knee. He gave me gin and ginger cake and kissed me on the mouth with lips that tasted of sultanas.

'Dat a big house you got for a likkle girl like you,' he said. 'An' a big book you was readin' up dere.'

He told me he worked as a bouncer in one of the nightclubs – a fact I didn't doubt once he'd made me touch the bulging scar on the side of his neck where, he swore, someone had stabbed him in the jugular. Since there was nothing to eat in his cupboards apart from packets of cake and chocolate biscuits, I took him back to ours to have beans on toast. He laughed at the fake burglar alarm, broke my mother's electric tin opener, and took me up to the attic because it was the only place in the house where we could lie on the floor to snog without setting off his allergies.

On his night off, Baptiste got us into Tiffany's for free, with half-price drinks. It can't have been much of a change of scene for him, but for me it was a distraction from the tedium of being stuck at home. My A Level results had come through, and although I'd done much better than they expected, neither Chad nor Peggy seemed to think this warranted any discussion about my future. I wondered if I'd end up marrying Baptiste just to piss them off. Failing that, I thought I could show my mother the photograph of Cherry Blossom Lane I'd seen in Baptiste's copy of the *Daily Mail* under the headline, 'The most burgled street in the country'. That nugget might be just about enough to make her spit.

I received a congratulatory letter about my results from my old English teacher, Mrs Edmunds, which gave me a little thrill. She was a small, neat woman in her late fifties, who always wore brown nylon tights and sensible shoes. Whenever she bent over my shoulder to examine my exercise book, I knew she was smelling my hair, because she'd make what I considered to be flirtatious remarks about 'the terrible habit of smoking' in an alluring gravelly voice. I sensed a kind of sadness in her that resonated with my own, and towards the end of my final year, when my mother reported that Mrs Edmunds had cornered her at parents' evening to tell her I was 'the light of her life', I braced myself to hear what Peggy had said back.

'Oh, you *stupid bitch!*' my mother had replied.

I caught the look of concern Mrs Edmunds gave me the following day and my devotion to her was sealed. I found her address in the phone book, took the *A-Z* out of Peggy's car, and walked the two miles to her detached house in the suburbs. I loitered outside for a couple of hours with wet feet and a deep yearning in my heart before giving up and dragging myself home.

Now she had invited me for lunch and we sat in deckchairs at a little table in her back garden eating ham sandwiches, even though I'd recently become a vegetarian. While Mrs Edmunds pointed out her campanulas and sweet peas, I admired her legs in the familiar brown nylon tights. It was interesting to see that she wore them on Saturdays also.

'You *must* go to university, Finley,' she said. 'You're too clever not to. If you go to university, you'll find a boyfriend and you'll have clever babies. You must have babies, a clever girl like you, because they'll be very intelligent.'

My head swam a little and I had a strong urge to fend off the subject of babies by declaring my infatuation with her. It was either that or let her know she'd said 'clever' too many times in a row. I kept my mouth shut and Mrs Edmunds seemed to take my silence to mean I was embarrassed by her indirect reference to sex.

'Oh, well,' she said, rather sadly. 'You'll get there, one day.'

Before I left, she handed me an application form for Oxford. I filled it in with a queasy sense of duplicity – even my name seemed a bit of a sham.

When the letter came through to say I'd been accepted into Charlotte College, I was in no doubt that this had been facilitated by Mrs Edmunds' claim that I was 'the most accomplished pupil she'd taught in over twenty years'. I wondered whether she was even more besotted than me.

My mother gave me a cursory hug and said that if I was going to go to university after all, I shouldn't be wasting my time with Baptiste. She must have thought his intellectual challenges might rub off on me, but she did him a disservice because Baptiste was both skilful and enterprising. When he found out I'd need a bike, he fixed up a racer for me within a week. I told him it was the lightest and fastest bike I'd ever ridden, and he laughed and shook his finger.

'Dat because she hot; she gotta get away quick!'

I stroked the elegant handlebars. I wasn't at all convinced that *I* was hot, but I was definitely going to get away soon, and quick.

Baby

My mother once told me that when I was about to be born, she was under the impression she just needed to have a shit. I began my entry into the world so quickly that the midwife barely had time to park her car before my grandmother was hurrying her into our flat in Meanward, Bradford. My father had scarpered for the day, and my brother had been farmed out to a neighbour so he wouldn't take advantage of the commotion to consume yet another bottle of orange-flavoured junior aspirin.

I wish I could add that Peggy had more to say about my sudden arrival. She claimed not to remember whether it was seven in the morning or seven at night, nor how much I weighed, nor whether anyone much liked the look of me. She reported only that she'd been badly bruised on the thigh where the midwife had gripped her while she felt inside.

'*And* she was introducing the risk of infection into the birth canal,' my mother said, in the clinical tone she always used to speak about anything to do with bodies. 'Silly cow.'

Even on such an occasion, it seemed, my mother's capacity for scorn remained intact. She had an equally brief though rather more graphic account of my brother's appearance two years earlier. Destined to have sensitive skin, he was red all over, with a livid birthmark down one side of his face. According to my mother, she took one look at him and wondered what on earth she had spawned. She stopped short of calling us maggots – a term she reserved for the children who came to her office for a psychology assessment – but my brother and I were fair game when it came to our general nastiness. When Charles finally left home at eighteen, she claimed never to think of him again from one end of the week to the other.

I cried non-stop during my first few years, apparently causing my father so much exasperation he nearly threw me out of the window. I imagine being lifted up between Chad's trembling hands, hearing his half-suppressed cry of rage while I enjoy the breeze at the open window for a few moments, until, suddenly remorseful, he returns me to my cot.

Babies, I have since learned, are remarkable beings. The number of connections between their neurons increases from around fifty trillion to one quadrillion in the first month, and thereafter a baby is making a thousand new connections a second between their brain cells. I sometimes wonder whether whatever ability I do possess is down to the extreme measures my brain had to take to cope with the quickly buried atrocity of those early years. I have read, too, that we are conceived with a resounding 'yes', but this can quickly turn into a 'no'. In the womb, I'd been relatively safe; out of it, I was at my parents' mercy. The gene for nurture didn't switch on in my mother until she was well into her sixties and I have a hunch I knew from the start that something was badly amiss in the Wilson household.

Peggy did eventually take me to the doctor about my constant wailing. This was back in the day when family doctors were a thing and, for the whole of my childhood, ours was a dour, solid Scot who dressed in tweed skirts and jackets and wore a terrifying pair of pince-nez. She operated out of a chilly Victorian house in the posher part of Bradford. I can still recall the creak of the white painted staircase and the pounding of my heart once I was old enough to approach the door of her consulting room on my own.

'She's fine; she just doesn't like being a baby,' the Scot told my mother, adding with an uncharacteristic stab at clairvoyance that I would be 'quite intelligent' when I grew up.

My not liking being a baby became family folklore and the wave of nausea that came over me every time this story was told only seemed to confirm it. It was just one of the many disagreeable facts that made me unlovable, and I didn't stop my bawling until I was taken out of the cot in my parents' bedroom and put into a bed of my own.

'You were fine after that,' Peggy told me. 'We didn't hear another sound.'

I couldn't help wondering what kind of mother sees her child's shutdown as a great result.

Yorkshire Pudding

Chad drove me down to Oxford in his Renault Fuego with the go-faster stripe, a car I'd long felt embarrassed to be seen in. Rain hammered on the windscreen and my father, red-faced and sweating, wore his usual expression of trapped exasperation. I was wearing one of Baptiste's vests underneath a shirt and braces, and a bowler hat in the style of *A Clockwork Orange*. I thought this get-up went well with my black-dyed, back-combed hair, which I'd had done by a punk hairdresser at Snipperfields Circus at the top of our street. One good thing about my parents: they weren't the types to criticise my outfits.

The only advice my mother had given me about leaving home was to pour a tin of vegetable soup over a packet of noodles for my dinner, and to keep hold of my supermarket receipts so they wouldn't accuse me of stealing. Before Chad and I set off, she'd also instructed me that it would be more correct to say I was going to 'college' rather than university, though I suspected this was another of her attempts to demote me.

'Keep an eye on yer bike, love,' Chad said, nodding at the rear window.

We didn't have a roof rack, and Chad had done a botch job with some bungee cord and a lot of screwed-up newspaper to protect the paintwork. I turned to see the front wheel of my bicycle slipping into view, giving me the feeling that this whole enterprise, with me at the centre of it, was lacking the appropriate resources.

Charlotte College had a fairy-tale beauty; two storeys of honey-coloured stone set out over three courtyards containing squares of manicured grass. My name was painted in white in the last entrance porch, alongside the eleven other female students, who had names like Felicity and Rosalinda. This brought tears to Chad's eyes.

'Bloody hell, love,' he said. 'Bloody hell.'

My room was equally lovely, with a parquet floor, wood panelling surrounding a recess with a single bed, and a heavy wooden desk set in the window. I couldn't wait for Chad to leave.

Our first tutorial was with a Dr Bothy, a kindly man in his sixties who I soon learned from the other students to call a 'buffer', though I couldn't help imagining this had something to do with correction fluid. I sat on the leather sofa next to a lad who introduced himself as Dan, and while I was enjoying the dappled light coming through the stained-glass windows and the waft of patchouli coming off Dan's denim jacket, Dr Bothy offered each of us a sherry. Then, as a congenial way to start our studies, he suggested we all read aloud together from T S Eliot:

'... *Except for the point, the still point*
There would be no dance, and there is only the dance.'

While the other students' 'dance' glided to a graceful end, mine fell as flat as a failed Yorkshire pudding. Everyone was too well brought up to smirk.

In spite of the waywardness of my vowels and the weirdness of my clothes, Dr Bothy took a liking to me. In my first one-to-one supervision, he made me read out my essay on Ruskin's fairy tale while he listened with his eyes shut, hands folded over his portly stomach. Each time I mispronounced a word I'd only ever read, never heard spoken, he didn't laugh, but with his eyes still discreetly closed, gently corrected: 'I believe it is pronounced *Proost*, rather than *Prowst*.' Halfway through the first term, he awarded me a book token as a prize for the best essay on 'The Miller's Wife'.

Our assistant tutor was less impressed. When we first met, he looked me up and down and languidly crossed his legs, as though doing his best not to laugh.

'Some people say Shakespeare would have been a better writer if he'd read more. What do *you* say?'

I mumbled something about Shakespeare's 'strong characters' and 'understanding of emotion', until I saw by the look on his face that it was time to shut up.

'You are more sensual than spiritual,' he concluded as he waved me towards the door. I mentioned his comments to Dan, who'd gone to school in London and was more switched on than the rest of our group, who were fresh out of the home counties. He had the good grace not to tell me Shakespeare had read *The Decameron*.

'What the guy really meant,' he said, 'is: "I have a fine, strong penis. Would you like to see it?"'

We fell about.

I wooed Dan by showing him a short story I'd written called 'Gin and Ginger Cake'. I must have impressed him with my northern credentials and robust wordplay, because he could have had his pick of the young men and women in our year, but it was me he invited round to the basement room he'd rented on the outskirts of town.

I stood in the drizzle holding various tools while he changed the tyre on an old black cab he'd acquired. I was already so convinced of his superiority I never thought to ask him how he came to own it. He drove me around Oxford, veering off the road across a sports field to avoid a traffic jam while I held onto his arm. As if this wasn't enough, he had white Egyptian cotton sheets, he could play the guitar, and he kept a collection of Keats' poems by the bed. I was a goner.

I didn't tell him that on the way to his flat, I'd climbed over a fence onto a patch of waste ground and sat there for fifteen minutes, staring into nothing. I had no idea what I thought this would do for me; I knew only that I was depressed, and that I mustn't on any account make Dan aware of it. We kissed and talked and got into bed naked and fell asleep with our foreheads pressed together. We woke at dawn and straightaway started kissing again.

'Shall I get a condom?' Dan asked.

I was thrown. Like a fool, I hadn't anticipated this. I'd got so used to messing about with Anish and Baptiste without things going this far. I couldn't think how to respond.

'Guess!' I said shrilly, like an imbecile.

To my surprise, Dan got up and went to his drawer and took out a packet of Durex. My heart thumped. I would have thought my idiotic answer would at least have led to a pause. But I made up my mind that I did indeed want to have sex with him, so I let him put on a condom and climb on top of me. He proceeded to kiss *between* my breasts in a manner I considered extremely sophisticated, and then he slowly and rather laboriously penetrated me.

It hurt like, well, fuck.

A few weeks later, when I was more in the swing of things, I admitted to Dan that that morning had been my first time.

'Oh, wow, it must have been rupturing for you physically and emotionally,' he said.

I batted this away; he wasn't to know I'd been using tampons for ages.

'I should have realised,' he went on, gently. 'You were so still afterwards, for a long while.'

'Was I?' I shrugged, trying to look unconcerned. I must have spaced out, though I hadn't been aware of it. No doubt it was the only option, since feeling anything at all would have entailed not only the joyful giddiness of having been made love to by a very sweet young man, but also an unspeakable onslaught of terror.

I'd never in my life spent a whole day with anyone, but Dan wanted us to do everything together. We cycled to the library to study, went to student gigs and theatre productions and anti-nuclear meetings, and hung out in the walled garden I'd never have discovered without my clever new lover. I was expected to have an opinion on everything we saw and did; the attention was relentless and exhausting. I was in love.

On the first day we were apart, when Dan nipped home for a cousin's wedding, I bought a bottle of wine and lay burping and drinking alone in my room. I could feel a familiar hopelessness beginning to take hold – a feeling I'd spent my childhood trying to keep at bay. I stared at the wine, and then at my sad, blank face in the mirror. There were only two ways this could go. I tipped the rest of the bottle down the sink.

It was a defining moment. I didn't touch another drop of alcohol for almost forty years; instead, I devoured packets of custard creams and cartons of orange juice to sugar-coat my horrible moods, and some years later, it would come to me that Dan, who always behaved towards me with the utmost respect and sensitivity, had misheard me that first morning. He thought I'd responded to his careful request for consent with an unequivocal 'Yes'.

Something Rotten

There are very few photographs of my brother and I from our early years. I've seen one of me in my so-called ugly phase, delicately holding a small rubber ball and gazing off into the distance, either preoccupied or dissociated. In another, I'm kneeling on a white sheepskin rug in a red velvet dress with my chubby fingers clasped together in supplication – a pose only an exceptionally sentimental adult would find appropriate for a two-year-old. My brother is kneeling behind me in his grey shorts, black lace-up shoes and a crisp white shirt, and is inexplicably clasping my velveted bottom.

I half remember this outing to a photographer's studio, though at the time I had no idea what was going on. I understood only that a man was squeaking a rubber toy and talking nonsense, and I wondered why he was trying so hard and so pointlessly to be kind.

There is one other photograph. I am at someone's wedding, sitting on a hard-backed chair in front of a white tablecloth in the same red dress and clean white socks. There is a bread roll on a plate in front of me and my lips are pressed into a pencil-straight smile. I was horribly anxious about that roll; I knew I wasn't going to be up to the job of eating it. My mother used to dunk my dummy in a packet of sugar to stop my screaming and, as a result, my milk teeth were a row of rotten stumps.

When another little girl with long orange hair approached to ask me my name, I wouldn't open my mouth. She crept her sticky fingers towards mine and I shrank away. I could tell this other girl was smugly comfortable in her hand-knitted sweater and clarting of chocolate. She was confident the world was going to meet her with open arms and she left me with the nagging certainty that I, on the other hand, wasn't quite the ticket.

Marry Me

Word got around college that I'd once spent a night at Greenham Common, and I was recruited to join a group of students who organised protests at a nearby airbase. We spent an afternoon in the chilly Quaker Meeting House, learning passive resistance techniques and what not to say if we were arrested. I was paired up with Marianne, a stunningly beautiful young woman with such a laidback manner I could hardly bear to put her in an armlock. While I pretended to read out her rights, she pretended to superglue her hair to the wall. I wanted her to marry me and I wasn't put off even when I found out she'd been to a school run entirely by nuns.

'Women slip in and out of relationships with each other all the time,' she informed me later as we watched a student sketch about what would happen if men had periods.

'Oh, I know,' I lied. Her breath smelt of nicotine and polo mints, and I was enraptured.

It didn't take many midnight raids on the airbase before Marianne and I became lovers. Kissing her felt like the gentlest of transgressions and she had a sophistication that surpassed even Dan's. She, too, had poems by her bed; she, too, had clean white sheets; and, to top it all, she'd been brought up in Libya.

'I've never been on holiday anywhere further away than Scarborough,' I admitted. She laughed as though she thought I was joking.

When we slipped off our jeans and jumped into her bed, it hardly crossed my mind that I was being unfaithful to Dan. I was well aware that I was rubbish in the sack; I had zero communication skills, plus I had no experience of being with a woman. Our attempts at lovemaking were sweet and unsatisfactory, and our romance was already in danger of slipping away from us when, during the end of term break, Marianne invited me to join her at her mother's house in Richmond for her twenty-first birthday party. I couldn't afford the coach fare and I thought my impoverished state was a good enough reason to say no.

'I don't get it,' Marianne said, sounding hurt and annoyed.

I was tempted to tell her I'd only just 'got it' that her parents must be swimming in cash to have given her a Coutts bank account, but she ended things between us before my sarcasm got the better of me. The next thing I heard, she was sleeping with a man. I was outraged even while I blamed myself and, only dimly aware of the irony, I tried to return to Dan. It was no good. He'd already moved on to an affair with the daughter of a politician, who no doubt thrashed around in bed in a much more exciting manner than I'd ever managed.

In spite of all the upsets, I continued to be close to both of them. It was Marianne who drove me to my first lesbian bar in London; Marianne who understood my frequent depressions; and Marianne who made me smile by calling the phone a 'telling bone' – a phrase I continued to use long after the novelty had worn off. It was Dan who introduced me to hitchhiking round Greece in the summer holiday; Dan who persuaded me not to take the Medieval Literature paper since it would mean being taught by even dustier old buffers than Dr Bothy; and Dan who informed me that most people lay face *up* in the bath, not on their front with their arse looming out of the water like I did. Dan and Marianne continued to be my best beloveds. They occupied my broken heart and broken dreams long after I'd broken off with them, and I counted myself unbelievably fortunate to have had my first grown-up sexual experiences with these two trustworthy young souls.

After my first year as a student, I returned to Bradford to eat and laze my way through the summer holiday. I telephoned Anish, who was back from Salford where he was deep in his biochemistry studies. He came straight over, and as soon as my parents took themselves off to their country friends' place for one of their all-night games of cards, he shaved the sides of my head so we could get into a Goth nightclub in the city centre. I was relieved almost to tears to be messing about with my undemanding Bradford boyfriend again. We danced like idiots and propped ourselves up at the bar to compare notes on Salford versus Oxford without bothering to be funny or clever. University had taken everything out of me and I slept like a log that night.

My parents came home in the early hours to discover that the house had been burgled while I was in bed. The thieves had gone all the way up into the attic and stolen my brother's collection of limited-edition Kate Bush LPs, as well as taking off with my parents' video player and a fair amount of jewellery and cash. Peggy was furious and, after that, no matter how often they changed the locks, they got burgled so many times that she and Chad eventually sold up and moved back to the suburbs.

My bedroom was the only room that was never disturbed, let alone ransacked. I don't think my parents ever cottoned on to who was behind it. No doubt Baptiste, who I never set eyes on again, was laughing into his gin.

Unschooled

I waited in the corridor of what I later understood to be the local primary school, listening to my mother's raised voice behind the headteacher's door. I was trying to manage my anxiety by examining a poster of the story of Humpty Dumpty. I lingered a long time over the final frame; I supposed I was meant to be delighted by that shattered head.

The world was troubling, this much I'd already grasped. It was astonishing how hard adults tried to introduce us to its horrors. There were already so many events that made my stomach churn: sour milk, Chad's scowl after a bad day, my mother's – well, pretty much anything my mother did. For the sake of shorthand, I'd come to call my reflexive cringing, 'the frights'. *It's the frights, Finley*, I told myself. *Because you're just not up to it like other children.*

My ears tuned in again to Peggy's shouting.

'You bloody well better sort this out,' she was saying, 'otherwise I'll be speaking to the chair of governors.'

I had no idea what such a chair might look like, but I recognised that tone. My mother had an insatiable need to be always in the right.

'You *wanted* to start school a year early,' she told me later, in the casual way she spoke to me whenever she wanted me to think she was stating the obvious.

I swallowed the majority of her fibs, but this one was so absurd I knew it couldn't be true. I was afraid of my own shadow. If, at four years old, I'd said I wanted to start school, it could only have been because I understood that going along with Peggy's wishes was less risky than the alternative. Whatever school turned out to be, at least it wasn't my mother.

Until now, there'd been short days at nursery. I was taken there on my tricycle, which Peggy pulled along by a rope attached to the handlebars. Various toys were unloaded from the nursery storeroom; there was a nylon hooped tunnel to climb through, a Wendy house to sit in, and a makeshift kitchen with pots and pans and dolls. Everything smelled of plastic and other children's bodies, and since touching these instruments of torture would also involve engaging with said other children, I was determined not to do it. I liked only the rudimentary black-and-white rocking horse; this, I would sit on for hours, rocking myself back and forth, feeling supremely self-contained.

One morning, not long after my mother's shouting episode, I was bundled into my anorak and walked at high speed down to the primary school, where I was put inside the front porch.

'Stay there and keep quiet,' Peggy instructed.

I huddled against the locked double doors, watching my mother hurry away down the path in her raincoat. She'd dropped me off long before any other children were due to arrive, on the pretext that she needed get to work on time. I knew with terrible certainty that she was going to forget to turn and wave, but I felt only a quiet sort of stoicism as she disappeared from sight.

The morning passed in a blur of screaming and urine and chalk smells and strange, frightening children who were bigger and much more adept at tying their shoelaces and putting their coats on pegs than I was. At morning break, we were taken outside to stand on a bit of a wet, grey pavement. Peggy had given me a sandwich that I was supposed to eat during this interval. It didn't matter that I wasn't hungry, it was just another of the tasks of living according to Peggy that must be got through.

I dutifully unwrapped my snack and took a bite. My chewing soon attracted the attention of a trio of little girls, who bustled over in their nice coats and demanded to know what I was doing – didn't I know that eating *wasn't allowed*? This was a new and startling dilemma. My mother's instruction to have the sandwich was very clear, but the announcement that I'd be breaking the school rules if I did was disconcerting. I gazed at the three little misses with their frowning brows, but no further information was forthcoming. I bolted down the rest of my snack, crusts and all, and stuffed the wrapper into my pocket. My tormentors gasped at my temerity and ran away.

It was some days before anything further came of it. We were to have a music lesson and we filed into a shady classroom where an ample, grey-haired woman sat to attention at an upright piano. I was feeling uncommonly self-assured for once and chose a chair at the front of the class, right by her elbow. The sound of her plonky piano playing had just begun when the door opened and the headteacher my mother had scolded came in. The music teacher stopped playing as the younger woman bent to whisper in her ear. I was on alert, stomach knotted. Secrets were a terrible thing. The headteacher straightened up, all pairs of eyes on her now.

'*This* young lady,' she said, pointing at me, 'has been bringing *cheese sandwiches* into school.'

I cringed, suddenly drowning in shame. The whole room had heard her. Why hadn't I sat at the back where I wouldn't have felt the sting of her criticism quite so much? I knew the injustice of it; I was only four and I hadn't made the sandwich myself, but since I'd eaten it, it seemed I was entirely to blame.

That brief dressing-down turned out to be the sum total of my punishment, but I was devastated and could hardly keep my legs working for the rest of the day. My mouth stopped moving altogether. It seemed to me that life was always going to be this way – painful and unforgiving. Even a cheese sandwich could tip me over the edge.

There is just one standout memory from my childhood, which is incalculably precious. Now, as then, it has a dreamlike quality to it. I'm sitting on a grassy slope in front of the one-storey red brick school and the sun is shining. I fancy the grass has been recently cut – the air is fragrant with it. I am picking daisies and there are two other little girls with me, chattering together. I don't say much, but it's magical that these little girls are content to sit with me in my loneliness, that they find me acceptable. I'm unable to believe it's quite real even as it is happening. It must be some other little girl who deserves these riches. But somehow, for that one brief period of time, on a single sunny afternoon, I experience an unschooled, unqualified happiness.

Sebastian Angel

It was only a matter of time before I would sleep with one of my lecturers. He lived in a pretty white house on a hill with his professor friend; he was small and beautiful with yellow curly hair; and he was a little bit French. I'll call him 'Sebastian Angel'. Oddly, his friend, also a freelancer, had the same name. The main difference between them, as far as I could tell, was that the other Sebastian was straight, while Sebastian Angel was bisexual. In his spare time, Sebastian Angel was the guitarist in a band that the other Sebastian managed, and they could often be found performing at local events, Sebastian Angel jumping around on stage like a flexible hobbit, occasionally singing in a rather flat voice, while the other Sebastian jumped around in the audience like a bigger and less flexible one.

I waited until Sebastian Angel was no longer teaching me to make my move, which meant sitting through a whole year of Old English trying not to correct his grammar. I felt honoured to be invited into his bedroom at last, having until now been tutored only at his dining room table. His sanctum sanctorum contained a queen-sized bed piled high with cushions in various shades of gold, and on the wall was a large William Morris peacock print in a silver frame, and there were more peacocks on the curtains. I eyed his pert behind as he removed the cushions from the bed and started to rearrange them neatly on the rug. I had to hold myself back from swiping them out of his hands.

It pleased me to kneel in front of this little man and suck his cock. He had a gleaming, circumcised penis to match his other shiny accessories, and as it was my first one of this type, it occurred to me that he might be Jewish. I had a vague idea that this was an inappropriate conjecture, but I couldn't let it go. At a suitable moment, I cupped his penis in my hand and looked up.

'Is – is your mother religious at all?' I managed.

Sebastian Angel tittered politely and said, 'No.'

To keep my mouth better occupied, I continued with his cock. I didn't feel in the least bit subservient; I could always remind myself of the time I'd come up with a more accurate translation of Beowulf than his. Besides, these were the days of intense attention to the language and practices of feminism. The male students called me 'Muzz', never 'Miss', and I was always a woman, never a sanitised lady or a diminished girl. Once we were installed in his beautiful bed, Sebastian Angel didn't ask whether he could fuck me. 'Would you like to embrace me?' he said and in the interests of equality, he suggested we do it lying sideways. By employing a breathy countdown, which I was encouraged to join in with, he was able to time his orgasm to coincide perfectly with mine.

I was too bowled over to fall asleep between his fragrant sheets. I lay awake, holding his hand, listening to him breathe and watching the gentle rise and fall of the satin bedspread. In the morning, he took me out to a cafe that served three types of croissant, and while I admired the kiss curl on his forehead and he called me sweetheart, I remained painfully aware that I was, in fact, the Beast to his Beauty.

All this perfection made me nervous, but our night-time congress continued anyway. Sometimes I went straight downstairs in the morning for my tutorial with the other

Sebastian, who was supervising my paper on *Ulysses* and thought I was a bit of a whiz. This ought to have given me courage, but I couldn't shake off the feeling that he knew in his heart that I was no good for his special friend, and I could hardly contain my anxiety at having messed with this musical dyad. Sebastian Angel continued to fall for my cute image, while I became increasingly aware that if he got too close, he'd soon discover I was all smoke and mirrors. And no one, least of all me, wanted to know what was going on behind that.

When, one day towards the end of my time as a student, he suggested that we ought to have the 'what next for us' conversation, I blindsided him with a long speech about Molly Bloom and made my exit as soon as I decently could. With my stomach growling with undigested porridge and panic, I tore my bike off the railings and pedalled away, picking up enough speed to be able to freewheel and fart all the way down the hill to my room.

Swinging

No one taught me my letters before I started school, but I quickly got the hang of it. By the time I was six, I was composing my own stories, recorded in thick pencil in a pocket notebook my grandfather had given me. He was a manual worker on the railway, a working-class socialist who believed in the value of education. His workmates called him 'Sir Herbert' because he thought enough of himself to go to night school in the evenings, and he gently encouraged me to always try my best.

When I was seven, an unusually enterprising teacher suggested we each write a nonsense poem and, at the end of the lesson, to my astonishment, mine was read out:

> There was a man
> Who lived in a flan
> Made of raspberry jam.
> He ate the floor
> Sat on the door
> And said I feel so sore.
> He went to bed
> For his pillow his head
> And in the morning
> He found he was dead.

'But how could he *find* he was dead?' the boy sitting across from me whined.

'It's just a funny story,' our teacher explained.

I wasn't so sure. We'd just spent Sunday visiting some friends of my parents, a bohemian couple called Barry and Barb, who had a large house in the countryside. I'd spent a long time standing alone in a bleak green field, as far away from my parents and brother as I could get, feeling utterly weary of life. I wouldn't have minded at all if I could drop dead just then, especially if I could do it full of jam.

I went on to write more poems and stories, about vicious cats howling on rooftops, aliens who ate up whole families, and a girl who tried to break her own neck. These stories were brief, stilted, staccato, and some years later one of my teachers told me she liked my style, though she thought the content was more suited to a boy. I said nothing. It wasn't a style; it was a suffocated scream.

By this time, we had moved out of the flat into a semi-detached house in suburban Bradford, with a garage made of corrugated iron for Chad's beloved Renault and a gloomy back garden. Our neighbours on one side were a retired couple who fended us off with their large blackcurrant bushes and a poodle called Muffin, and on the other side a woman who was a dinner lady at my school. Whenever she was serving, she gave me an extra helping of the piped mashed potato that tasted like misery.

I don't think my parents liked our house any more than I did. Every weekend, they drove off to Barry and Barb's to have dinner and play cards on their patio. Peggy started copying Barb's habit of leaving her blouse half unbuttoned and she learned how to cook *boeuf stroganoff*, and what to do with garlic. Sometimes my brother and I got the leftovers the following day, but once I'd overheard my parents talking about sitting naked in each other's laps at Barry and Barb's dining table, I couldn't help associating the creamy, sour taste of that particular dish with Barry's booming laugh and Barb's bouncy cleavage.

For my eighth birthday, Chad bought me a swing. He erected it after I'd gone to bed and when I first set eyes on this apparition through the kitchen window, its slender blue legs and orange plastic seat almost stopped my breath. The surprise was spoiled only because I couldn't help thinking of my father cursing and sweating in the dark, trying to get the thing to stand up. That someone would do such a thing for me was heartbreaking.

Chad disappeared back upstairs, overcome by his generosity, and I slipped outside in my nightdress and bare feet and had a few goes before Peggy could catch me, then went back inside to help myself to a bowl of cereal. I was tucking in when my mother came down and threw her coffee cup into the sink, blatantly forgetting to wish me happy birthday. Charles trailed in behind her in his pyjamas. He pulled the paper packet out of the Weetabix box, tore it open and huffed.

'Can you please not take just *one* Weetabix,' he told me with all the authority of a ten-year-old whose younger sibling has got out of hand. He'd fallen for the optical illusion that promised a final pair of biscuits, only to discover there was only one. I covered my bowl so he wouldn't see I wasn't guilty as charged; his weedy little sister was actually scoffing a celebratory three.

Charles stomped away into the front room and I leaned against the cupboards, wondering when my mother would remember there was a packet of Curly Wurlys from my grandparents hidden behind the Golden Syrup. Peggy picked up the kettle and took a few steps towards the stove, unaware that she was splashing a stream of boiling water across the floor. I saw it coming a split second before it poured over my foot. I flinched, but it didn't occur to me to cry out. I waited to see what would happen next.

Peggy shouted for Chad, and he carried me upstairs and dropped me onto their bed.

'Don't upset yer mam about it.'

I rubbed my heel against the sheets in silent agony while my father opened and closed the bureau drawers, searching for the antiseptic. His face was red and the soft folds of his double chin were wobbling. He made things worse by spreading a thick layer of cream over the top of my foot and sealing in the heat. In between the rushes of lacerating pain, I pitied him for being so rubbish.

My mother didn't come up to see me. Sometime later I heard her downstairs, saying angrily, 'No, Chad, I've burnt her!' I didn't know what my father had been suggesting, but it was thrilling to hear Peggy admit to what she'd done. Within a couple of days, the burn had turned into an enormous, fluid-filled blister that prevented me from putting on a sock, let alone a shoe. My father telephoned our dour doctor, who told him to open up the blister. With a pair of nail scissors. In the shape of a triangle.

I sat on the yellow tiles in the bathroom, with my foot surrounded by toilet paper to mop up the anticipated flood. Chad knelt in front of me. He repeated the doctor's instructions and paused, looking into my face as though he half hoped I might offer to do the deed myself. I couldn't help thinking my father was a bit of a sissy.

Once the blister had been drained, I still couldn't get my shoe on.

'You can't stay off school just for that!' Peggy shouted when I explained the difficulty. Becoming suddenly inventive, she tore open the top of one of my brother's old slippers, put my foot in it and yanked a thick elastic band around the whole thing.

The humiliation of limping to school in this get-up was worse than being burnt in the first place. I stood in my usual spot by the playground wall, my leg bent up behind me, attempting to hide my monstrous footwear. After dragging myself from lesson to lesson all day, I hobbled home exhausted and threw myself onto my bed. That one short afternoon on the grass with those two amiable little girls seemed very long ago.

The front door slammed and, a moment later, I heard my mother running up the stairs. She burst into my room.

'You didn't do the veg!'

'I know.'

'What's the matter with you?'

'Just a bit tired.'

'Oh, stop your moaning.' She snatched up yesterday's knickers that I'd forgotten to put in the laundry and swept out.

After tea, I took myself out to my swing. The back-and-forth motion made me queasy, but I persisted. Back and forth, back and forth until my head banged and there was bile in my throat. Back and forth, knowing my father could see me from his armchair in the lounge. When he finally left the room I came to a stop, clinging to the chains as I stood up, waiting for the world to come to a standstill.

The swing lasted two years before it corroded. Two years in which I went silently back and forth every night after school. Back and forth, nauseous and heartsick, wearing a muddy furrow into the grass. Back and forth, letting my father know I was grateful to him for trying to love me.

Nunnery

The news from Bradford was that Chad had started using cocaine, and although I didn't think he'd any behave more erratically than usual on Class A drugs, I didn't really want to find out. Feeling like a fraud, I told Dr Bothy I couldn't go home after my finals. He looked stricken and said he'd arrange for me to stay on in my room for the summer.

The next time I saw him he said I'd 'won an award', and not only could I continue to live in college rent-free for a couple of months, I'd be getting a daily allowance to cover my food and study materials. Dan told me he must have applied to the university benevolent fund, but was too tactful to say so. I bought Dr Bothy a shiny, oversized thank you card to big him up for being such a gent. He held it thoughtfully between his fingertips while it sprayed glitter down the front of his trousers.

Not long before our final exams were due to start, Marianne invited me to join her on a week's hitchhiking trip to Germany. I jumped at the chance. It would help me avoid the difficult conversation with Sebastian Angel, and since things always went Marianne's way, I trusted I'd be in safe hands for my first trip abroad.

We hitchhiked to the Dover ferry and on through France, then crept our way in fits and starts along the autobahn until we bagged an eight-hour lift from a young German woman, who drove us right into the centre of Koln. It was 10pm by the time she dropped us off and since we had no idea where to stay, the best option seemed to be to spend the night in a public toilet. We dumped our rucksacks in the sinks and pulled on all clothes we could manage, not so much for the warmth but as a barrier against the unsanitary conditions.

I tossed and turned on the hard tiles, trying not to inhale the smell wafting from the cubicles. This wasn't quite what I'd been expecting of my resourceful friend with the Coutts bank account.

'I hate going to sleep,' Marianne whispered.

I admired her optimism; I wasn't convinced sleep was an option.

'Why's that?'

I heard her swallow as she rolled her face close to mine. Her usually minty breath was sour.

'I get this feeling,' she said. 'Something's touching my leg. Just as I'm about to figure out what it is, I lose it again.'

I put a hand on her shoulder. We didn't speak again, but her fear reverberated a long time inside me.

A clattering of boots startled me out of my trance. Two policemen kicked at our legs and we scrambled to our feet. We sat dazed and silent in the back of their car. My German was too rusty to make any sense of where they were taking us or what they would do to us once we got there. I had visions of being thrown into jail because we couldn't afford the fine for whatever law we'd broken, and I wondered how this would affect my chances of graduating. In fact, they dropped us off at a convent – a piece of luck I put down to Marianne's Catholic credentials. We were put to bed by nuns and slept soundly until dawn when we were invited to go to morning prayers, at which point we made our swift and ungrateful exit.

We travelled on to West Berlin and spent the week strolling through the graffitied streets and sitting in cafes trying to explain that we wanted milk with our tea, which was then produced in two glasses for which we were charged extra. The day before we were due to set off for home, we queued for what felt like half a day at Checkpoint Charlie so that Marianne could visit a penfriend in East Berlin. Once we'd been thoroughly searched and my copy of *Outwrite* had been confiscated, we were let through the barrier.

The friend was sharing an apartment with some shady-looking young men. One of them worked as a translator for the East German government and had excellent, over-precise English. He asked us why we did not take the train back to the United Kingdom instead of wasting our precious time hitching lifts. I told him we were skint. He giggled, repeating the word carefully, and then disappeared into a back room. An hour later, he returned with two booklets containing forged copies of train tickets from West Berlin to the port, two ferry tickets to Dover, another pair of train tickets to London, two underground tickets and two train tickets from London to Oxford. Marianne's usual nonchalance fell away for a moment as she asked if we were likely to get caught.

The translator touched a corner of one of the ticket booklets with his fingernail. 'Just here the line is a little too thick. That is the only mistake.'

We couldn't believe our luck. We boarded the first train trying to actually look like we'd just come out of a convent, and once our tickets had been punched without a second glance, we relaxed into the luxury of our free ride home. Less than a day later, we sailed into Oxford, and three days after that I sailed into my finals.

Slipping

My mother decided Charles and I should be sent to the rougher of the two middle schools in our catchment area. She could have chosen the more well-resourced, aspirational affair with some halfway decent teachers and a regular bus service – the one all the other kids on our street were sent to – but Peggy, with a kind of perverse altrisum, declared that, 'Smallwood badly needs some kids who can achieve.'

It was the only time she gave any indication that she thought my brother and I might have more than half a brain between us. I wondered whether she also thought we needed toughening up, that her general indifference to us wasn't quite enough to prepare us for life's disappointments; Smallwood would have to finish off the job. Charles began there when he was nine; since I was a year younger than my classmates I arrived when I was eight.

Smallwood was on the edge of a council estate, not far from the highest point in Bradford where the water tower stood – and in autumn, it got extremely windy. At break time, I always tried to find a sheltered spot by the wall, where I would rub my frozen hands together like a cartoon miser. Even in summer I had terrible circulation, and in winter chilblains were inevitable. One day, I was suffering the indignity of a particularly itchy one on my nose when a group of girls bounded across the grass and came to a halt in front of me. The ringleader laughed and pounced to fling up my skirt.

'She's got blue knees!' she trumpeted.

Her friends hooted in delight and dragged her away, leaving me to examine my legs. The skin above my socks was indeed turning a sickly shade of purple. Something had to be done. I'd heard a rumour that there was an underground playground somewhere in the school grounds; either Chad had mentioned it or my brother had been boasting. It made sense to me that this shelter would be where the puny children went. I imagined finding another little girl there – perhaps one who was prone to a runny nose and incompetence like me – who could be my friend.

I set off in search of the special playground, following the boundary fence right around the perimeter of the school grounds and then doing another loop round the building itself. I trudged with single-minded determination, kicking at the scrubby grass and silently chanting 'Warm soon' to the rhythm of my scuffed shoes. There was a poster Blu-Tacked onto the wall of our classroom, a picture of a man with a pointed beard and a stiff white collar, which read '*I have never known any suffering that an hour's reading could not allay*'. I wondered whether thinking hard might also do the trick. I tried to conjure up a happy thought to set straight the painful chaos of my mind, but all that came to me was an image of our tomcat's jaunty testicles.

There was no sign of a hidden entrance. I discovered only a concrete walkway with rows of pillars supporting a first-floor extension to the school. It was mystifying and I was too timid to ask for directions. When the lunch bell rang, we were made to queue up on this walkway to re-enter the school by the back door that led to the dining room. The other kids jostled and yelled, and a teacher with an angry face called the boy in front of me a 'dirty Arab' for spitting. As the boy ducked his head, I saw right inside his wax-filled ears. I tried to find something else to look at, but there was only concrete. It suddenly occurred to me that this corridor of hell was, in fact, the so-called underground playground. I was outraged; my brother might be dense, but I would have expected my father to get his words right.

'It's an under*cover* playground,' I muttered to myself, 'not *underground*.'

Just at the height of my indignation, the wind picked up and I was smacked in the face by a football.

Lunch was a desperation of tough beef, spotted dick and more screaming, and I could hardly wait for the bell to call us back into the safety of the classroom. I was in Mr Jolly's class and, true to his name, he was a genial man who never told us off. When he met my father at the end-of-term parents' evening, he laughed heartily at Chad's truculence and terrible jokes.

'What are you going to give your dad for Christmas, Finley?' he asked me the following day.

Chad loved salted peanuts, so I planned to take myself to the corner shop to get him half a pound of them in a brown paper bag. 'Some peanuts,' I said quietly, not yet having learned to obfuscate, and not understanding that peanuts were, well, peanuts.

'Peanuts!' Mr Jolly cried in delight. '*Peanuts*?!'

Feeling culpable, I shrank away, but on the whole Mr Jolly was like a better, much more relaxed and loving version of my father, and because I liked him so much, I knew it couldn't be his fault that it was during one of his lessons that I first caught myself slipping out of my body.

I was watching autumn leaves scudding past the window and wishing my feet weren't so cold, when I simply slipped sideways and hovered somewhere over to my left. At first, I was only mildly worried. I was curious about being outside myself; I hadn't known a person could do such a thing and still be alive.

It was only after some time that I began to panic. Who was running my body if I wasn't in it and, more importantly, what if I couldn't get back? Suddenly, I didn't like it at all. I wanted to be where I belonged. And then, just as suddenly, I was back.

This slipping sideways continued to happen from time to time, when everything got too much. I always felt the same initial curiosity and then the sudden dread of staying that way. A couple of years later, in a rare moment of courage, I decided to tell my mother about these incidents. She was standing on the dining room windowsill with her back to me, cleaning the Venetian blinds. I hovered by the door, ready to flee if it went badly.

'Sometimes, Mam, I have this weird feeling like I've come out of my body, like I'm not in it at all. I'm just sort of *next* to it.'

'*As though*, not *like*,' she said, flapping her cloth. 'Oh yes, I used to get that when I was cycling to school.'

I waited, stock-still, as she ran the cloth along the slats. I could hardly believe my mother and I had something in common.

'I used to cycle past your grandfather; he'd be walking to work and, for a whole year, I never said hello. I just went numb.'

I was stunned; this was the most my mother had ever told me about herself. 'So, wh-when did you start talking to him again?'

'When I left home,' she said, still with her back to me. 'I got a summer job as a cleaner in a boys' school and he took me there on the train. Thank God I got into college; I was so unhappy at that place, my periods stopped.'

We seemed to have got off the point of our shared dissociation, but I was so surprised to hear my mother use the words 'unhappy' and 'periods' that I forgot what it was I'd wanted to ask her. Neither of us mentioned the subject again.

Result

Dan and I drove to Southend to stay in his dead aunt's flat while we waited for our degree results. As we sat in the seafront cinema watching the matinee screening of *Indiana Jones and The Last Crusade* with the blue rinse brigade, it occurred to me that Marianne's exams had been scheduled a month later than mine. She would have had time to put in a fair amount of revision after our trip. Going to Germany had meant I was in no danger of peaking too early, and in an attempt to cut down on the amount of original thinking I'd have to do for my poetry paper, I'd memorised and reproduced an essay I'd written the previous term. I hadn't considered that the tutor who marked it first time round might also mark my exam and I began to panic.

'What does it matter?' Dan said, as we walked back to his dead aunt's flat to wait for the phone to ring. 'No one really cares what result you get if you went to Oxford.'

But I cared, a lot. I still remembered Peggy telling me I wasn't bright enough to get in. I wanted to have done something that would amaze her.

The phone call came while Dan and I were lying on his dead aunt's bed discussing whether or not it would spoil our friendship if we had a shag. Dan let me answer the call first. After a couple of pleasantries, Dr Bothy told me I'd not only been awarded a first-class degree, I'd come out with one of the highest marks in the whole year.

'Oh brilliant!' I said, grinning from ear to ear. 'Brilliant!'

'Yes, you are indeed brilliant,' Dr Bothy agreed, not understanding my vernacular.

I hugged Dan and danced about the room, noticing that for the first time since he read my short story, he was looking at me as though he hadn't quite got the measure of me. I could only hope that Peggy would be even more gobsmacked.

It took a good few attempts to get hold of my parents. The phone rang and rang, and I imagined them getting stoned with their middle-class friends, or already in bed, having forgotten it was results day. I wondered whether the past decade of dope smoking and sleepless nights had scrambled their brains, while mine, it seemed, had turned out to be awesome. Sometime after midnight, my father finally picked up, and on hearing my news, his voice broke.

'Oh love, you're going to feel special for the rest of your life.'

It was the most generous thing Chad had ever said to me and I almost believed him. Oxford had been such an antidote to Meanward, it almost made me think I might get past my demons and do something worthwhile with my life. Almost. Little did I know quite how 'special' I would turn out to be.

My father put Peggy on. She asked how Dan, and then Marianne, had got on. I told her they'd both been awarded 2.1s.

'Ah, so all the clever people came second,' she said. 'Their ideas were too original.'

I slammed down the phone, promising myself I'd never again try to impress my dreadful mother.

Jennifer Jane

I n my third year at middle school, the girls in my class began a campaign of harassment against a girl they used to be friends with. They tied the sleeves of her coat in knots, sniggered when she came into the classroom and yelled insults at her in the playground. I wasn't shocked so much by the concertedness of their bullying as the fact that they hadn't picked on me or Jennifer Jane.

Jennifer was, unbelievably, smaller, paler and even more subdued than I was. It was like being confronted every day with an even worse version of myself, and if I'd known the expression, I would have whispered 'There but for the grace of...' every time I looked at her. Jenny got more than her fair share of grief from the teachers; they seemed rattled by her in a way I somehow managed to avoid, especially the one with the angry face who'd made the racist comment in the dinner queue on my first day. He was Mr Dunn, our music teacher, though he didn't seem to think music ought to have any joy in it. It was like the time of the cheese sandwich all over again. Dunn liked nothing better than to tell us that men should be men and girls should be girls; that men doing ballet, wearing tights and dancing to Tchaikovsky and so forth, was revolting and unnatural. During one of his mirthless lessons, he handed each of us a percussion instrument – a triangle, a drum, a tambourine – and we were told to make one sound each in turn. Jenny had a tambourine and when it came to her turn, she froze.

'Shake it,' Dunn commanded. 'Go on, shake!'

Poor, frightened Jenny didn't move a muscle.

'Get out,' he said, without missing a beat. 'Either shake it or get out.'

Jenny's shoulders jerked, causing her tambourine to rattle. Anti-music. Dunn had won and his attention moved on, but I lingered on Jenny's face, watching the small, secretive smile emerge. It was something I'd witnessed several times before when Jenny was in pain, and it was obvious to me that she'd learned to find a wretched sort of pleasure in her own humiliation. I wondered why no one ever helped her, why no one saw what I saw. It seemed to me that Jennifer Jane and I were in a category all of our own, we both carried some secret burden, some inarticulate pain. And somehow, little and fragile though we were, we did not break.

Falling

At the end of the summer, Dan moved back to London to take up an administrative role 'in publishing'. I packed up my things and, without a word to Sebastian Angel, and with the handle of my saucepan sticking out of my suitcase, I got on a coach for Salford. Ruby was living in the student nurses' wing of the hospital and Anish was still at the university, embarking on a postgraduate course. They were as close as I had to a decent sort of family.

Ruby met me off the bus in Pendleton. Now that I had a degree, she looked at me as if I must be carefully handled, as though I might start quoting John Donne in the middle of the shopping centre. As she led me down the stuffy corridor to her room, I tried to ignore the posters of silly-looking kittens and sentimental God quotes sellotaped onto every student nurse's door. It was clear that Dickens and Shakespeare were too clever by half for the real world, thank you very much.

I slept the night on Ruby's carpet, inhaling large amounts of Shake n' Vac, and the next day, since I was penniless, she took me to The Dutch Pancake House and treated me to a pancake the size of a bathmat. She told me shyly that she had good news of her own; she was engaged to be married. I'd first met her young man when she brought him round to my parents' house. Charles had called him 'totally characterless', mimicking his sappy voice, but since he'd once given me a Delia Smith cookbook, I'd tried hard not to agree.

I kept my mouth shut while Ruby showed me pictures of her wedding dress. It wasn't long since Princess Di's wedding, so I thought she should be forgiven.

'And this will be for the bridesmaids,' she said, sliding a picture of a ruffled pink monstrosity across the table.

'Mm!' I said, trying to hide my relief that she hadn't asked me to be one of them.

Anish found me a room on campus, which a friend of his had temporarily vacated while he recovered from glandular fever. He took me into the city centre and introduced me to Elphick's Palace, an indoor emporium crammed full of stalls selling second-hand clothing for hippies, stainless steel jewellery for various hippie body parts, and tiny bottles of scent with names like 'Vanilla Nights'. I bought 12-inch singles of the Sex Pistols' 'God Save the Queen' and Art Garfunkel's 'Bright Eyes', and tried not to take it personally when Anish made fun of my 'blatant identity crisis'.

Throughout the autumn, it rained all day, every day. After signing on, and with nothing much else to do, I knitted myself a patchwork quilt while bingeing on apple turnovers from the local bakery. Anish had his wrist strapped up in a splint because he'd snapped some tendons during a game of squash, but we still managed to have oral sex on my bed whenever he had the time. When his friend was due to return, I gave the bedding a good wash and tried to think about finding somewhere else to live. I had no idea how to go about it. Chad and Peggy seemed to have abdicated any remaining responsibility for me and three years at an elite university had done nothing for my practical know-how.

In the end, I took the first job I was offered, as a residential worker in an eight-bed hostel for homeless people. I wasn't sure why they picked me, unless no one else had applied. I had nothing to recommend me except for the fact that, by this time, I looked pretty much like a rough sleeper myself. I'd discarded the short dresses of my sixth-form days when I realised I couldn't decently get on the racer in them and my hair was a tangled, half-dyed mess. I didn't even buy myself proper underwear. I'd acquired some old Y-Fronts that used to belong to Charles, and a couple of pairs of second-hand trousers that I hitched up with the braces left over from my *Clockwork Orange* days. Both the braces and the underpants had long ago lost their elasticity, and on my aimless treks around the streets of Salford, I regularly had to duck into a phone box to sort out my builder's bottom.

I didn't relish the prospect of working in the hostel. Whenever I'd come across someone sleeping rough in one of the dirty little squares in the centre of Bradford or, more rarely, begging in the Oxford shopping arcade, I had a disconcerting feeling that I had something in common with them. They reminded me of the time our middle school Humanities teacher had wanted to impress upon us what it took to lead a healthy life.

'No one can survive alone on a desert island. We need other people,' she declared.

I wasn't an expressive child, but she caught my look of disbelief.

'You don't agree,' she added, smiling.

It wasn't just that I disagreed; I'd been surviving in a kind of emotional destitution for as long as I could remember.

I was given a makeshift room on the lower ground floor of the homeless hostel. Originally, it had been the entrance hall, and it was now used as a store cupboard for any non-perishable food items donated to the residents. A sagging single bed had been wedged between the wall and the unused front door, and each morning, while my face burned in a burst of heat from the Economy 7 heater, the day's post would land on my feet.

I managed to slide a broken wardrobe door underneath the mattress to firm it up and I reorganised the shelves to make it feel a little less like living at a primary school harvest festival. After that, my days consisted of doing nothing much until around noon, when the residents would start to appear in various states of undress, demanding mugs of instant coffee and trying to cadge cigarettes. They were mainly men in their forties and upwards, many of them ex-army or ex-service industry – jobs where their accommodation had been tied to the work. One or two gave me their tales of woe; others barely acknowledged me except to say my vegetarian lasagne made them want to heave. I figured they were used to a big turnaround of staff and it would go better for all of us if I stayed out of their way.

I shopped and cooked and did laundry, and in my spare time, I took myself off to the municipal swimming baths. I'd hardly been able to swim when I left school; I'd hated the whole chilly, chlorinated experience, especially the piercing screams and the red faced woman with the long pole who used to haul out anyone who looked like they were about to drown. But I liked the feeling of being submerged, and after a few weeks of following the rhythm of other swimmers in the municipal pool I got the hang of it, working my way up to ten lengths before getting out to have a cry in the showers.

One of the youngest residents, a wiry Glaswegian in his thirties who'd run away from the Foreign Legion, caught me alone in the kitchen one morning. He sucked on a Marlboro while I buttered his toast.

'Ah'm Danny,' he said, eyeing me up and down. 'Dan, fer short.'

The incongruity of that wasn't lost on me.

'You're a cute lassie, you know,' he said. 'If only you didnae dress like a wee orphan.'

I felt a surge of desire and abandoned my attempt to keep a low profile. We went out for a walk along the canal, where, he said, the keenness of the wind 'makes ye know ye's alive'. On the way back, he bought me a cheesecloth skirt and a pair of tasselled socks in the market. 'Go to yer room and put them on, then I'll come down there and take 'em off for ye.'

Fifteen minutes later, he was sitting on my bed with his jeans round his knees. He'd already spotted the Oxford University ID card I was using as a bookmark and secreted it away in his pocket. When he took out his front teeth to demonstrate how thoroughly he'd be able to lick my anus if only I would let him, I thought of Sebastian Angel's clean fingernails and delicate lovemaking, and realised with a pang just how far I had fallen.

Bully

When I turned ten, Peggy sent me to ballet lessons because she wanted me to turn out ladylike. This seemed to me to be a fanciful idea, unless she also wanted me to take after my father. Chad was the one who did the ironing, owned a set of watercolour paints and knew how to make custard from scratch. And, by his own admission, he had the prettiest feet. But I did as I was told and began to spend every Saturday morning prancing about in pink satin, pretending to eat curds and whey and to be scared of spiders.

Incensed by my anxiety masquerading as good behaviour, the other girls wiped snot on my ballet shoes, called me a 'fucking baby' and sniggered at my plastic tambourine. I was so shutdown I hardly noticed and this proved all the more infuriating to their eager young minds. I endured their Chinese burns, the sudden tugging down of my knickers when I was trying to change, and the careful spreading out of their coats and bags so there was no room left for me on the bench.

This despotism stopped only after the biggest bully appeared on the allotments behind our house one weekend, and we sat together with our feet in the ditch and showed each other our privates. She seemed to have mistaken my helpless endurance for something more heroic and we became friends for a while. She went as far as to show me her guinea pig and her collection of Robertson's sax and drum-playing gollies, which I pretended to like, though I had a vague feeling that there was something much more disturbing about these hideous figurines than the sight of my own hairy triangle had been to her. She only showed them to me once and she later claimed it was by accident.

I'd just started to think I was safe from predators when the girl who'd noticed my purple knees in the school playground began to pay attention to me again. Her name was Mandy Skinner; her elbows and knuckles were covered in eczema and she had copious amounts of dandruff, which she sprayed across her desk whenever she wanted attention. She'd set her sights on my newly beloved, a placid girl called Julie from the local estate who had thick wavy hair and a lovely mole on her cheek. I was surprised and gratified when Julie came to sit with me at the one desk left over after everyone else's had been fitted together into threes. Without Julie, I would have been left adrift in my usual isolation.

Right under my nose, Mandy began to pass Julie notes saying things like 'I am your best friend' with the 'I' thickly underlined. She pilfered my rubber and covered it in ink with aggressive concentration; she hid my pencil case in her bag and smacked me on the head in the corridor. Her attentions escalated until, one day, carefully observed by a small audience of little girls, she decided to pinch me long and hard with her fingernails. I refused to react, though the pain was searing, and when she finally let go, my skin was puckered into two small red welts.

'Are yer alright?' one of our young audience gasped.

Jolted out of my trance, I nodded curtly. It hadn't occurred to me that I was tough; I was simply a person who was used to absorbing pain. Julie was soon seduced by Mandy's attentions and I went back to my solitary corner of the playground, fed up of being shoved around every time I tried to play with the pair of them.

I was still hurting at the absence of Julie's loveliness when, one break time, I spotted Mandy among the crowd going down the stairs just ahead of me. Without thinking, I pushed my way in between the kids and grabbed a fistful of her hair. I yanked it hard. 'That's for stealing my stuff!'

Mandy shrieked as her head snapped back. Given the shrillness of the noise she made, I was certain one of the teachers would catch us, but no one did. It was one of the few times in my life I got away with something. I felt not a jot of guilt about my rage and Mandy never bothered me again.

My mother, too, must have dimly intuited that there was a line she shouldn't cross with me. I once overheard her in one of her fits of temper yelling at Charles: 'Do what you like, *I* don't care!' I couldn't believe my brother's luck; she'd just handed him carte blanche. I was even more aghast that he squandered this opportunity by doing nothing with it. Though he could be cheeky at school; though he flunked his exams after contracting pneumonia; though he once crashed Peggy's beloved, souped-up Mini when he was waving at a friend while inching forwards in a traffic jam, Charles was never really a rebel. I prayed for our mother to give *me* that same permission, but Peggy never relinquished her hold over me. If she'd ever just said the word, loosened the reins one tiny bit, I was in no doubt I would have wreaked havoc. I dreamed of smashed furniture, torn clothes, unbridled screaming and a final, longed-for escape.

One day – *one day* – I would be that wild thing.

Careful

I returned to the hostel after a swim to find Peggy sitting in the hallway outside my room. She had a holdall with her and, for a moment, I was terrified she'd come to stay.

She jumped up, looking put out. 'I've been waiting *ages*. Come on, let me in for a cuppa!'

I could hardly picture my mother in my room. Peggy liked to be in charge of her environment and this peculiar corner was all mine. I unlocked the door and waved her in. Her eyes darted around, looking for somewhere decent to sit before she settled for the side of my bed. It didn't seem to occur to her to ask why I was living in a lobby surrounded by shelves full of tins of fruit cocktail and meatballs.

'Oof, what a week I've had,' she said, twisting her wedding ring. 'Your brother's gone to live in Italy, apparently.'

'Oh?' The last I'd heard he was working in Croydon.

'Hmm. And then yesterday I came home to find your father *fornicating* in the front room. I should have known,' she sucked in her breath. '*I should have known!*'

I got the feeling that being kept in the dark about these goings-on upset my mother more than the goings-on themselves. Peggy lived her life battling to be always in the know, always right. More than once, as a kid, she left me at the shops and drove off home, and when I returned, foot sore and weary, she never admitted she'd made a mistake.

'He's extremely difficult to live with these days, your father. High as a kite one minute and then miserable as sin the next. And he won't talk to me! If he'd talk about it, we might get somewhere, but, no, he says it's private.'

I thought of the Swedish exchange student my father had invited to stay with us one summer. She'd given me a game called 'The Hooker' and she and Chad had sniggered together, casting glances at Peggy, who was deploying what I'd come to call the 'Bradford silence'. All the same, I wasn't in the mood to join in with my mother's string of complaints and eventually she broke off.

'Now, look, I brought you some things.' She pulled a plastic bag out of her holdall and dumped it on the floor. 'You can sort through that later. Do you need any money?'

I shook my head. Peggy lived in a fantasy world when it came to me and my finances. Once, when I'd been running late to catch the train back to Oxford, she said she'd pay for a taxi. She'd given me 20p.

'I don't know if the cutlery belongs to you or your brother,' she said, nodding at the plastic bag as though she couldn't quite get her attention off it. 'You may as well have them. He just takes himself off without a thought, whereas you're virtually on the doorstep. How did I end up with two such different children?'

'I guess it's...' I ran out of steam.

'You need to let go, spread your wings. You were so clingy as a child.' She shot a glance at me and her voice went low. 'Be careful or I might tell you something in a minute.'

The room swayed a little and, for a few moments, I slipped out of myself. From a distance, I observed my mother's thin legs in the dark trousers, the short hair brushed back off her forehead, the sharp nose that used to frighten me as a child. My mother, always more powerful, more knowing. I had a disconcerting feeling that I did indeed need to be careful, that I could never hope to get the better of her.

When I tuned in again, Peggy was rattling on about a neighbour who took up all the parking space and whose children threw cigarette butts over the fence, burning holes in Chad's Astroturf. She was going to have to have a serious word. I nodded, my mind still scrambling away from whatever it was she'd hinted at. She ended the visit as unexpectedly as she'd arrived, declaring that the meter would be running out and she didn't want to get a fine. Something in the way she picked up her holdall made me feel certain she was going to return to Chad, rather than throwing herself on the mercy of one of her lovers. She left behind a cloying scent that had me shoving open the window and breathing in the traffic fumes.

I sat down on the floor and peered into the carrier bag. She'd brought me a packet of plastic picnic knives, a Pac a Mac raincoat in a polythene sleeve and an unwashed pair of size eighteen knickers. I wondered whether they belonged to Chad's lover and how my mother could possibly think my arse was that big. I shoved the bag under my bed and went in search of Danny.

During the next few months, while Danny was receiving his unofficial resident's perks, one of the morbidly obese residents fell into the bathtub and had to be hauled out with ropes, another knocked his front teeth out on a beer glass and a third appeared on the front page of the *Salford Herald* under the headline 'Floral Fall: Man drives wrong way up motorway before crashing through florist's window'. I'd had no idea he owned a car. By spring I'd had my fill of this bunch of slurring, lying, belching and tunelessly crooning men. Danny had been promised a bedsit in Birmingham, which would get him off my hands; I was confident Anish would be perfectly happy whether I was there or not; and Ruby was taken up with her colourless husband. I suspected babies would soon follow and I definitely didn't want to be around for that. I decided to move to London, where the lesbians were.

Rocking the Bed

When my brother turned thirteen, in an attempt to be liberal without actually having to engage with him, my mother bought him a book about teenage sex called *Make it Happy*. He rather pointedly left it untouched on the coffee table where she'd given it to him.

By this time, I was getting up before everyone else at weekends. I would go downstairs into the curtained lounge, which still smelled of alcohol and cigarettes from my parents' Friday evening card game, to pick at the leftover cheese crackers, sniff the dregs in the wine glasses and poke about on the little bookshelf. It was here that I read Kafka's *Metamorphosis* and *Goodbye Mr Chips* in one sitting. I also attempted some Freud, which freaked me out, and one of Peggy's textbooks on child development, which declared that if a child under the age of five is deprived of its basic needs, the damage is irreversible. I slammed the book shut and instead absorbed myself in reading *Make It Happy*.

This wasn't my first introduction to sex. Years earlier, I'd gone into my parents' bedroom one morning to put yesterday's underwear in the laundry basket and spotted a magazine lying face down beside their bed. I was obsessed with pictures of cats at the time, which I was pasting into a scrapbook. I picked up the magazine, hoping to find one or two more to add to my collection. They weren't quite the kind of pussies I was expecting.

I particularly remember Juicy Lucy, who featured on several pages with her private parts raised up very close to the tongue of another happy-looking young woman. I examined these pictures carefully and a seed was sown. I wasn't exactly turned on, not to begin with, only surprised. But for the remainder of my years living in my parents' house, whenever I felt horny, I rifled through the collection of *Playboy* magazines I'd found hidden on the left-hand shelf of my parents' wardrobe under a scarf. I would choose a magazine I'd not seen before, squirrel it into my own room, and lie on the musty carpet between the two single beds and give myself a really good wank.

This solitary activity had started at a very young age. I know this because my brother and I slept in bunk beds until I was six years old, after which he was given the little box room and I had the bigger front bedroom to myself – one of the rare times I got the better deal. I had the top bunk and one night, when Charles climbed into bed below me a bit earlier than usual, I was still occupied with my special face-down technique of rubbing my bunched-up nightdress vigorously over the general area of my clitoris.

My brother soon lost patience. 'Can you please stop rocking the bed?'

I have no idea whether he knew what I was doing, though I suspect not. I doubt he was wanking yet and even if he was, it wouldn't have involved the whole room shaking. I considerately put aside my own needs so he could get some sleep, but his rebuke did nothing to dampen my enthusiasm. I tried to teach my technique to a couple of the neighbours' kids, describing with scientific precision the response you could get from touching 'down there'.

'And,' I added generously, 'I have tried to do it by touching my bottom, but that doesn't work.'

They looked at me in bewilderment, clearly too young to understand. It took reading *Make it Happy* for me to learn the proper word for what I'd been doing all this time, that it wasn't just me who liked it and it wouldn't make me go blind. It was good to know.

Stopcocks

I slept for a couple of nights in the front room of Marianne's expensive new flat in Earl's Court, next to the pair of pedigree cats she'd bought with the remainder of her trust fund. We hung out in Leicester Square eating slices of pizza and watching the crowds, and in the evening we sat on Marianne's patio drinking mugs of tea in front of the chimenea.

'So, how long would it take me to cycle from one side of London to the other?' I still had no idea of the scale of the place.

Marianne looked at me with a raised eyebrow. 'Do you want to kill yourself? Take the tube.'

While we were living at such close quarters, I thought she might tell me more about the night-time apparition she'd mentioned in Koln, but she seemed relaxed and untroubled, though she couldn't decide what she wanted to do with her life.

'I might apply for a fine arts course or I might get a job in the wholefood shop,' she said vaguely.

I supposed it must be tricky when you didn't actually need to work for a living. I got her to tell me about the gay bars she'd been going to and Jezebel's, the local dive for lesbians. And the lesbians.

'You have to have a short back and sides to be a proper one, which counts you out,' she said. 'And a decent shirt.'

I smoothed down my crumpled top. I was aware of how

much my appearance had deteriorated since Oxford, but I didn't seem to have the wherewithal to do anything about it. Marianne told me my best bet for finding somewhere to live was on the basement noticeboard in the Last Out café off Oxford Street, so the following afternoon I pushed past the couples smooching at little tables under the dim lights and copied down the phone number for a room in a house owned by two 'lesbian separatist wimmin'.

The address was in Newham, which explained the cheap rent, and the woman who answered my call sounded eager to get me over there. Since I didn't want to kill myself, I took the tube. I wore an old brown leather jacket Danny had offloaded onto me, which smelt overwhelmingly of an aftershave I knew wasn't his. I thought about the massive pivot I was doing, presenting myself for a women-only house share so soon after my recent exploits with him and Anish. But I reasoned that if I had no idea who I was, then, in all fairness, I couldn't be accused of faking it.

The semi-detached house was a stone's throw from a scruffy bit of common land. There was a sign on the gate that said 'Big Swingin' Melons' and while I was grappling with the latch, a wiry-haired woman in a purple vest and leggings and no bra opened the front door.

'Hi, I'm Sam, come in.'

She showed me into the front room, which was crammed with two tired sofas and smelled of mud and incense. A Dobermann stared at me from a dirty beanbag. While Sam ran upstairs to get her girlfriend, I sat down gingerly and looked around.

The floor was strewn with cups and plates, tatty bits of clothing and crumpled magazines. Someone had created a grotesque collage of dried leaves and feathers that hung on the wall above the gas fire, entitled 'On the Seventh Day God

Rested, On the Eighth Day She Created Something Better'. The
rust-coloured frame, I was told, was painted with menstrual
blood. I wasn't impressed; given the state of my own periods, I
could easily have redecorated the whole room.

Sam came back with Robbie, a tall, dark-skinned woman
in her late forties with multiple ear piercings and a severe face.
Since my mother's impromptu visit to Salford, I'd come to realise
I was scared of older women. I smiled vacantly at them, pressing
the palms of my hands onto the sticky seat cushion and willing
myself not to space out. The dog jumped up and folded her bony
front legs into my lap. I gave it an awkward pat.

'Oh good, Sappho likes you,' Robbie said, pulling Sam onto
her knee. 'Right then, what's your story?'

'Oh, I just moved to London and I'm staying with a friend
while I find somewhere permanent...'

I tailed off. Sam was licking Robbie's ear.

Robbie pushed her face away. 'So you're homeless?'

I nodded. Sleeping in Marianne's plush living room hardly
made me feel like a down-and-out, but I got the impression I
should agree.

'We don't have any men across the threshold, okay?'

I nodded again.

'No fuckers or breeders,' Sam whispered into Robbie's hair.

'I'll be looking for work,' I put in, before they could ask
whether or not I could afford the rent.

Robbie told me she was a driving instructor for BSM, which
explained the sign outside. Sam cackled and added that she
worked in lesbian porn and was currently putting together a
series of photographs of women's vulvas for an exhibition.

'So if any of your friends would like to get involved in that,
let me know. Or you.'

'I – okay.'

'And you're definitely a lesbian?'

I seemed to have lost a grip on where this was going. I said yes, since the only other response I could think of was to say not exactly, but that my ex-girlfriend was.

'Shall I show her round?' Robbie said.

Sam leaned back and spread her arms, grinning.

The kitchen faced onto a small garden with a blown down fence and masses of nettles. The back door was half off its hinges, letting in spatters of rain. Robbie lit the gas burners on the stove to demonstrate how to get rid of the damp. She explained they drank a coffee substitute called Barleycrap, and she showed me jam jars full of sprouting mung beans and bottles of home-made sauerkraut and kefir – names that struck me as scary and exotic. There seemed little prospect of the fried eggs and chocolate I'd been living on in the hostel.

Robbie tapped a list of numbers pinned to the wall by the telephone: Stopcocks the plumber, MsGuided Trips the cab driver, Happy Bitch & Happy Pussy the pet sitters.

'Someone will have a job for you if you want. You can do a ring round once you've settled in.'

Standing among the clutter with Sappho sniffing my crotch and Robbie's musky scent in my nose, I felt almost like a proper lesbian already. All that remained was to keep Dan at arm's length, and since he was now a published writer and my envy knew no bounds, I didn't think I'd have much problem doing that.

Quick

I was given a room at the back of Sam and Robbie's house. Marianne borrowed her mother's car to give me a lift across London with my suitcase, and as soon as she left, I turned on the Calor gas heater and got into bed. I lay on my back watching the condensation sliding off the windows, feeling wiped out. I could hear Sam and Robbie having sex in the bathroom; they groaned and splashed about, thumping the wall. I needed a pee and they were spending so long in there, I started to think I might have to relieve myself in the garden. I hauled myself up and tapped on the door.

'Sorry,' Sam said, as they emerged in their dressing gowns. 'What do you call lesbians who make love for three hours?'

I shook my head.

'Quick.' She winked at me and they hurried down the landing to their room.

Within a couple of months, I'd found myself a part-time job as an administrator in the local community centre. It was my speedy touch-typing skills that swung it rather than my fancy degree, and I felt sure I'd be fired as soon as someone realised I'd never progressed to punctuation. But almost as soon as I started work, I got sick. On the Friday morning, I woke up dry-mouthed and numb, with hardly enough energy to climb out of bed to get a glass of water. Shooting pains flashed through my head, and by the afternoon I was getting crippling waves of period pain and enough bleeding to saturate my mattress.

This heavy bleeding had been building up over the years. My sheets and underwear were all hopelessly stained, and I didn't stand a chance of wearing anything a shade lighter than navy. I treated my period like a bothersome stray dog; something to be ignored as much as possible until it went away. Marianne came and sat with me when she could, and Sam and Robbie took turns to bring me bowls of 'spicy arse pip' soup and mugs of tea. At the end of the week, I struggled downstairs, trying to look chirpier than I felt.

Sam was in the kitchen, washing up. 'Hi, Fin, how're you doing?'

'Getting there. I just wish my periods didn't knock me out so much.' I was embarrassed I'd turned out to be such a dud.

'You could get help with that.'

'I don't want medication,' I said warily. I thought northerners didn't take painkillers and my mother had always treated illness as a sign of incompetence. She'd never given me so much as a hot-water bottle. The only remedies allowed in the house were Chad's Rennies, because she didn't like the sound of him burping.

'Of course not,' Sam said, 'you don't want to kill the messenger. We'll have a think for you. Are you a survivor?'

'A what?'

'A sex abuse survivor. If you are, that can mess up your cycle.'

I almost wished I could say yes. I knew Sam and her best friend had both been abused by men in their families. They saw their therapists on the same day, and returned to the house afterwards with bottles of wine and cartons of Indian takeaway. The more they ate and drank, the more hysterically they laughed. I hesitated and then I told her something I hardly ever thought about.

'My father used to fondle me a bit, down the back of my knickers. Not – not genitally. I stopped him eventually.'

Does that count? I wanted to know. Chad's groping didn't compare with what Sam and her friend had been through, but there was something about it, now, that made me uneasy.

Sam took her hands out of the suds and wiped them on her vest. 'My therapist says there's a fine line between affection and abuse.'

'I don't know...' Her response didn't satisfy me, but I felt too unwell to care. My head drooped and I grabbed the edge of the counter. Before I could stop myself, I sank to the floor and passed out. Sam must have helped me back up the stairs, because sometime later I woke to a blast of foul breath. Sappho was pinning me to my bed with a look of silly delight on her face.

Woo-Woo

If I'd learned anything at all at university, it was that you should do your research no matter how dubious the material and reach your own conclusions. It was in that spirit that I agreed to try whatever woo-woo my housemates suggested. I thought maybe I'd be able to find someone who could explain why I was incapacitated with exhaustion and a low mood half the time, even if they couldn't sort it out.

I began with acupuncture, which was offered in a Chinese herbal shop just off the local high street. The practitioner was a squat, frowning woman in a pair of oversized pink overalls. She spoke little English, and after nodding at my list of symptoms without any sign of comprehension, she took me by the shoulders and drew me to sit in front of a large mirror on a couch covered with polythene. She seemed uncertain where to insert the first needle, so I pointed out a couple of aches and pains that could do with attention. She stabbed me deftly in the shoulder three or four times and this seemed to give her momentum. I took off my top so she could insert needles rapidly one after another all the way down either side of my spine, then she wound up what looked like an egg timer and, with strict instructions to 'No sit back!', she disappeared down a curtained hallway.

I twisted round to survey her work. She'd made me look like a frightened porcupine. It occurred to me that if a well-trained nurse wielding a large needle couldn't always draw blood from a bulging vein, there wasn't a lot of hope for anyone attempting to hit an invisible spot with a tiny one. I'd also looked into the existence of so-called energy lines. There were thousands of the things – meridians and sen lines and nadis and so on – and although you could kill a pregnant woman by pressing on certain points in China, if you pressed the same points in Thailand she'd most likely produce twins. Perhaps the acupuncturist had the right idea in the first place, randomly sticking needles into me wherever I wanted.

After twenty minutes, the egg timer began to play jingle bells and the woman returned, pulled out the needles and told me to get dressed, adding that, 'Everything fixed now.' Though she was Chinese and I emerged from her shop into blazing sunshine, I felt I really ought to have wished her a 'Happy Christmas'.

I threw away the bag of brown leaves and twigs she'd given me, and made an appointment to see the Western medical herbalist who was next on Sam and Robbie's list. Her consulting room smelt of cupboards and was filled with amber bottles full of murky liquids. She asked if I'd had any stress before the age of five; when I told her I'd been in full-time education by the time I was four, she looked appalled.

'In Austria, nothing until six, nothing!' she shouted. 'That is only reason why I have no stress at all!'

She recorded my personalised recipe in a tiny notebook, telling me it was essential to keep a detailed account of what she was prescribing because the doses must be fine-tuned to keep up with my changing monthly cycle. She soon lost track of these calculations, with the result that when I got diarrhoea after our fourth session, she couldn't work out which herb she'd added at the time. Fearful of shitting myself to death, I gave up on her.

Next up was the reiki-reflexologist, who was keen to do a home visit. I lay on my bed while she unfolded her stool and took my left heel in one hand, staring into my eyes. I was just beginning to wonder why on earth I'd thought a foot rub would help when she pronounced that I 'presented like a teenager'. This wasn't far off the mark, since I now bought all my clothes from the boys' department at John Lewis. Clearly she'd never heard of tax-free shopping for the smaller lesbian.

'How do you feel about your body?' she asked, attempting to stare into my soul.

'I love it.'

'Look me in the eyes and say that.'

I tried to peer through her glasses. I wasn't going to let her think I was deficient just because the label in my sweater said 'Age 12-14'.

'*I love it.*'

She sniffed, looking disappointed, and while she waved her hands up and down over me, I nodded off for a bit.

'So!' she said at last, startling me awake. 'We must find the fire, not just put out the smoke.' She jabbed what looked like a miniature poker into the sole of my foot and I snatched my leg away, almost knocking her off her stool. It was time for her to leave.

Osteopathy, cranio-sacral therapy and kinesiology all followed, all with zero success. It seemed no amount of pricking, prodding or poisoning was going to help me discover what was wrong with me. I didn't think these people were charlatans, exactly; I simply had the unnerving sense that they were attending to scratches while I endured a mortal wound. It was also galling that everyone else in my life seemed to be getting on with things. Marianne had decided to train as a social worker and was dating a woman who worked for the United Nations. Dan, as far as I could gather, was rapidly establishing himself as a successful children's author, and even Sam and Robbie were settled in their own chaotic way. They talked of one day moving to Todmorden to open a bookshop and adopt a child, which struck me as a terrible idea. Meantime I was going through the motions, barely managing to hold things together, and all the while feeling quietly more ineffectual than all the woo-woo practitioners in East London put together.

The one alternative treatment that stuck was yoga. I found an Iyengar instructor with a whispery voice and a beatific expression, though when I told him I was hoping the class might help with my heavy periods, his smile faltered a little.

'Are you on your period now?'

'Not exactly.'

'I don't know what that means!'

'You know,' I said, trying to be helpful, 'menstrual bleeding doesn't turn on and off like a tap. It kind of fades away...'

For a moment, he looked as though he might fade away himself. He livened up once the class started, bending over each of us in turn and whispering things like, 'Do your practice and all is coming down the path; don't let pain define you – sweat it out, drop it onto your mat.'

It was the closest I'd ever come to a sadomasochistic experience, but he did indeed set me on the path. His lessons gave me a shot of endorphins and calves to die for, and I always looked forward to the final class of the week when our fastidious teacher would give us each a chair to climb on so we could hang ourselves off the wall ropes while he briskly hoovered the floor.

In the end, I pretended to Sam and Robbie that I was feeling better, and their next suggestion was that I should explore the scene to find a girlfriend. They told me to pay a visit to the women's sex shop in Hoxton first to get some equipment. Finally, a plan I was eager to carry out.

I rang the doorbell and waited while the staff at OOh! peered through the peephole to check I looked like a lesbian before they opened the door. I was given a plateful of pink wafers to snack on while a woman in thigh-high boots and a red lace-up bodice flicked through a range of sex toys hanging from a rail.

Since I was a beginner, she recommended a slim silicone dildo, which had the added advantage of being dishwasher proof and a lubricant made from grapefruit seeds, which was safe to swallow. She also recommended a sensible doctor at the lesbian sexual health clinic in Whitechapel, who could fit a coil to dry up my periods. Not only did this lovely woman put the coil in; she gave me two Valium and an extra two to take home 'for later'. By the evening, I was so tranquillised I treated my housemates to a breezy demonstration of what I intended to do to any big swingin' melons that came my way. With my bloody flow dried up and the messenger effectively silenced, if not quite killed off, I was ready to meet Filchie.

Arrested

In my second year at middle school, I was adopted by a pair of gigantic, flaxen-haired twins who seemed to think it was their Christian duty to rescue me from my playground isolation. They were the only truly middle-class children I came across at Smallwood; their father was a professor and their mother, a German. Between them, they must have been ignorant of the British class system, otherwise they would have got their children into the right sort of education.

Like Peggy, the twins' parents were too preoccupied to realise there was a free school bus and at the end of each day, we were the only kids who waited at the public stop. I would lean into my new friends' uncomplaining bulk, soaking up the warmth from their woollen coats and the smell of baking that rose off their skin. It was difficult to follow the conversation with their heads so far above mine and the northern wind whistling round my ears, but I didn't mind much. Whenever they argued about whether to buy wine gums or lemon sherbets, I had the deciding vote. I prided myself on being able to tell which of them was which and whose turn it was to win without even having to look. It was dizzying to have such power.

Peggy had no idea about my new security guards and it didn't occur to her that perhaps I shouldn't be making the journey to and from school, alone, at such a young age. She and Chad drove off early in their separate cars, and Charles went out to kick a ball around before sauntering up the road to the bus stop at the last minute. I was left in charge of feeding the cat and putting him out for the day, with instructions to prepare the veg for tea if I still had time on my hands before I locked up.

Our cat distressed me more than the forced labour of potato peeling, even though he was supposed to be mine. He was unvaccinated, unneutered and so flea-ridden his fur was falling out in lumps. Before his kittenhood had been entirely destroyed by living with us, I'd wanted to call him Michael, but Peggy told me that was a ridiculous name for an animal. The name Charles came up with wasn't ridiculous, apparently, and so our constantly pooing and pissing little bundle was called Fluffy. He grew up to be even less worthy of the name.

On the last day of term, I was desperate to get home because I'd forgotten to open a tin for him and I had no idea how long a bruiser like Fluffy could last without food. As I rushed across the main road between the heavy traffic, I was spotted by a police car and promptly picked up. By the time the placid officer dropped me off at home, I was sobbing. I thought this time I must have done something truly criminal.

I told Chad the awful news as soon as he got in.

'But what's the matter, love?' he said irritably. 'You're always safe with a policeman.'

It was obvious my father was almost as unnerved as I was that law enforcement had been to our house. Months later, when I realised he was pursuing his own mildly criminal activity in the greenhouse, I understood he'd been more concerned about his tender crop of cannabis than he was about his feral daughter.

Sometime after my arrest, a neighbour cornered my mother in the street to ask what had been going on that day, why I was brought home by the police. Being left in the dark had clearly been killing her.

'Oh, give over. It was a fuss about nothing,' Peggy bristled. 'They obviously thought she was much younger than she is.'

I supposed that must be true, since I was small for eight.

Filchie

I'll call her Filchie, for that was her name. She looked just like Honey Lee Cottrell in her infamous self-portrait 'Bulldagger of the Month', which I'd found in a collection of lesbian erotica I came across in Sam and Robbie's front room. It was one of the many startling educational collections I was treated to while I lived with them and it was a personal favourite. Underneath the photograph, the reviewer had written: 'Honey Lee's dark eyes burn holes right through Amerika's worst fears for their daughters'. Just what I was after.

Filchie wasn't my first real lesbian. By this time, I was accustomed to cruising the bars and clubs, and I was seeing a number of women, including a friend of Marianne's – a paramedic whose best friend was a Russian aristocrat. We got together when the Russian was conducting research on female sexuality for a documentary and needed volunteers to share their experiences. With her eyes fixed on mine, my new medical friend recounted how she used a hole in her pocket to pleasure herself on long train rides, and when it came to my turn, I told them about my childhood method of using my bunched-up nightdress to bring myself to climax. To which the Russian replied that it was a wonder my mother never said anything about the creases.

Being oversexed was a desirable trait on the London lesbian scene and so when the paramedic learned I was having my wisdom teeth removed at the local hospital, she offered to take me home afterwards, even though my face looked like a hamster's and I couldn't stop dribbling. When she gave me a sweaty hug and I pulled away, protesting, she told me that while I'd spent the afternoon on intravenous drugs, she'd been rushing an epileptic child to casualty. She was kind, solvent, highly functioning and not really my type.

'I want to meet a nice butch,' I told Marianne as we lay on her bed the following evening. She was packing for a weekend away by reaching for things in a drawer without looking and throwing them at her suitcase. 'You know, a woman with balls and a strong right arm.'

'Go back to Jezebel's; it's full of dykes these days,' she said. 'You can walk there from here. Stay the night and feed the cats for me. And change my sheets when you're done.'

The entrance to the club was hidden between an Indian takeaway and an off-licence. The walls of the stairway down to the basement were covered in large black-and-white photographs of naked women and the sound of thumping music vibrated along the handrail. I descended into the dark and leaned against the bar to order an apple juice. I was still off alcohol, and I was indifferent to drugs, though I sometimes got asked for them when people saw me slugging bottles of water and dancing like a maniac.

I took my drink over to the dance floor to scope the lesbians. These days, I was beginning to understand what I liked; I wasn't interested in women like me – deceptively healthy-looking and just about able to pass for straight – I wanted someone who'd been around the block and knew who she was. I didn't care if feminism had passed her by, I just wanted a dyke who could fuck. I clocked Filchie almost immediately. She was standing in a corner, holding a pint and grinning at the throng of women. She was well built, with high cheekbones, deep-set eyes and a lived-in look. She had on a black silk waistcoat, dark jeans and a thick leather belt with a biker's buckle. I didn't need to check the length of her fingernails to be confident she could fuck for England.

I eased my way across the room until I was standing next to her. She didn't look at me, but her smile widened. A group of women jostled past and we were pushed together. Filchie snaked her arm around my shoulder. I leaned in. She smelt of beer and chip fat.

'Alright?' Her voice was low and husky.

Oh, yes.

'What's yer name then?'

'Finley.'

'Never heard that one before.'

'What do you do?' Stupid question; I cringed as soon as I'd asked it. At this point, I wouldn't have cared if she was a contract killer.

'Forklift truck driving. I'm qualified up to the hilt. You?'

I mumbled something about my job. When I stopped talking, she pulled me in and kissed me for a long time. She tasted sour and mature. My response was so strong I almost buckled.

'You gonna go with me tonight then, Finley?'

Oh yes.

She kissed me again and we stayed pressed together, and I knew the deal was sealed. I thanked my lucky stars that Marianne had offered me her flat; we needed to be alone for this.

Filchie swaggered into Marianne's place without a glance at the concierge. She renamed the cats Useless and Shitty and booted them out of the way. While I ran the oversized bath, she counted the row of expensive shirts hanging on the airer.

'How many people live here?'

'Just one,' I said sheepishly.

My butch wasn't quite so alluring without her clothes on. Her breasts sagged, there were large rolls of fat around her middle and she had quite a lot of difficulty getting herself into the tub. All the same, I was excited.

'You're perfect,' she said, gazing at my hirsute legs under the water. I slid lower, spreading my knees and holding her gaze while a flush of desire ran over my thighs.

She fucked me all night with her skilful, blunt fingers while I shook like a leaf in a thunderstorm. She went at it with such uncomplicated enthusiasm that I orgasmed more times than I thought biologically possible, and in between the bouts of lovemaking, she smoked roll-ups while I basked in her dirty laugh.

Her father, she said, was Māori. He came over during the war and had disappeared before she was born. Her mother once went to prison for stealing half a dozen placemats from a department store, and since she omitted to mention that she had a nine-year-old daughter at home, Filchie spent two weeks alone, stealing food from shops. She switched carrier bags to confuse things: an Asda bag in Woollies, a Co-op one in Tesco. 'So the stupid fuckers got done over twice, innit.'

She said she was into 'Egyptology' and I still didn't care when it transpired that her expertise amounted to reading a few pages of a book she'd pinched from the library the week before. I felt too ridiculous to mention my own education. With Filchie, I didn't think for a moment I'd come low. This time, I had landed.

At dawn, when I was sore and sated, she finally orgasmed, silently squeezing my ears between her thighs. Afterwards, she lifted her head to look at me, sucking in her bottom lip.

'Christ, no one ever done that to me before. Feels like I been hit over the head with a spade.'

I grinned. I had flipped a stone butch. When we got up, we discovered we'd pulled the bathtub right off the wall and Filchie asked me to be hers.

Luton

It turned out that my new lover didn't live in West London as I had supposed, but in Luton. Filchie was 'between places' and sleeping on a camper bed in her best friend's downstairs room. I made the journey to visit her the following weekend, timing my arrival just as the pubs were opening. I bought us pints of beer while she taught me how to play pool. She lined up all my shots, grasping me by the hips and telling me where to aim, and within half an hour she'd managed to get me to bounce a ball off the cushion and pot two in one go. A couple of solitary men eyed us from the bar, disgusted and entertained.

After a few weekends of this, I began to play in the backrooms of the London gay pubs, giving the butches and the gay boys a decent run for their money. It was all foreplay to me and Filchie, just something to while away the hours until we could go to bed. We fucked so hard I got nosebleeds and cystitis and a rash round my mouth, but no amount of fallout was going to slow us down.

On my fifth visit to Luton, while we lay naked and crushed together in Filchie's camper bed, I made up my mind I wanted to spend the rest of my life with her. I had no idea how delusional I was. Around noon, just as I was beginning to wonder where my underwear had got to, there was a tap on the door.

'*What?*' Filchie bellowed.

A young boy came in with two mugs of tea on a tray. Filchie

sat up and I snatched at the duvet to cover my breasts.

'Hiya, son, wotcha got for us?'

The boy knelt down by my side of the bed and put the tray on the floor. Now that his face was level with mine, I could see he wasn't a boy at all, but a grown man about my own age.

'I forgot you was coming to mend the television,' Filchie said, smacking her forehead.

'It's dead, ma, sorry. Nothing I can do.'

'Oh well, bugger off then, and don't let the door slap you on the arse.'

With a cheery wave to me and a pretend fart for his mother, he left us.

'How – how old is he?' I stuttered. 'I mean, how old are you?'

Those cheekbones had a lot to answer for. It turned out my bulldagger was twenty-five years older than me. Once the shock had worn off, I realised I didn't mind; you couldn't get sex this good with a novice. In fact, I could have forgiven Filchie almost anything and, over time, it turned out there was a lot to forgive: her vulgarity, her prejudice against her Asian neighbours, her criminal acquaintances. This was a world even I couldn't mess up and I was only dimly aware that my obsession with her was a furious rebuttal of my mother – a joyful attempt to oust Peggy by having a woman who actually liked me, in me.

It came as a surprise when I woke myself up sobbing in her bed in the middle of the night, overwhelmed by a baffling despair.

'Am I clamping you, babe?' Filchie asked, always ready to take the blame. 'I never seen you like this.'

I had no idea what was wrong. My lover couldn't figure me out either, but she held me and talked cheerful nonsense until my kaleidoscope of pain subsided.

When her friend moved a man into the house, Filchie stayed

for a while in a women's hostel until she was offered a council flat in Bushmead on account of her asthma and a dodgy knee. That lasted a few months and then she told me she'd moved to a room above an empty shop back in the centre of Luton. I never questioned these sudden transitions. As long as I could find her, as long as she would let me in, grab me by the belt and take me in her arms and whisper 'Babe' in that husky voice, I was content. I never for a moment doubted she'd be faithful to me, until, one day, I turned up and she wasn't there.

I arrived outside the shop and pressed the upstairs buzzer a few times, expecting her face to appear between the dingy net curtains. The flat stayed silent and still. I hammered on the door, shouted up at the windows, roamed the streets and eventually went back to her friend's. There was no answer there either. I spent the rest of the day walking up and down the shopping mall, searching the park, asking in the Jobcentre. When it got dark, I caught the train back to London, feeling exhausted and ill. I had lost her.

For the next few days, I lay on the sofa with Sappho, eating Sam's sweet potato casserole and crying. Marianne came over with a spinach pie, looking mystified. All this time, she thought I'd been having one of my meaningless flings, albeit an impressively long-lasting one.

'I mean, it was sex in a vacuum, wasn't it?' she said.

I hid my face. Oh, Filchie of the cheekbones and the blazing eyes, how could I ever explain you to my cultured friend? Nothing had ever worried Filchie; no amount of fucking was too much. It was the most thrilling, healing and wildly inappropriate liaison I'd ever had.

Some years later, one day when I was feeling nostalgic, I looked my bulldagger up on Facebook. There was just one post, a photograph taken in Maidenhead. She was standing in a yard in front of a washing line, wearing a Fair Isle jumper and a pair of sweatpants. She gazed unapologetically at the camera, hands in pockets, looking almost as I remembered her. At her feet was a basket of puppies.

My uncompromising butch, my lover who'd helped me simply by being the polar opposite of my mother. I messaged her and then I messaged her son, also on Facebook and now living with his boyfriend in Barcelona. Each time I checked, my messages remained unread. I couldn't help thinking Filchie must be ill or dead, and I mourned for her all over again.

Bleeding

Since my mother never told me about periods, it was left to the school to volunteer the bad news during a health education class. First we were taught the basics of digestion, which only added to our bewilderment. Our teacher drew a pink tube on the blackboard and then put in a scribble of green cabbage. A rather plump little girl held up her hand. 'Does your dinner and your pudding go down the same way?'

'Oh yes,' came the airy reply to groans of disgust.

The information on periods was met with silence. No doubt some girls had already started to bleed and others were in shock. We were told we must tell our mothers what we'd learnt and so, being an obedient child, I reported to Peggy that I now 'knew about periods'. She didn't respond, but the following weekend after the grocery shop, I found a packet of sanitary towels on my bed. It was over a year before I needed them and meantime they remained at the back of my underwear drawer, an uncomfortable reminder of what was to come.

When my first period finally arrived, Peggy showed me how to secure a sanitary towel to the special pair of knickers she'd bought. The knickers had press studs dangling from short lengths of plastic and the sanitary towels had holes punched into each end, through which the press studs could be snapped. The knickers were impracticably white, with a fake lace panel and a waterproof gusset, and since I only had one pair, I had to rinse out them out each night and try to dry them on the bathroom radiator before the following day. Peggy refused to buy me a second packet of towels when I asked.

'One lot should be more than enough for the month,' she said in a tone that implied I was being greedy.

Since I was still bleeding heavily when I got down to the final towel, I wrapped a plastic bag around the gusset of my knickers to make it last longer. The bag chafed the tops of my thighs, but at least it prevented any leaks. I used this method successfully every month until Peggy started buying me cheaper towels. Then, one afternoon, during Geography, I bled steadily through the thin towel, over the edges of the plastic bag, through my not-so-waterproof-after-all knickers and onto the back of my skirt. I watched the clock, feeling the blood ooze across my bottom and dreading the moment I'd have to stand up. Even now, if anyone asks me anything remotely geographical, I want to run away and hide.

When the bell rang, I got up carefully. There was a puddle of blood on the seat of my chair. I rubbed it with my fingers, leaving behind a grisly handprint. One of the more perceptive boys in the class noticed the state of me and gazed into my face with some concern. I hoped he thought I'd sat on the map pins.

I tied my jacket round my waist and got myself home as fast as I could. I washed out the knickers and my skirt and hid them in my wardrobe, along with the disgraced plastic bag, and spent the next seventeen hours dreading the dried blood I'd have to face on my school chair the following day.

When I pulled my chair out from my desk in the morning, the blood had disappeared. I felt faint with relief and I'll be forever grateful to the observant cleaner who must have dealt with it.

Jay

As soon as I felt better, I moved on to a job in a women's centre at the north end of Newham. The centre was at the top of a four-storey Victorian house on the high street and it was as unlike working in an office as it could have been. I loved the tiled fireplaces, the lofty ceilings and my spacious desk, which was set in front of one of the long windows looking out onto an ornate iron balcony. We had a collective of volunteers who planned the schedule and a seventy-year-old receptionist who protected us from out-of-hours punters with the ferocity of a mouse fending off a disgruntled cat. I often heard her reedy voice floating up the stairway: 'No, you may *not*, and I don't care how many times I have to tell you. I assure you I have nothing better to do with my day.'

My colleagues were a young and beautiful Muslim woman who translated for the Sylheti-speaking clients, a Nigerian housing advisor who wore a different wig every day of the week, and our white working-class manager who shared all her marriage troubles with us and let us go home early on Fridays. In lunchbreaks, the four of us sat round the gas fire with our jacket potatoes, putting the world to rights. Our manager tried to persuade me to train as an advisor, but I didn't want to do it. I felt safer typing up other people's pronouncements; even my mother couldn't have faulted my minutes.

At my first collective meeting, the room was packed three rows deep. I scribbled furiously, trying to keep up with the barrage of requests while trying to hide my disappointment. None of these women seemed interested in learning anything remotely feminist; they wanted bring-and-buy sales and cake-decorating classes and Spanish, not self-defence skills – let alone advice on self-insemination. When they began discussing an over-forties support group, I lost patience.

'What about one for lesbians?'

A ripple of discomfort went round the room.

'That's a bit niche, isn't it?' someone said.

'Newham does have a large population of lesbian women, apparently,' a middle-class voice came in. 'But I'm not sure...'

'Really? You never see them.'

'That's because they're all couch potatoes,' someone at the back said. 'And when one of them does go out, she sometimes forgets to write 'lesbian' on her forehead.'

The woman cackled and I craned to see. She was leaning back in her chair with one foot propped up on her knee, and when she flipped back her fringe, I couldn't ignore the tumble of curly hair. As I was gathering up my papers after the meeting, she came over to give me a pen I didn't remember dropping. She was short and stocky, with a cheeky grin and wide green eyes that matched her dungarees.

She stuck out her hand.

'Jay. Can I give you a lift home on the pretext of talking about the AGM?'

I looked at my watch. 'I don't finish for another couple of hours.'

She waved an arm. 'All that crap can wait until tomorrow.'

'Yes but—'

'I'll wait for you downstairs, big brain.' She gave me a piercing look and left the room.

Jay drove her Ford Fiesta as though she owned the road, which she may as well have done since the other drivers gave way to her. At Plaistow, she pulled out halfway across the junction, forcing a whole line of traffic to a standstill, and threw back her head to laugh. She boasted that she'd lived in Newham all her life and knew all the shortcuts, all the scams. I felt myself shrinking to accommodate her. Before she let me out of the car, she dug around in her bag for some flyers she wanted me to distribute. A tangled leather harness tumbled out onto the gearstick.

'Oops,' she said, giving me a fake innocent look.

I smirked awkwardly, fumbling with my seatbelt. She reached across to release me, her large breast nudging my arm.

'See you very soon.'

She did a rapid three-point turn and sped away. It was only as I was shutting the front door that it occurred to me that I'd never given her my address.

Hooked

The following week, we met in Last Out for a date. I arrived a few minutes late because Sappho had hidden my favourite hat.

'What time d'you call this?' Jay said, drawing up a chair. Seeing my face fall, she laughed.

She said she'd been on the shortlisting panel for my job and had 'virtually memorised' my CV. She thought I ought to have applied for the manager's job rather than 'just being a typist'. She was funny and assertive, and when I discovered she had her own flat and a good job with the council, I crossed my legs and simpered before taking myself off to the toilets to give myself a slap.

Jay got three fingers into me that night and as we lay naked on top of the duvet afterwards, I noticed two parallel scars down her breastbone.

I brushed my fingers across them. 'What happened here?'

'When I was a kid, my bones kept dislocating. I've got pins and screws all over the place. I would've been more like six foot if I hadn't come out of joint all the bloody time.'

I didn't know what to say.

Jay made me dress better, in tight-fitting T-shirts I never would've chosen for myself, trendy low-slung jeans and Converse trainers. She gave me advice on dealing with difficult situations at work and coaxed me into eating fish, which I'd always disliked, because she said every lesbian ought to enjoy it. My education began with a warm smoked salmon and cream cheese bagel with lemon and pepper from Ridley Road, followed by pair of whole rainbow trout, also from the market. Jay named them Tracy and Tanya before deftly cutting off their heads. Then we both got bacterial vaginosis and finally understood the real meaning of the poem about a dissolute lesbian who ends up 'with a fish smell all in her clothes'. Even gorging ourselves on strawberries didn't mask our nasty odour.

My lover introduced me to baked cheesecake from Brick Lane, Guinness punch and escovitch fish from the Plaistow Caribbean takeaway, and a place in Soho that served the biggest plates of fresh pasta I'd ever seen. These marathons of eating helped my anaemic, exhausted body; I put on a bit of weight, got my hair cut into a slick short back and sides, and felt sexy and loved.

Sam and Robbie were alarmed at how enthusiastically I was embracing this new affair.

'Don't make yourself too vulnerable too soon,' Robbie warned.

I wasn't worried. Jay didn't need to know I was a mess inside and if she, too, was pretending, I didn't want to know about that either.

Marianne was keen to meet my 'new permanent lover'. The three of us spent an afternoon in one of the arcades in central London, bashing frogs' heads and spinning fluorescent tokens across a backlit table. Jay treated my friend with a careful respect and when we went back to Marianne's for tea, she paid full attention to the cats, dragging them into her lap and forcing them to stay there – one bemused animal squashed firmly onto each of her solid thighs.

'You've gone up a notch with this one,' Marianne said when we were checking in over the phone afterwards.

'I hope so,' I said darkly. 'She's going to have to meet my mother soon.'

Joy

I'd come out to my mother just the year before. She was driving to Kent for a meeting and had dropped in on the way. She took a sharp breath at the state of Sam and Robbie's kitchen.

'Ooh – I couldn't live like this!' She began opening the kitchen cupboards, poking about for a dustpan and brush. 'What a mess.'

'Mam, it's not my house. You can't really start cleaning.'

She let the brush clatter to the floor and said she'd sit in the garden while I made her a coffee. I watched her through the window as I waited for the kettle to boil. My mother, adrift in an old deckchair, shielding herself from the weeds and the dog shit with her newspaper.

I took a tray outside and put the coffee down at her feet, kneeling beside her. My chest was thumping. I felt small on the grass, like a supplicant. I'd been building up to this for a while.

'Mam, I just want to let you know I'm a lesbian.'

There was a short pause; then, without lifting her eyes from the paper, Peggy said, smugly, 'I know.'

I was crushed – nothing I'd ever said to my mother would have given her any clue about my personal life. She didn't know Dan and Marianne had both been my lovers; she had no idea about Filchie or all the other women I'd been taking to bed over the last few years. I'd always imagined she thought I was too dull to be having sex at all.

I pulled myself up. I wasn't about to let her take the wind out of my sails. 'You know, the first time a lover put her fingers in me, it was such a joy—'

I stopped, shocked at what had just come out of my mouth. I couldn't believe I'd said something so personal, let alone to my mother. I glanced furtively at her. She hadn't reacted, her eyes were still on the article she was reading. I waited. After a moment, she shook out her newspaper and turned the page as though I hadn't said a thing.

The Bradford silence had descended.

Darts

I'd only gone back to Bradford once since I got involved with Jay, when Chad and Peggy were away on holiday. It had given me time to recover from lesbian London without having to deal with my parents and it was an easy train ride to Salford to have lunch with Ruby and catch up with Anish. This summer, my father was taking himself off to a hotel on the coast to learn how to swim and Peggy was going to Dudley to meet a friend she used to work with, before she and Chad caught a flight to visit Charles, so I offered to house-sit again. My brother was still living in various parts of Europe, where, Peggy told me over the phone, he was building an empire as a property mogul and dating one of Italy's top female bankers. She reckoned he'd be a millionaire soon.

'He's really come good,' she said, with a mixture of grudging admiration and disbelief. I thought of the photograph she'd shown me of a tired-looking man with sad eyes and a collapsed chest. He looked like he'd sold out.

My housesitting plan was almost spoiled when Peggy said she wanted me to break my journey to Bradford to meet her and her friend for dinner. I'd come to realise that while my mother criticised me to my face, behind my back she boasted about her Oxford graduate daughter working in the metropolis. I couldn't live up to that for a whole evening, so I told her it would be too much of a detour to travel to Dudley.

'You're letting us both down,' Peggy said, angrily. 'But I suppose if you won't, you won't.'

I offered a compromise. If Jay agreed to come to Bradford with me, we could drive to Birmingham to meet Peggy for lunch and still get to the house before dark.

'If that's all you have time for, I suppose it will have to do,' my mother sniffed.

On the way up the motorway, Jay interrogated me about my parents. The more I shared, the more delighted she became. I told her about Peggy's distaste for small children and the long-running affair she'd been having with the headmaster of a school she was now working in. My father was oblivious; he'd once told me he was banished upstairs while Peggy and her headmaster 'worked on the equal opportunities policy' in the lounge. It was only when Jay snorted that I saw the funny side of it. I was about to tell her about the Greenham debacle, too, when I was distracted by the spectacle of my lover removing her tampon at sixty miles an hour. She whooped as she threw it out of the window at a boy racer.

We got to Birmingham in good time and while Jay looked for a parking space, I went into the station to find my mother. She was standing by the departures board, looking irritated. She wouldn't meet my eye.

'Where is she then, this woman you seem to think so much of?'

Jay appeared on cue. She strode over and gave me a firm kiss on the mouth. She'd changed into cargo pants and a florid shirt and I could feel Peggy taking in her size and almost, but not quite, blenching. I couldn't help thinking that Jay was the polar opposite of my mother: cheerful, charismatic and fat.

My lover held out her hand with an amused expression. 'Hello, Peggy, how are you today?'

'Very happy to see my daughter,' my mother said, sounding anything but.

'She's lovely, isn't she?' Jay grinned, turning to me. 'Want a cigarette, Fin?'

'You're not smoking?' Peggy glared at me.

'*She* got *me* into it,' Jay lied. 'She loves having one in the morning, after—'

She clamped her lips together, eyes twinkling. Peggy looked apoplectic. She grabbed my sleeve and began to steer me out of the station.

'Where are we eating? Come on, I'm starving.'

Outside on the concourse, she pointed at a glass-fronted restaurant that had a salad bar in the window. 'That'll do.'

I looked round for Jay. The sight of the restaurant had wiped the grin off her face. '*It's for tourists*,' she hissed.

'I know.' I disentangled myself from Peggy so I could speak lower. 'But the quicker we find somewhere to eat, the sooner we can leave.'

Peggy had already disappeared into the restaurant. When I caught up with her, she began talking to the air in the way she always did when she was trying to wrest back a sense of control.

'What they're doing to Bradford town centre is appalling and our MP is an absolute shit. I cannot abide him.'

I wasn't listening; I was thinking of what I'd said to her in the garden when I came out to her. Why the hell had I told her that?

Jay had already signalled for the waiter. He showed us to a table and the pair of them began dissecting the progress of the local football team. Peggy raised her eyebrows at them and pinched my arm.

'How's Marianne and Dan? Such lovely people. They're both working – doing well, I expect? Is your friend here going to join us any time soon?'

Jay glowered, snatching up the menu. She ordered *spaghetti alle vongole* and a hot chocolate, followed by apple pie with ice cream.

'A salad,' Peggy snapped when the lad turned to her. He slunk away, chastised. My mother pulled a newspaper out of her handbag and tried to make me help her with the crossword.

'Give us a clue, Peggy!' Jay said.

Peggy ignored her.

'Jay's good at this sort of thing, Mam,' I tried, pawing at her arm. I was falling apart.

Our meals arrived and my mother launched into a long diatribe against John Major, while Jay slurped on her spaghetti. Whenever Peggy paused to get my reaction, Jay waved a forkful of her dinner in front of my face. All three of us ate at top speed and, as soon as our plates were cleared, and before Peggy had chance to order her customary coffee, Jay asked pointedly if she needed a lift anywhere.

'No, thank you. I thought you said traffic was bad.'

'So I did,' Jay laughed.

Peggy got up and pushed her way to the counter to pay the bill. I went after her, leaving Jay to tip the waiter. My mother had her back turned, but I caught sight of her reddened nose, the glistening of a tear.

I was horrified; I'd never known Peggy to be vulnerable.

'Mam,' I said softly. My heart was suddenly breaking and at the same time I felt a sliver of hope. If Peggy was this upset, perhaps she'd understand how awful I felt all the time.

'Mam...'

'What?!' She wheeled round, stony-faced.

'Nothing,' I murmured, suddenly afraid.

She stuffed her purse and her newspaper into her bag and gave me a brittle hug. 'I suppose that's it then. Two hours' journey for an hour with my daughter. Well, look after yourself.'

Before my mother was quite out of earshot, Jay announced loudly that she was desperate for a shag.

We spent the week in Bradford playing darts in the lounge

and having sex in every room. To Jay's delight, there was a photograph of Peggy and her headteacher lover on a motorbike, pinned up next to a map of the Pennines. No doubt Peggy had calculated that she could get away with it, since Chad had sketches of Barb next to a barn tacked up all over the place. Jay scoffed at my father's work, calling it 'daubs' and imitating what she imagined to be my father's whining: 'Peggeee, I want my cereal! I want my toy-toy, Peg-peg!'

I giggled and told her it was short for Peggotty.

'*Peggotty!* Maggotty Peggotty – oh, that's *priceless!*' She laughed her forced, insolent laugh and I suddenly wished I hadn't said anything.

At the end of the week, Jay threw a dart that missed the board by several inches and tore a hole in Peggy's lover's head.

Jesus

In the summer holiday before I moved on to high school, I had an invitation from the twins to go to an afternoon barbecue. My pre-teen horniness had been growing at the same rate as my hormonal fluctuations and who knew what a person could get up to in a wood.

The twins arranged to meet me at the shopping centre in Manningham, where we were to wait for a private coach that would take us to the forest park. It was the same bus stop I went to after my ballet classes, directly opposite the entrance to the precinct. The body of one of Peter Sutcliffe's victims had been discovered on nearby wasteland and while all the other parents were ushering their precious children into cars, I strolled along the unlit walkway in my ribbons and pink tights to wait for the number 96 bus, less than quarter of a mile from the murder scene. Peggy had started reading *Spare Rib* and fancied herself a bit of a feminist.

'The police shouldn't be telling women to stay at home,' she parroted. 'It's *men* who should be kept in; *they're* the ones under suspicion.'

It reminded me of the time I'd run away to Heaton Woods to avoid being taken for a haircut. Just as I was about to disappear in between the trees, a comfortable-looking woman in an apron had called to me from her front gate. She asked if I was new to the area and didn't I know there were strange men about? I said I liked playing by the quarry. She shouted after me that she hadn't wanted to seem interfering; presumably that would have been a worse fate than my abduction.

The twins were already waiting when I arrived. They had freshly washed hair and sensible shoes, and they frowned at my pencil skirt and messy new perm. I'd had it done after Peggy tried to prettify my hair in a brief fit of interest, ineptly tying up my split ends in a bit of white ribbon while I rolled my eyes. I'd pulled the ribbon out the minute she turned her back; it didn't match the ugliness inside me.

We boarded the coach, which was already full of pink-faced, eager-looking kids wearing transparent rain capes and chunky sandals. I didn't know which school they were from, but they had no dress sense to speak of. It wasn't until we'd turned into a country lane and were getting off in the car park that I took in the full extent of the corduroy. We gathered around a clearing on the edge of the woods and while two of the older lads began to pile up branches to make a fire, a couple of the adults produced guitars. The whole group sat down and, right on cue, everyone started to sing.

> *What a friend we have in Jesus*
> *All our sins and griefs to bear...*

Subterfuge! I'd been brought on false pretences to a Christian camp! The corduroy was explained and I was outraged. My parents were atheists; Charles and I had been brought up not just to dismiss the idea of an afterlife, but to view people with any kind of spiritual belief at all as completely dim-witted. Much as I knew the twins wanted to save me, I'd never imagined they'd dare to try and convert me.

There was no way I was going to sit through an afternoon of sappy God songs, so while the twins were unpacking tubs of pasta salad from their rucksacks I made my escape into the woods. I thought I'd get as far away from the camp as I dared while still being able to find my way back when the coach was due to leave, since I had no idea where we were. I wandered a little way along a path between the trees and sat down on a fallen tree trunk. I felt sullied by this unexpected rendezvous with Jesus and I was still attempting to re-establish the Wilson sense of invincibility, when I became aware of shouting somewhere beyond the trees.

Four or five lads appeared, thrashing their way through the nettles. I felt a shiver of relief. It wasn't the Christians coming after me, just some local louts. They tossed a couple of sticks in my direction and when I didn't react, they moved closer and began to mess around near my tree trunk, shoving each other about and exclaiming in Bradford accents so broad even I couldn't understand what they were saying: 'Ayeaye, 'ere'sanuttergadabout!'

I felt my hair being whipped up from behind, and one of the lads leapt over the trunk and sat down next to me, plonking his hand into my lap. I shot up and pushed him away, but as I turned to leave, he reached an arm round my waist and grabbed hold of me between the legs, growling 'Owsabow'tit' like a junior Jimmy Saville. I stumbled for a moment, then elbowed him off and took to my heels.

They didn't come after me, though I could hear them whooping and crashing about beyond the trees. I slowed to a walk and began to giggle. I supposed I ought to have been scared – there were several of them and only one of me – but I only felt a hysterical sort of elation.

For the rest of the weekend, I was in a frenzy. This was even better than my fantasies about Juicy Lucy; a real boy had actually groped me. I lay on the carpet, hidden between the old twin beds, the same bit of carpet where I'd spilled orange squash and poster paints and biscuit crumbs, and masturbated myself into oblivion. The twins' civilising attempt to bring me to God had provided me with the biggest burst of sexual arousal I'd ever experienced.

Undone

Before long, I was spending so much of my time with Jay that I hardly saw anything of Sam and Robbie. If I came across them in the kitchen making Barleycrap, they were distant and polite, tying their dressing gowns and hurrying back upstairs as though I no longer deserved to be treated to the sight of their lesbian breasts. On the rare nights I wasn't out with my lover, I lay on my bed listening to their laughter and the hiss of beer cans floating up from the back garden. Sometimes they had friends over and lit candles or built a fire, and someone would strum on a guitar. I had the uncomfortable feeling I wouldn't be welcome to join them anymore, especially not if they overheard what my lover called them when they wore their identical plaid shirts.

'Aw, don't worry about it,' she said. 'You don't need the amoeba. They're so loaded they don't need to work, you know. They just do it to look cool. They don't care about you or anyone else.'

I opened my mouth to protest, then shut it again. Jay seemed so sure about everything and it was true she had enough friends for us both. I was invited to everything: clubbing nights out with rowdy women and Eurovision nights in with gay men and junk food. Wherever we went, Jay chatted to everyone. I watched her tease and flatter, and it was a while before I realised she didn't actually like anyone. In private, dropping the charm, she was scathing.

'Load of idiots, the lot of them. Total losers.'

I tried not to think how much she reminded me of Chad.

My bike was another thing Jay thought I didn't need. She changed the brake blocks and gave it a thorough oil, and suggested we sell it. There was no question, these days, of me cycling anywhere, not even to the tube to go and see Marianne. Jay collected me from work and drove me wherever I wanted to go. She would come in and lean over my desk to check my schedule. 'Oh no, you've got a meeting with Jobsworth Suckyface tomorrow, hahaha.'

We went to Amsterdam, San Francisco, Hebden Bridge and then to Eressos, Lesvos, where Sappho was born. *'The poet, not the dog,'* we explained in unison to friends. I didn't tell Jay how much I struggled with headaches and depression during these trips, nor that I was starting to feel like I didn't know where I ended and she began. I didn't even tell her when I got the monthly period pain that had me doubled up in bed, though she loved it if I asked her for help. Once, after I'd mentioned I had nowhere to store my books, she turned up with a drill and some MDF to make shelves for my room. She bore steadily into the wall, snickering when she discovered she'd gone right through into the bathroom and pretending she could see Sam and Robbie in the tub. I stood by, sick to my stomach with an anxiety I couldn't fathom.

On my birthday, when I told her I didn't like marzipan, she dumped the cake she'd bought me into the bin. She persuaded me to get my nipple pierced as her present to me and was annoyed when I said it was too sore for her to play with. She said she wanted to watch me having sex with a friend of ours 'as a treat'. I said I didn't fancy it.

'I didn't think you'd be so uptight,' she countered. She said she used to leave her previous lover tied up while she went to watch a show in the West End and they were both gagging for it by the time she got back. I cried and said maybe we should split up, and Jay replied calmly that she'd take her own life if I ever left her.

After one particularly bad argument and a bitter round of make-up sex, I returned to an empty house and a note from Sam. She and Robbie had gone on holiday, and someone would be coming in to feed Sappho. I sat in the front room, tearful and shivering. I had no idea when they'd be back and I hadn't even been trusted to look after their dog. Also, I didn't know how to turn on the central heating.

For the first time in months, I phoned Dan. I thought I could ask him to sit in my room while I sorted through the pile of clothes that had accumulated on the floor. I couldn't face doing it alone and Sam and Robbie need never know a man had been in the house. Dan sounded distant and vague; he had plans for the evening already – things in the air.

'Anyway, I don't understand this way of life you've chosen,' he added. 'I can't go to the clubs you go to and, most of the time, I'm not even welcome in your home.'

I felt a stab of remorse and when I put the phone down, I couldn't help feeling I'd thrown away something precious.

'Aw, poor chicken,' Jay said when I reported back. 'Tell him you would pop into one of his rich white man's clubs, only you might choke on the privilege.'

The following afternoon, while Jay was taking her car for a repair, I took Sappho out for a walk. I thought I could at least prove I was capable of doing that, though she was so mad to get to the squirrels I had to wrap the lead round my waist to avoid being dragged straight out into the traffic. I unleashed her on the common and as I watched her tear away across the grass, I had the queasy sense that my life was unravelling.

I turned away to look for a bench and saw a familiar figure coming towards me with a tiny white dog on a lead. His face lit up as he got closer.

'Finley, oh my goodness, it's you! How are you?'

'I'm good, good...' I lied.

Sebastian Angel shook his finger at me. 'First-Class Honours – well done, you! It's what we all expected of you.'

I stared at my feet, embarrassed. That seemed like a lifetime ago.

He bent to unclip his dog and the tiny piece of fluff made a few half-hearted attempts to hump his leg before tripping away to sniff at a twig. I surveyed my old lover out of the corner of my eye as we ambled after her. The same angelic hair, the same silver rings and manicured fingernails, and the same neat blue jeans. He'd hardly aged at all, whereas I felt about two hundred years old.

He told me he was doing childcare for his sister's kids for a couple of days. I smiled awkwardly; I'd had no idea he had a sister, let alone that she lived in Newham. He said he'd almost given up lecturing and was now 'a pianist and a potterer', still living in the same house with the other Sebastian. As a sideline, he made personalised wedding hats.

'It sounds idyllic,' I said, trying not to sound upset.

'Yes, I suppose it is.'

I lied about my wonderful housemates and my interesting job. I didn't mention Jay.

'Well, here we are.' He indicated a house facing onto the common. 'Quick cup of tea? The boys won't be back from school for a while yet.'

I nodded, feeling shy, and we retrieved our dogs.

The house was open-plan, airy and immaculate. Sappho scuttered round the kitchen and living room, then settled down on a doormat by the French windows. The little bit of fluff sat in Sebastian's lap while we drank our herbal teas.

Sebastian Angel tutted, leaning forward to put her on the floor. 'Silly thing, you're getting hair all over my trousers!'

I gazed at the nape of his neck, feeling a stab of longing. It occurred to me that I was incapable of being alone with him without wanting to suck his cock. The odds were good that he'd be incapable of resisting. He sat back and my hand was on his thigh, helping to brush off the dog hairs. It crept to his flies and, before long, we were both undone.

His timing was still impeccable. We were finished and decent again, and sitting decorously at opposite ends of the sofa by the time the door opened and two teenaged boys tumbled in. They threw down their sports bags and kicked off their shoes before they spotted us.

'Ooh, look at the lovebirds,' the bigger boy said with uncanny intuition.

I felt myself flush and, as soon as the boys had disappeared upstairs, I made my excuses to leave. I hesitated at the door.

'Can I see you again?'

Sebastian Angel shook his head, dropping his gaze. 'You hurt me. You left without saying anything and I was depressed for a whole year. I can't go through that again.'

My gut twisted. I'd never imagined I could have that effect on anyone.

'But I'm older now. It would be different.'

The plea was out of my mouth before I could stop it. It was unfair of me to ask; I was no more stable now than I had been ten years ago and I was in no doubt at all that I'd mess him about all over again. But I'd panicked, feeling him starting to withdraw. I wanted so much to be the kind of person who could make it work with this delicate little man.

'We could at least try,' I looked at him imploringly, feeling him clamp shut.

'No, this has to be a goodbye.'

Shamefaced, I gave him a last, dry peck on the cheek. Suddenly, I couldn't wait to get away. I prayed he wouldn't tell the other Sebastian about me; the bad penny that had turned up again.

Back in my bedroom, I unearthed a page of calligraphy Sebastian Angel had put under my door when we first became lovers. I cried, pressing his words to my face. The past, without me in it, looked so wholesome. The following day, I tweaked the wording a bit and sent it in to a competition I'd seen in one of Sam's magazines for the most romantic love letter.

I won fifty pounds.

Move

The day after my transgression with Sebastian Angel, Jay came to pick me up. We were supposed to be meeting some friends of hers in the pub, but as soon as we'd driven out of sight of Sam and Robbie's, I asked her to stop the car. I told her what I'd done.

'Okay, okay...' She stared straight ahead, clutching the steering wheel. 'He's gone now though, so we'll be alright.'

'I don't know, Jay. We need to talk.'

She turned in her seat to face me. 'Move in with me.'

My mouth fell open. 'No, I—'

'Let's go back now and get your stuff.' She gave me her fake innocent look. 'Yes. Move in.'

I couldn't help laughing; she was like a child asking for more sweets, but even while she held my hand, I got the feeling I was treading on eggshells.

'Okay,' I patted her arm, trying to buy myself some time. 'Let me sort my head out tonight and we can meet up after work tomorrow and figure it out.'

To my surprise, she agreed and let me go. As the car sped away, I felt suddenly bereft. Without Jay, I had less idea than ever who I was.

In the morning when I wheeled my bike out of the gate, I saw her car parked opposite. She was staring at me through the driver's window. I tapped my watch. I needed to get to work and we both knew it was quicker by bike at this time of day. She indicated that she'd follow me.

I got on my bike and cycled off, feeling her at my back all the way through Newham. My heart was thumping by the time I got to work. What the hell did she want? She parked up and came over holding out a piece of paper with an address scribbled on it. I noticed a large bruise on her arm.

'It's nothing, Aikido practice. Here, let's just see a therapist and sort this.'

I let out a sigh of relief. A therapist. Why hadn't I thought of that myself? Jay had made us an emergency appointment for the following day.

The therapist was a small, soft-looking woman, wearing a flowery dress and a long string of beads. She led us into her consulting room, where she'd given herself a large armchair, and pointed us to two rickety folding chairs. As soon as we sat down, we started to snigger. The therapist frowned and we fell apart, shoulders shaking like naughty schoolchildren. Once I got a grip on myself and saw that Jay wasn't going to take the lead, I decided to take things into my own hands. I thought if I explained to this dumpy little woman that there'd been something deeply wrong with me for as long as I could remember, she would discover what it was and put it right. I didn't care how she did it, as long as it didn't mean I had to wear a dress like hers.

I recounted one of my earliest childhood memories, of sitting on a chair in front of the bread roll, feeling profoundly anxious.

'Something to do with the breast, perhaps?' the therapist said, sounding grave.

Jay rolled her eyes and I had to work hard not to start laughing again. Was she really going to pathologise us for liking breasts? It was the kind of Freudian interpretation my mother would have loved. I began again, telling her what a difficult, unhappy baby I'd been.

'Were you colicky?' she tried.

'Oh, for fuck's sake,' Jay muttered, wiping her arm across her mouth so the therapist didn't hear.

I may not have known what I was reaching for, but I knew this woman was way off the mark. I wondered about telling her about Chad's hand down my knickers, to see how she'd react to that, but I thought better of it. She might decide I was a lesbian because of my father. I changed tack.

'I feel a bit stifled; me and Jay do everything together. I guess I want more space.'

The therapist looked at Jay.

'I *try* to give her space,' Jay said.

The therapist reached into her pocket and threw a bunch of keys on the floor near Jay's feet. 'Try to pick those up.'

I stiffened. It was a bad move, attempting to outsmart my lover. Jay bent down, but instead of scooping up the keys in her hand, she unlaced her trainer, removed it, took off her sock and tried to hook the keys between her toes. It was impossible not to watch. I gritted my teeth, overcome with mirth, and the therapist looked like thunder.

'Alright,' she said after a few moments. 'Point taken.'

This surrender had a strange effect on Jay. She began to open up. She talked about her childhood in a block of flats overlooking Clayton Pond, the chess games she'd pretended to know how to play with the neighbour's son, her solitary tree climbing. She went on to describe how, at twelve, she discovered that she'd been adopted by her grandmother, that the girl she'd believed to be her older sister was, in fact, her mother.

I was astounded. I'd met Jay's supposed mother many times, seen the birthday cards that always read *'To my Dear Daughter from your Loving Mum'*. I had a sudden suspicion that Jay enjoyed making her revelation this way, knowing I'd be too embarrassed to admit it was the first I'd heard of it. I felt a quiver of fear. I'd entered a roomful of family secrets and I was in danger of getting shut in.

At the end of our fifty minutes, the therapist said we had a lot of work to do and that this was only the beginning.

'Yep,' Jay said brightly. 'Lots of work to do.'

I knew from her tone we wouldn't be going back. I was still trembling as we got into the car.

'That was a pile of shit.' Jay switched on the ignition and revved the engine, and we both sniggered again.

Back in my room, we threw ourselves into sex, wiping out the disapproving gaze of the therapist, but our lovemaking was more disconnected than ever. Jay's eyes looked empty and cold. As soon as we finished, she began to cry. She told me she suspected that her much older brother, now in jail, was actually her father. It would explain why she'd had such a problem with her joints: the bad genes.

I held her hand, shocked. 'What can I do? This is serious, Jay.'

'Nothing, don't touch me. I wish I hadn't told you.'

She turned her back on me and as she fell asleep, I heard her mumble something that sounded like, '*I could punch you black and blue*'.

Something inside me stilled and went numb.

Legacy

My father grew up in a rural village in the East Riding, where his parents worked as farm labourers. Peasants really, he used to say, shaking his head. They were both dead before I was born, but Chad once showed me the only photograph he had of them, taken on my parent's wedding day. My grandfather is a little man with a humped back and a sun-darkened face; only the top of his forehead is pale where he has removed his cap. My grandmother is also very short and her white knitted cardigan is hanging off one shoulder. Beside them, my mother's parents look smart and cross.

Chad wasn't yet twenty-one when he met my mother. He liked to tell me in a tone of fake dejection that he'd 'had to get a letter from his mum' to marry her, because he hadn't quite reached the age of majority.

He had one sibling, a brother, twenty years older than him. His brother had a bad war and was found dead in a bedsit surrounded by cigarette butts and empty beer bottles. I suspected that Chad carried some shame about this, as well as the discovery that my grandparents had married only three months before his own birth, making him precariously close to being a bastard. He told me that although his father could name all the plants that grew in the fields and hedgerows, he hadn't been able to read or write. He was a man of few words and when

Chad's mother died, he'd said only, 'She's gone then, boy.'

It was no wonder then that my father, though highly emotional himself, couldn't bear for me or Charles to have any feelings. Peggy was the same. If either us let slip any sign that we were angry or unhappy, the Bradford silence would descend. Chad's heart and Peggy's face would close down as though a curtain had fallen, and my brother and I would be left to manage our upset for ourselves, bewildered and unseen.

But my father loved to tell me stories of his own childhood. He was allowed to run in and out of the neighbours' houses as much as he liked, and at one time he owned a pet raven whose leg he kept tied to a tree branch. He was taken every year to the cinema in Pocklington, where he once laughed so hard a toffee flew out of his mouth and stuck in the back of his aunt's hair. He fell hopelessly in love with his cousin Dottie. I had her eyes, apparently.

'The Wilsons always had rugged good looks,' he told me, half tongue in cheek, half wanting to believe it.

When he was fourteen, his mother had a stroke and lay alone on the bathroom floor until nightfall. After that, Chad was sent to live with his aunts and uncles who ran the village pub. He drank beer out of the slop trays, developed a talent for darts, and learned to keep backgammon scores in his head because the old men trusted him more than they trusted each other. Just once, he admitted to me that no one had ever hugged him.

When Chad was accepted into college to train as an art teacher, my grandfather understood that his son would need books, and so he bought a set of twelve encyclopaedias from a travelling salesman. For the whole of my childhood, these heavy volumes, with their dark-green cloth covers and faint columns of tiny print, sat unread on a home-made bookshelf outside my bedroom door – a legacy of my grandfather's greatest attempt to love his son.

Siege

I told Jay over the phone that I wanted us to finish. She sounded reasonable about it and ended the call more quickly than I'd expected. I felt the sinking sensation again; I was back on my desert island, isolated and exposed.

The next day she was waiting outside when I finished work. She'd had her hair cut and was wearing a new pair of skinny jeans that didn't suit her. She barred my way.

'Four years! Almost four fucking years you're going to throw away?'

'Don't, Jay. Leave me alone.' I hurried to unlock my bike, half dragging it to the kerb while Jay tried to grab hold of my back wheel. As I pedalled away, I knew she was following me in the car. I jumped a couple of red lights and lost her in the traffic. Five minutes after I got home, she was hammering on the front door. Sam appeared at the top of the stairs.

'What's going on?'

'Oh gosh, you're back. I've broken up with Jay and she's losing it. *Please* don't let her in.'

I hid in my room until the hammering stopped. An hour later, when I went down to retrieve my bike from where I'd flung it down, I saw she'd punctured both tyres and gouged holes in my saddle. I thought of the pen knife she kept in her pocket.

Sam and I nailed an old blanket over the door so she wouldn't be able to peer through the frosted glass if she came back. The next morning, half the blanket had been pulled out through the letterbox and cut to shreds; the spare T-shirts and boxer shorts I kept at Jay's flat were strewn across the path.

Over the next few weeks, she turned up at all hours, banging on the front door and the bay window, throwing stones up at Sam and Robbie's bedroom and yelling for me to come out. I went to stay with Ruby for a few days to get a break. When I got back, Marianne told me she'd come home late one night to find an old crate in her lobby, surrounded by cigarette butts. Jay must have persuaded the concierge to let her in and waited there for hours, thinking that was where I would go. I thanked my lucky stars I'd never told her about my friends in Salford.

'You've got to leave,' Robbie said eventually, hard-faced. 'Our bedroom is at the front of this house and we're living under siege.'

I wasn't going to argue.

The housing officer at work helped me to apply for a council flat on the grounds that I couldn't stay where I was due to harassment.

'We all knew there was something wrong,' she said, tutting as she went through the forms. 'You been lookin' so stressed these days.'

I spelled out Jay's surname and she gave it a male prefix. All this time she'd somehow remained oblivious to the fact that my lover was one of the women in the collective. When she began her supporting letter, I asked her to correct it.

She paused and stared at me. 'I thought we was dealing with a big man!'

'People get confused,' I said, hating myself, 'because she looks like a man.'

Queensway

I was given a temporary bedsit in a square just off Queensway in West London, about as far away as I could get from Newham and Jay's fury, and just three stops from Marianne. It was on the first floor of a dilapidated Victorian house, in between the backpacker hotels and the sex workers' flats. When I strolled up through the crowds of tourists to sit in Kensington Gardens, I had the old, familiar sense of a double identity: I felt like a wretch and yet there was an Italian strawberry ice cream in my hand.

I didn't have a clue what to do with myself. I paced the streets, trying to convince myself that this was a holiday, that I didn't feel lost or weirdly fizzy inside. The only thing I felt sure about was that I was never again going to let someone bully me like Jay had.

Sam and Robbie forwarded a letter from her. It told me in no uncertain terms to return everything she'd ever given me. I jumped into action, upending rucksacks and holdalls, snatching up her expensive gifts and stuffing them into a bin liner: the patterned boxer shorts because she'd liked the way my arse looked in them, a silk vest to show off my yoga arms, a dressing gown because I'd never had one as a kid, argyle socks for my permanently cold feet. Once I'd purged my belongings, I sat on the edge of the bed and scanned the room with the nervous tension of a sniper. I had a feeling there was one last thing. I looked down at what I was wearing; my vest and jeans, my rings, my boots – what was it? I leapt to my feet to tear off my belt.

Without Jay, I couldn't even keep my own trousers up.

Meanwhile, Marianne was going through her own turmoil. One evening, as we sat on her patio, she told me she was taking anti-depressants and had been seeing a therapist for over a year. She hadn't wanted to tell me while I was in the middle of my relationship meltdown. It made no sense to me that my clever, cool friend, who never seemed fazed by anything, should be having such difficulty. She explained she'd come to recognise the shadowy shape that seemed to touch her leg when she was falling asleep.

'It was a flashback, Fin. It was my uncle.'

I hugged her, feeling her quiet distress and my own guilt. All this time, while I'd been lavishing attention on my troublesome lover, Marianne had been going through hell. I promised to get her a copy of the survivor's self-help book we had in the women's centre.

'Anyway,' she said, putting it all away. 'How are you?'

I took a breath. 'With everything you're dealing with, do you ever feel suicidal?'

'No, I've never thought like that.'

I despised myself for feeling disappointed. But if Marianne never felt like taking her own life after what she'd been through, why the hell did everything feel so unbearable to me?

There's an upside to depression if it lets you stay in bed wanking all day while normal people go to work. Back in Queensway, I treated myself to a fresh bottle of lube and some lesbian porn from OOh! and in between the bouts of numbness and fear, I had a reasonable time of it. It helped that my temporary accommodation turned out to be attractive to guests.

Ruby managed a brief visit and I finally admitted to the number of lovers I'd had over the years.

'What on earth have you been looking for?' she asked, astonished.

I had no idea. Ruby had grown into herself these days and would never understand my disordered life.

Dan came over and told me about his new bike, his new Latina lover, his soon-to-be-published book of poetry. 'I've got more energy than anyone I know,' he said. 'And I understand what makes a good poem. And I feel very relaxed about sex these days.'

If I hadn't been so exhausted, I would have thumped him.

Anish said he would have visited, too, but he was working in a lab that kept him up all night with his hands plunged into vats of inexplicable gunge. I comforted myself with the thought that this was a tribute to the home-made concoctions I used to force him to drink when we were kids. Then, even Peggy threatened to come. I spoke to her from a phone box stuffed with business cards displaying cartoon pictures of women that looked like Barbie.

'I could drive down right now. She won't dare bother you if I'm there.' She seemed to have forgotten that Jay hadn't been in the slightest bit intimidated by her. Either that or she wanted to get away because Chad was having another affair. I tried to think of an excuse, but she beat me to it.

'Hang on, though – would she slash my tyres?'

'Oh, probably.'

Having avoided a solo visit from my mother, I agreed to fly out to France to meet her and Chad and my brother at an apartment Peggy had booked for the week. A family holiday could hardly be weirder than the way things were going for me already.

Ponce

For such a dysfunctional household, our family Christmases had very little melodrama. Chad would wake me and Charles at 5am, almost as excited as we were about opening our presents. He wore his green towelling dressing gown with a white trim for the event, and with his veined cheeks and bristly beard, he looked like an off-colour Santa Claus. He bought me good stuff: a box of pipe cleaners in various sizes and colours to twist into animal shapes, a plastic contraption that could be made to weave wool into long scarves, a set of paints.

When my mother came down, she would scoff at these treasures and tell Chad he'd spent far too much, but the arguments and the door slamming were put on hold for the day. Chad would drive over to Wetherby to pick up my mother's parents and the turkey and puddings my grandmother had spent days preparing. I can picture her in her tiny unheated kitchen, nose dripping, fingers red from the cold, making sweet pastries and pies while my grandfather sits by the fire in the front room with his crosswords and the television. He loved watching Formula One motor car crashes; the more catastrophic the pile-up, the more he shook with suppressed laughter.

At lunch, my grandfather would praise the tenderness of the meat and my grandmother would fall asleep in her paper hat, wanting only the Queen's speech to make her day complete.

Every year, when my father leapt to his feet to mock-salute the national anthem, my grandmother would startle awake like a bewildered gnome.

She was a nervous woman, with furtive black eyes and Raynaud's – a circulation problem I seemed to have inherited from her. She'd escaped from a family of ten with an alcoholic father to marry my grandfather on the same day her sister, Amelia, was admitted to the asylum where she would spend the rest of her life. My grandmother begged Peggy to let her take me to visit, but my mother always said no – I could only go if my father agreed. She knew her mother would never dare ask Chad.

'She's frightened of men,' Peggy told me smugly.

My mother's childhood was more opaque to me than Chad's. I knew she was an only child and that she'd always wanted to be in charge. My grandmother told me Peggy used to corral all the kids in the street to sit in front of her toy blackboard and recite the alphabet, while she waved her arms about and told them off.

Peggy hated being working class. Although there were various great aunts and uncles living just twenty minutes away in Armley, we didn't visit them and they were never invited to ours. If I had other relatives, cousins nearer to my own age, I never knew of them. My mother had to feel superior; it was bad enough living in a less-than-middle-class street – our vulgar relatives would only bring her down.

'Look at scruffy Jean O'Reilly,' she would say in a pleased voice when she saw our neighbour going past with her shopping bag. 'See how old she looks.'

'Ponce!' my father would ejaculate if Mr O'Reilly appeared in his salmon-coloured trousers.

I knew that 'fuck' and 'shit' and 'turd' were words reserved for my parents' use only, but ponce sounded so comical I didn't have it in the same category. The first and only time it came out of my nine-year-old mouth, Peggy looked at me as though I'd just told her I wanted to be a prostitute when I grew up.

'Finley Wilson!' she cried.

I clamped a hand over my face.

Groping

The Italian apartment was a spacious, three-bedroom place in a gated community overlooking the sea. I got the basement room next to the garage, which suited me fine. My brother arrived in his expensive car with his expensive Italian girlfriend on his arm. She spoke no English, called him *Sharl* and looked me as though I was a lapdog that might still turn out to have a nasty bite.

One thing I can say for my mother is that she didn't lack the imagination to cater for guests. There were board games, CDs, spare sun hats and slippers, and clean towels in all the bedrooms. Every morning, the breakfast table was spread with cheeses, ham, melon, olives and a fresh pile of baguettes and butter. After what seemed like hours of showering and hair drying, everyone gathered in the living room smelling of aftershave and sunscreen to discuss who should go to the beach in which car. If it wasn't for Sharl's girlfriend's insistence on wearing a flared white trouser suit and stilettos, there might even have been a sense of normality.

I practised my yoga on the terrace and went on long walks with Chad, who was going deaf these days and didn't feel any need to talk. I sat with a book while he sketched and wondered whether anyone was ever going mention what I'd just been through with my ex.

About halfway through the week, I crashed. I spent the day in my basement room with the door locked. Peggy knocked a few times, calling my name in a wheedling voice I'd never heard her use before. I stayed put, wishing she'd go away, but also quietly enjoying her torment. I'd watched her at the breakfast table trying to control the conversation, pointing a finger at the person speaking, interrupting when she'd had enough, holding up a warning hand to anyone she wasn't ready to hear from. She must be hating it that I'd worked out how to use a key all by myself. When I finally went upstairs to make a cup of tea, she cornered me in the kitchen.

'Come on, love, let me do that. What's the matter?'

'Nothing, just let me make a drink.'

She snatched up the mug I'd put on the counter, dropped a teabag into it and tried to take hold of the kettle.

'Let me do it!' I shoved away her hand.

I lifted the kettle and began to pour water into my mug. Instead of leaving me alone, Peggy began to rub my back. I was about to tell her to stop when her hand slid downwards. Without warning, she was rubbing my backside. I slammed down the kettle and grabbed her wrist, removing her hand. I was trembling with shock.

'Don't *ever* touch me like that again!'

She looked chastened and I let her arm drop. A wave of confusion came over me; that was what *Chad* used to do, not my mother. From what I could recall, she'd barely touched me as a child.

'This, and this,' I indicated my face and my arse, 'is for my lover, *not* for you.'

Peggy's face was blank, as if she wasn't there. I turned on my heel and walked out, and for the rest of the week my mother kept her hands to herself.

Split

In the Easter half term before I turned sixteen, my mother took herself off to Croatia for the week. She went with Barry and no one apart from me seemed to think it was a bit off that Chad and Barb had been left behind. Shortly before her trip, I found a pair of lacy knickers in the glove compartment of her car. She'd just spent an hour driving me around Bradford in a blustery storm, telling me we must look out for a flat to rent because she was going to divorce my father. This was brilliant news and I was surprised only that she seemed to think I'd be going with her. If it was a choice between her and Chad, I was in no doubt which parent was less of a catastrophe.

Having failed to find anywhere charming enough to put in an offer, Peggy parked in our driveway and ran inside. I stayed in the car, feeling hideously desperate for her to disappear from my life. When I searched around for a travel mint, the discovery of the packet of knickers only made her seem even more repulsive. Whatever was going on between her and Barry, I knew she'd lie about it. I'd once been mystified by a girl at school who told such outrageous fibs that only a total idiot would believe them. Against my better judgement, I'd sought enlightenment from my mother.

'Why does she do it, Mam? I mean, no one believes her.'

'If you tell a lie for long enough, you start to believe it yourself,' Peggy said.

It was the only psychologically astute answer my mother ever gave me, and she was so quick to produce it, I was left in no doubt at all that she was speaking from experience.

The day after she left with her ticket to Split, I began to get shooting pains in my head that were so intense they made me throw up. By the third day, I was still vomiting even though I had nothing left to bring up but bile.

'Your eyes have glazed over!' Chad mocked, pointing. I heard the edge of panic in his voice and when the filmy glaze couldn't be wiped away, he was frightened enough to take me to the doctor. Peggy had taken her car to the airport, together with the sexy knickers, and Chad's must have been at the garage, because he made me run for the bus – bursts of pain hammering behind my eyes.

Our dour Scot lay me down on her chaise longue and gently moved my head this way and that, attempting to make casual conversation with my father. The more she said about the weather, the more I thought she must be checking for something terrible. Meningitis? A broken neck?

She decided I had a neurological virus and wrote out a prescription, telling my father to wrap me up and take me straight home to bed.

For the next few days, I lay in my room, gently hallucinating. Then I began to spasm. The contortions jerked my head backwards and sent my eyebrows up to my hairline. Chad laughed, before hurrying away to call the doctor again. She told him I must have had too much medication for my weight, and to stop giving me the pills immediately. I cried into my pillow, wondering how long it would be before my body stopped going rogue and I could have my Easter egg.

Plus, I'd just found myself a boyfriend – a lad called Patrick who was head of our year and far too wholesome to know what he'd got himself into. All he wanted to do was take me for walks.

My mother had sniggered the first time she saw him coming down the street to fetch me. 'Look at the daft git, he's got his coat zipped right up to his chin!' Patrick and I were meant to be going on one of our walks that weekend, but there was no way I could let him see me like this. I didn't even want him to hear about it. What sort of girlfriend spends the holiday drooling with her eyes rolling up into her head? I asked Chad to telephone him to let him know I was a bit under the weather.

'Can't you tell him?' my father whined.

I tried to shake my head without setting off another round of seizures. I could hardly see, never mind get myself downstairs to the phone. Besides, Chad had just admitted to eating my egg, so he owed me. I listened to him talking to Patrick's father on the phone downstairs. He was over-explaining, making things worse. I cringed and pulled the covers up over my ears, Patrick would never forgive me for this.

The day before Peggy was due home, I suddenly got better.

'She was only ill because I went away,' I heard her telling Chad as she rinsed out her knickers in the sink.

If she was right about that, it wasn't because I'd missed her. In the safety of my mother's absence, my mind, which had long been in a kind of stasis, had started to reorganise. That night, I wrote a poem in my diary. I knew it was dire.

Something is coming, something is going to break through.
A clash of realities, a mind split in two.
Please, please make it all be true.
And let me be a writer.

I blushed when I read it over, pressing a hand to my forehead. It wasn't just the crushing embarrassment of my own drivel; my brain was creating a fresh firestorm of shooting pains. I threw down my diary and groaned to a non-existent God to please,

please make it all fucking stop. I returned to school weaker and none the wiser, and Patrick never spoke to me again. My father's pronouncement that he was a little shit did nothing to alleviate my heartbreak.

That holiday, while my mother was away with Barry and I suffered quietly in my room, my father began to paint. He laid out a thick sheet of cartridge paper on the dining room table and set to work with his oils. The result was a triptych abstract of bark and rock and sand – one of the boldest pieces of work he ever produced and my favourite. He would go on to spend the next few decades of his life painting picture after picture of rivers and skies and old farmhouse buildings, as though trying to recreate the idyllic childhood he always believed he'd had. Chad maintained there were no shades of grey in life, whereas Peggy taught me that grey was all there would ever be. It seemed to me that, one way or another between the violent storms, my father had found his place in the sun, while my mother stood forever alone and unreachable in the shadows.

Damage

Sitting on the folding chair again, in front of the therapist Jay and I had laughed at, made me feel worse than ever. She frowned at me through her spectacles, waiting. I wanted her to understand my terror and deep sense of inadequacy, my inability to choose an appropriate lover, the awfulness of spending time with my family.

'I don't know where to start.'

'Just start,' she said. 'You look as though you need to.'

I tried telling her about the massive arguments my parents had when I was a child, and the year my brother and I hardly saw Chad because no one in Bradford would give him a job and he had to drive to Edinburgh to spend the week teaching in a school that couldn't find anyone else – a job that lasted only until he was signed off with nervous exhaustion. It was a mystery to me why no one would employ my father; I could only imagine they'd discovered his drug habit. I told her, too, that Peggy was obsessed with reading her daily newspaper and couldn't be spoken to until she'd finished it. And even then she didn't listen.

'Your parents sound like very damaged people,' the therapist said.

I don't know if she noticed the look of shock that flickered through me. I thought I must have over-egged things, given her the wrong impression. I'd only had an ordinarily miserable childhood; the problem was my inadequacy, my inability to love my mother.

'That must have been a more peaceful time in your life, while your father was away,' she went on.

I looked at her dubiously. Without the parent who'd managed at least an ounce of love for me, that time had been bleak. I changed the subject, offering her something easier.

'I've been out clubbing a few times since me and Jay split up, but I don't feel attracted to anyone.'

'Are you surprised?'

It hadn't occurred to me that anyone could hurt me so badly I wouldn't want to have sex anymore.

'You must feel terribly angry.'

Now I was frustrated. Anger wasn't an emotion I could recall ever feeling; I had no idea what it was even for. I simply wasn't an angry sort of person. I was just a bit crap. Since we didn't seem to be getting anywhere, the therapist suggested I lie down and she would read my energy. This time, she saw the look on my face and hurriedly changed tack.

'Or I could do a reading for you. I have the I Ching.'

I shrugged. I wondered what it must be like to believe you could solve someone with a book.

She threw down her little wooden sticks, turned the pages looking for the right section, and read out something so lyrical and abstract I let it flow straight in one ear and out of the other.

'My goodness.' She looked at me doubtfully over her spectacles. 'You have one of the best possible readings. *Everything converges*.'

'Oh. That's good, then.'

She'd sounded disappointed so I tried not to look too pleased. It must be galling to be overruled by the Chinese.

'Good luck,' she said as I left. I wasn't quite sure who'd washed their hands of who.

On the tube back to Queensway, I felt the fizzy sensation again. My arms and legs felt distorted, too thin and far away. I held a hand in front of my face, moving my fingers one at a time. They felt like balloons, fat and empty. Perhaps this was what therapy was supposed to do, to make you feel like you weren't quite yourself.

Bournehill High

I could walk to high school in less than ten minutes, which meant I didn't have to freeze waiting for the bus anymore. My parents had become increasingly negligent when it came to my clothing, and for the last couple of years, I hadn't owned a proper coat. There was an upside to this; I loved the cheap, oversized cotton jacket I'd bought in the Army and Navy Stores. Even now, when I think of it, it reminds me of the one time in my life when I genuinely thought I looked quite cool.

The school was so huge we had to have five minutes between lessons to get from one classroom to another. It had started out as Bradford Mechanics' Institute before it was divided into a boys' school and a girls' school: two long, dark brick buildings in the same grounds, with an old swimming pool and a dining room between them. Finally, in the early seventies, it became a mixed comprehensive. Inside the identical buildings, all the stairs were concrete and there were iron railings to prevent anyone falling down the stairwell and breaking their legs. If you leaned against any of the brickwork, you got a dusting of yellow mould on your clothes, but this was a better option than getting your arse pinched by the adolescent boys barging past.

Kids came to Bournehill from all over Bradford, including some from the classier middle school down the road from Smallwood. When our new teacher asked for volunteers to bring in extra chairs, several of the boys' hands shot up and I had to stop myself from snorting. I'd expected a hammering of feet, a growing hum of rebellion. At middle school, we'd once made a teacher flee weeping from the classroom after she'd had the nerve to ask if someone could help her to open the window.

Two girls, who signed their names 'Linzi' and 'Xtine', became interested in me for about five minutes when they discovered we'd gone to the same dance studio, and at lunchtime they introduced me to their friend, Ruby, who I suspected was their charity project. Ruby was a timid girl with a warm Jamaican accent I immediately fell in love with, perfect cornrows and a face covered in scabs. I never asked her what the problem was, because by this time I was struggling with terrible acne myself and I wouldn't have wanted anyone to comment on that. It was bad enough having to put up with Chad's hilarity. The only time I bunked off was when my spots were so inflamed I couldn't bear the thought of anyone looking at me.

Since we could never hope to be as fascinating or beautiful as they were, Linzi and Xtine soon left me and Ruby to our own devices. My new friend lived in a council house with her mother and a large Alsatian dog that drank out of the sink. They had no phone and no car, which meant I spent a lot of time wondering where Ruby was when we were supposed to be meeting up, but I forgave her lateness because her father, a factory foreman, had died the year before after getting his overalls caught in a machine. She told me he'd left her fifty pence on the kitchen table that morning and she never got the chance to say thank you.

I suspected Ruby had loved her father with same the kind of hopeless pity I felt for Chad, and she became my most loyal and trusted companion – my only real friend. Between lessons, we walked the length and breadth of the school together, whispering about everything under the sun; namely David Bowie, homework and cheap skin creams.

The dreadfulness of my acne was partly made up for by the appeal of our new school uniform. It was an adolescent's wet dream; we could wear anything we liked, as long as it was black. I put together a sleeveless black mini dress that went with my worn-out ballet shoes, one of my brother's oversized jumpers that came halfway down my thighs, and a charcoal waistcoat I'd picked up in a charity shop. Charles was into punk at this stage and since the school hadn't specified acceptable hair colours, I used his bottle of food additive to dye strands of my hair dark-green. Anything to take attention off my face.

Around this time, my mother decided I should start using tampons. I was keen because it meant the days of the plastic bags and stained underwear might come to an end, and my father wouldn't have to spend so much time unblocking the toilet. The only instruction Peggy gave me, delivered in the hard, offhand tone I'd come to expect from her, was to soap my fingers and stretch myself so I could get one in.

That wasn't going to happen.

At least our bathroom door had a lock on it by now. For most of my childhood, we'd barged in on each other to wash our hands after peeing, and I'd often come across my father lying on his back in the steam using a water pistol to try and dislodge the sponge he'd propped up between the taps. He always had his flannel neatly arranged over his groin and it was years before I realised this wasn't what all men did in the bath; he'd specifically arranged himself that way to protect his modesty when he heard me coming.

I knew that my father worried that his penis was on the small side, because I once found a half page of a short story he'd attempted before he lost it down the side of the sofa. It began, 'The young Picasso was daydreaming again...' and went on to describe his liaison with the Swedish exchange student. She wanted him to fuck her, but Chad had refused due to his size issue and offered to go down on her instead. It was clear this wasn't fiction, because he went on to compare the Swede's pubic hair to Peggy's in forensic detail. I urgently wanted to tell him he should leave the creative writing attempts to me.

I took my box of tampons into the bathroom, slid shut the bolt and sat down on the bathmat to read the instruction leaflet. It included a diagram of how things were supposed to look inside, which I studied carefully, unclear quite how it was supposed to help. I gently touched myself where I imagined my opening might be. Nothing. Just dense folds of skin. I nudged around a bit and wondered if I'd have to write to the agony column I'd come across in the *Jackie* magazine Chad had bought for me when I was sick. That seemed a little desperate, so I decided to wait and try again another day.

I don't know how many attempts it took, but eventually I was able to nudge aside my labia and ease a finger in. For just a second, the world went black. It was as though one frame of a film was missing, just one moment of disconnected silence. My mind – my clever, faithful mind – protected me once again and that brief moment of blackout was over so quickly, I hardly thought about it afterwards, though I never forgot it.

With a tampon successfully inserted, I could use a belt-and-braces approach to tackling the heaviest days of my period: a super plus-sized tampon, as well as a sanitary towel. Better still, I could get a decent night's sleep without waking up to sheets that looked like I'd committed murder. I felt as innocent as a cherub.

Cake

I was rehoused back in Newham, in a block of flats managed by The Arnold Trust. The estate was on the edge of Elizabeth Park, which was a rundown area, full of boarded-up squats and derelict shops. I was the youngest resident in the block by about fifty years, and my elderly neighbours gave me tea cosies and net curtains and made sure I understood the ground rules: 'We're all friendly, but we don't go inside each other's houses.'

I discovered, too, that word had gone around that I was a nurse, which explained the sympathetic smiles they gave me when they caught me returning home in the early hours, red-eyed from a night of clubbing.

On my first weekend in the flat, I bought myself a four-layer chocolate cake at the corner shop. I lay on the lino in my unfurnished front room, pressed my fist into the centre of the cake and stuffed a wodge of sponge and oozing buttercream into my mouth. Then I wanked myself silly. Afterwards I rolled onto my back with my pants round my ankles and stared at the ceiling. I hadn't given anyone my address yet and the landline was disconnected. No one in the world knew where I was. The thought was thrilling.

'Yes, get the fuck away from me,' I told no one in particular. 'Get. The. Fuck. Away.'

I bought a fridge and a cooker, and paid a couple of dykes

to lay carpet after the pensioner downstairs complained about hearing my footsteps all bloody day long. Apart from the tension headaches and continuing bouts of low mood, I thought I was doing okay.

It helped that I had to get out of bed each morning and cycle to work, though I got the feeling my manager was picking up on my fragile state. She'd recently enrolled on a five-year training to become a psychotherapist and when she wasn't reading books with titles like *Transitional Objects and The Meaning of Play*, I'd noticed her frowning at me. I wondered if she was using me as a case study for one of her essays. Every so often, she wrote in the staff diary that I was doing a home visit and let me take the afternoon off to go to the cinema, and when her divorce came through, she took me out for a drink to celebrate. While I knocked back my non-alcoholic cocktail, she told me the director of her psychotherapy school had organised a week's retreat for trainees in the south of France.

'We're going to do a bit of group therapy, obviously, but it'll be a holiday, too. Why don't you come? We're one person short and they've said we can ask around. It'd be a chance to clear your head.'

Something about this proposition filled me with dread, though I couldn't think why. And on the other hand, I didn't want to be stuck in the flat on my own all summer. Without a regular lover, I was desperately lonely and, confusingly, my heart kept breaking for Dan, for Sebastian Angel, for that old life of subdued, cerebral pleasures. If a week of psychoanalysis would sort my head out, I might be able to get on with my life at last. It was worth a try.

I had a brief interview with the assistant director, an older woman with a limp and a patronising manner. She asked what I did for a living and when I reminded her that I worked for one of her trainees, she nodded approvingly. I didn't have to pretend that I never lay on my sofa wanting to kill myself, never picked up random women in dodgy nightclubs to distract from my inner turmoil, never slept away whole afternoons because I couldn't face how I felt. In her clean, orderly office with the orchid and the attractive wooden blinds, those parts of me simply didn't exist. I smiled and said all the right things, and she saw only what everyone else saw: a rather pale-looking young woman who could do with brushing her hair.

She offered me a place on the retreat and told me I would fit in well.

Touching

A few weeks into my third term at high school, I was bounding down one of the staircases with all the vigour my innovative new menstrual wear allowed, when I almost collided with a boy coming the other way. My heart turned over. It was Anish.

'Alright, Finny.' He grinned, tapping my arms to put me straight before continuing on his way as though the world hadn't exploded at all, while I tried not to pass out.

Anish used to live at the top of our street. He played football with my brother, and when Charles wasn't around, I would lean out of my bedroom window to admire him riding his Raleigh Chopper up and down, waiting to be invited to join in. There was an old bike in our garage that had no brakes and as soon as Anish gave the signal, I'd rush downstairs, jump onto it and career out across the pavement. I dreaded the moment I'd need to stop because my feet couldn't reach the ground. Short of crashing into a wall, the only way I could get off was to run the front wheel into the grass verge and tip myself over, but it was worth the bruises to spend time with Anish. I'd never in my life met anyone so relentlessly good-humoured.

Sometimes he took pity on me and let me have a go on his Chopper, and I repaid his generosity by making special drinks for him out of Ribena, Chad's sweeteners and toothpaste, which he pretended to enjoy. I loved him for that. Whenever I'd tried to buy my brother's affection by making him paper aeroplanes, he crushed them under his slipper.

Anish's family had come to the UK from the Punjab and his parents ran a shop on the outskirts of town. It was from Anish that I first heard the mysterious phrase 'cash and carry', discovered that you could get a pint of Coca Cola in a plastic bottle, and got the impression that all corner shops sold fairy lights and thermal underwear all year round. When I was ten, they moved away to Huddersfield, taking their trays of mangoes and my broken heart with them. Their Bradford house stood empty and every day on my way to school, I gazed through the window into the half furnished, abandoned front room, longing for Anish to come back with a bottle of Coke.

Much as I was elated to see him again, I couldn't imagine why his parents had decided to send him to Bournehill when they lived so far away. There'd been several stabbings at the school and at least one of the teachers was having sex with pupils. If it was because they knew my brother would be there and they hoped he and Anish would resume their friendship, they were going to be disappointed. By this time, Charles had become quite abnormal.

My brother had adopted a permanently glazed expression and would stride past me on the way to school without a word, except for the occasionally muttered 'Weed'. Although his attempts to demonstrate his innate superiority were soon to peter out, he never spoiled his hard-man act by being nice to Anish.

I, on the other hand, pursued Anish like the devil. I cornered him after school, I wrote him poems I thought were deep, and invited him to go and watch the newly released *Grease* at the Bradford Odeon with me. It didn't occur to me that he still saw me as his friend's little sister and he was too high-minded to cradle-snatch. I was politely rebuffed and spent the next few months pining for him. When I read *Wuthering Heights* for my mock O Levels, I found it full of parallels with my own situation. Like me, Cathy was a Yorkshire lass with messy hair; like me, she had an aggressive sibling and an ineffectual father; and like me, she was in love with a boy who was, to all intents and purposes, her brother. I was on a romantic high and since Heathcliff and Cathy were finally united before she died, I didn't see why the same thing shouldn't happen to me.

Around this time, just as I was turning fifteen, the thought of 'sleeping with another woman' also occurred to me. I don't know how I came up with the idea, unless it was a throwback to my time spent with Chad's porn collection. This was 1978, long before the first lesbian kiss on Brookside. There had been a post-watershed drama on BBC2 about an affair between two women five years earlier, but it lasted only half an hour and, being only ten at the time, I'd missed it.

As soon as I'd imagined touching a woman 'down there', I knew I was going to do it, though I felt certain it would only be the once. Mrs Edmunds became the target of my Sapphic affections, and while other disengaged teachers droned on, I thought of the enactment of Macbeth she was letting us do on Friday afternoons. She was very frank about the fact that she'd chosen me for head witch 'because of the state of that mop', which is how she liked to refer to my sexy perm.

The only other halfway decent teacher was a tiny woman with a swollen nose who taught us German. She took her job very seriously, and would come running into the room crying, 'Eyes on the blackboard; we have just thirty-*seven* minutes!' She had the good grace to smile when the whole class sniggered on learning that the German word for father was pronounced 'farter', even though she must have gone through this debacle every year.

When my talent for languages could no longer be denied, my mother informed me that I had a way with words only because when she was pregnant with me she'd been 'lecturing'. I couldn't imagine what kind of lecturing a twenty-six-year-old psychology trainee could have been doing, but I admired her sudden belief in the possibility of a prenatal connection between us. The actual phenomenon of lived experiences in the womb was something I wouldn't come to appreciate until much later on in life.

Following up on this pronouncement with one of her more disingenuous lies, Peggy told me I wouldn't be able to go to university unless I learned Latin. This involved staying on beyond the end of the normal school day because only wimps wanted to learn a dead language, and there weren't very many of those at Bournehill. I only lasted one term of this ridiculousness, during which I took advantage of the empty corridors to pin up notices suggesting that various lessons had been moved to classrooms at the far end of the building. This was mainly as a favour to Ruby, who hated her nine o'clock Religious Education class. I enjoyed hearing how they'd all trooped off together only to be marched back again after their teacher had run from one end of the school to the other to round them up. My Latin teacher figured out I was up to no good, though he didn't quite know what, and he told me not to bother coming back. His touching excuse was that he didn't like the way I wafted my ruler.

Ruby and I counted the days until we'd be done with our O Levels and would no longer have to endure hours of physics and biology and all the other subjects we were useless at. This unimaginable level of freedom was slowly approaching, and we sat tight and waited.

Mr Frame

The psychotherapy retreat was held in a large, rambling house set in its own grounds, not far from the coast. There were about thirty trainees, all youngish-looking women. It turned out that the director, a guy in his late fifties, who liked to be known as Mr Frame, was dating one of them. She sat on the floor at his feet while he delivered his welcome speech.

I was given a room with a woman a little older than me who seemed nice and dull. The group I was put into was going to work with Mr Frame, while his assistant worked with everyone else, including my manager. They'd clearly decided we needed to be separated.

At the morning check-in, we sat outside on a circle of chairs on the shady side of the house and Mr Frame asked us how we were feeling. I said I was nervous and, with winning insensitivity, I added that I wasn't used to being around such a lot of strange women. That last part was obviously a lie, but Mr Frame looked disarmed and told me to ask lots of questions: 'Where shall I sit? Can I share that juice? Shall we talk?' I supposed I could make use of his chat-up lines to keep a harmless version of myself going for the week.

I felt a quiver of anxiety when I realised we weren't doing group work at all; each of us was going to have a one-to-one session with Mr Frame while the rest of the group observed and, presumably, tried not to look too judgemental. Every trainee cried in her session, complaining about herself and her relationships and copying down Mr Frame's pearls of wisdom about setting better boundaries, trusting female intuition and surrendering to wholeness. I was pretty certain I couldn't do any of that. To get a break from all the percipience, we made a few trips to the beach, and at dusk we chopped vegetables, took turns to stir the soup and ate our communal meals at a long wooden table we carried outside. Inevitably, I got a crush on one of the women. She used to be a miner and she could play the penny whistle and crack walnuts in her bare hands, which helped to pass the time.

The day before we were due to leave, Mr Frame asked who was yet to do a piece of work. I put up my hand, thinking it was about time I got my money's worth. He offered to record my session on his portable cassette player so I could listen to it afterwards and it crossed my mind that he was going to enjoy flexing his therapy muscles on someone so green.

'So…' I began. My mouth was dry.

Mr Frame made an encouraging gesture as though batting a balloon into the air.

'I've never really got on with my mother. I guess I was an anxious child. I didn't really speak much.'

'And now?'

'I still don't like her. I still find things – hard.' I ground to a halt, trying to swallow. It wasn't enough; it was too much.

With the air of a conductor singling out a soloist, Mr Frame told me to stand up and say one thing about my mother to each of the women in turn. I got to my feet and tried to concentrate. I told them about Peggy's disparaging comments, her refusal to believe that I was smart, the time she burned my foot and hadn't seemed to care. I said that by the age of three, she was leaving me alone in the house while she went off to the shops. Halfway round my circle of truth-telling, I paused shakily. The women murmured their sympathy, their faces swimming in front of me. Chad would have called them wussy Southerners; Peggy would have been withering. I could hear my mother's voice: '*Oh, for fuck's sake, talk about navel gazing!*'

'I don't feel safe.' I heard the crack in my voice.

'Beg pardon?' Mr Frame said.

'I don't feel very safe.'

'Yes, sometimes it feels like that when there's something you need to push through. Keep going!'

Keep going. I felt floaty and unreal, and my mind was spiralling away, but I did as I was told. I continued recounting my story until I got to the last kind face, then I sat down, feeling very odd indeed. Mr Frame fiddled with the cassette player and handed me the recording. He appeared to be congratulating me.

'Your work, your contribution to others will benefit very much from your insight. Your path will be one of compassion.'

I felt a flicker of confusion; he'd forgotten I wasn't one of his trainees.

He guided us through a closing meditation, telling us in a hypnotic tone to focus on 'just lines and shapes, lines and shapes', and I returned to my room feeling even more abstracted. A football chant started up in my head.

You're not gri-inning,
You're not gri-inning,
You're not grinning anymore.
You're not griiiinnnninggg ANYMORE!

The evening meal passed in a blur, and I tossed and turned on my bed. There was no way I was going to get to sleep. 'Is there a window open?' I asked the woman I was sharing with. 'Is someone trying to get in?'

She went to find Mr Frame's assistant. The older woman sat on my bed and listened while I sobbed, recounting my childhood sorrows all over again. She patted my arm, concluding that I'd had 'attachment ruptures', and heaved herself up to hobble away for a hot chocolate.

I was in freefall and I couldn't find the brakes.

Splatter

Bournehill Sixth Form was in a separate, modern block at the far end of the two older buildings. We didn't have to wear black anymore, though we were told we should dress 'as if going to work in an office'. That was never going to happen. Clothes were cheap in Bradford and I could save up enough pocket money to buy a new outfit every few months. My favourite was a drop waist dress, pale green, short sleeved and printed with golden dragonflies. I hennaed my hair a deep chestnut and clarted my eyelashes with mascara, which I smudged into what I hoped was a smoky, come-to-bed look. I was all grown up and, at last, Anish noticed me.

One Friday night, he drove over from Huddersfield in his parents' car with a bottle of wine and the keys to their empty house. The place smelled damp and the electricity was off, but we threw down our jackets and lay on them in the dark. Anish's curls fell over his eyes as he taught me how to wank him. It was the most gorgeous thing I'd ever done and I knew this was the beginning of a wuthering love affair, which I intended to pursue with all my might before I got ill and died. Anish was everything I'd never had and always wanted; he liked me and he paid attention to me, and he wasn't to know I'd just wiped my fingers on his scarf.

As our affair continued, Chad and Peggy's reluctance to take any responsibility besides feeding me and making sure I came home at night meant we could sneak up to my bedroom, close the door and switch off the lights, confident that no one would disturb us. My father was too occupied with his cannabis and Peggy was too occupied with her headmaster.

I'd found out about my mother's affair when I heard her playing a recording she'd made of her lover being interviewed on Look North to discuss the state of education. He only said about three words, but Peggy kept re-running his ten seconds of fame, lusting so repetitively after his boyish good looks that she wore out the VCR.

At weekends, my parents still drove out to Barry and Barb's country pile to play crib and smoke hash and do whatever else they got up to, and they didn't come home until the early hours. My parents' lifestyle had an inhibitory effect on me; even when I smoked cigarettes, I didn't inhale, and no matter how horny I got, I wasn't planning to have intercourse any time soon. I did get horny, though. Anish always wore the same pale blue mohair jumper when he came to see me, perhaps as a kind of medical buffer against my earrings, which looked like fly hooks and left red scribbles on his neck. Whenever I needed a respite from all the snogging, I would bury my face into this gorgeous garment, grinning like an idiot.

One day, in a typical lapse of judgement, I picked up Fluffy and dropped him from a height onto Anish's chest, where he sank his claws into the unsuspecting mohair. Anish yelped, scolded me for my stupidity and fled, vowing never to return. A couple of days later, when Peggy left a sheet to dry on the banister, I couldn't understand why I was so turned on I had to keep retreating into my bedroom to masturbate. Finally, the penny dropped; she'd switched washing powder brands and the house was filled with the enticing smell of that jumper. It was my first experience of erotic nostalgia.

To keep my mind off this rupture with my childhood love, I

knuckled down to my studies. I'd chosen Biology, German and English Literature to study at A Level and it wasn't until halfway through sixth form that my mother told me Chad was upset I hadn't chosen Art. After taking a year off sick, my father had progressed from selling insurance to teaching in a borstal. He boasted that he had his class under control from day one by telling them that if they ever got on his wick, he'd splatter them all over the walls. He also reported that the lads took bets on how many minutes into the lesson it would be before he said, 'Shit.'

Since Chad had been too busy with these well-bred young men to talk to me about what subjects I might take, let alone to notice my teenage divorce, for once I didn't feel particularly responsible for his feelings. Now that I didn't have to copy pictures out of the Sunday supplements anymore, which was all Bournehill art lessons had ever amounted to, or do sums, or remember facts about anything, life at school was almost pleasant. I whupped my classmates in every language test we were given, my nipples stood to attention whenever Anish breezed past, and Ruby's scabs finally began to clear up.

I soothed my broken heart with a new infatuation. Wendy Knowles was brown-haired, brown-eyed and brown-skinned, although it was difficult to know whether that was from a lack of washing or her actual complexion. I sat next to her when Ruby chose Domestic Science and I was doing English Literature, and once a week, while the rest of us were discussing Jane Eyre's secret love for Rochester, Wendy would make an urgent request to go to the toilet where she had an appointment with her unemployed boyfriend. She came back ten minutes later, smelling of cheap hand cream and spunk, and my English report that year said only, 'She would do better to change the company she keeps.'

But to my mind, Wendy was a bewitching creature. I didn't quite know whether I wanted to be her, or be with her, and my confusion only added to the intensity. My favourite children's book was Rumer Godden's *The Diddakoi* and, like the protagonist Kizzy, Wendy seemed to have no family apart from a grandmother she once took me to see in her bungalow. For the duration of our visit, the grandmother lay in silence in a single bed in the corner of the living room with a tin of Quality Street resting on her bosom, while Wendy and I played snap and ate bowls of sloppy Angel Delight. This happy state of affairs was beyond my wildest dreams.

A couple of months after Wendy dropped out of school, Charles bumped into her at the bowling alley. They dated for a while and I once caught sight of them messing about in our back garden, wrestling each other to the ground, all skinny arms and thrashing legs. I was so annoyed I had to stop myself from taking after my father and going out to splatter the pair of them.

Messiah

I travelled back to London with my manager and a couple of the other trainees without anyone noticing how mad I'd gone. They were used to me being the quiet one and they weren't looking into my eyes. I got myself home to my flat, dumped my bag on the floor and lay on my bed to stare at the lightbulb. I had the feeling I was being watched. Could someone have broken in while I was away and hidden a camera up there? I tried to shake off the idea, getting up carefully and going to the kitchen to make a drink.

A neighbour passed the window, saw me and waved. I shuddered. Perhaps they were in on it, too.

I began to hear voices. People calling my name, sometimes kindly, sometimes with menace. A chattering started up that I couldn't make head nor tail of. A cat meowing. I searched the flat for Fluffy and sobbed when I couldn't find him. Why had he run away from me again? I was trembling and went to lie down in the front room. I was being watched from this lightbulb, too. I liked it; I hated it. I couldn't tell. At least I wasn't alone.

A tsunami of images came over me; Chad touching me, Peggy touching me, Charles watching and judging. Did Charles touch me, too? I couldn't tell. Something inside me was cycling back and back to a preverbal memory that Mr Frame's pushing had threatened to expose. *Keep going.* I wandered from room to room, unable to sleep, unable to rest. I found an old whistle in a drawer and gave three sharp blasts: *Emergency, emergency here! Keep coming!* Nothing happened.

I took off my clothes, put them on again and gazed out of the window while strange shapes merged and separated before my eyes. Was I God? Was God this lonely? I couldn't tell.

Thoughts of sexual abuse kept tumbling in. There was something there. Was it Chad, coming into my room, perhaps raping me gently? If it was, it didn't hurt. What if Charles did it? No, no, it wasn't that. What was it? *What was it?* If only I could get to it, if only I could understand and get it out, whatever it was. The voices continued. It was my birthday, Marianne was going to give me her flat. I was young again, innocent. I was the Messiah. I was thirsty.

I filled a bucket from the bathroom tap and tried to drink, spilling water down my chest and onto the floor. My socks were drenched. I would get to it, I would get it out, if only I could remember.

I was the Messiah.

Embrace

Once I'd received my acceptance letter from Oxford, Peggy seemed to take a sudden interest in me. She told me she wanted to take me to Greenham Common for the three-day 'Embrace the Base' event, part of an ongoing protest against cruise missiles. Bradford had an active network of radical feminists at the time – she must have seen one of their angry posters.

Several of these women were also tutors at Bradford University, which would have impressed my mother. They ran the women's centre, housed in an old cricket pavilion on the edge of the university grounds. I'd wandered in there one day thinking I might volunteer. The woman at reception was wearing a man's suit and Dr Marten's boots, and when I whispered, 'Excuse me,' she thumped her feet onto the desk and gave me the once-over. I supposed it was helpful to know what I'd be dealing with if I ever decided to become a lesbian myself.

My mother drove us down to Greenham in the driving rain and we set ourselves up by one of the gates. A group of women invited us to sit round their fire and gave us sheets of lyrics so we could join in the singing:

You can't kill the spirit,
She is like a mountain,
Old and strong, she goes on and on and on...

'Shut the fuck up!' a voice bellowed from the other side of the fence.

I watched my mother curiously; her cheeks were flushed and her eyes were bright, and she leaned into the conversation, charming and animated and not at all judgemental. My heart softened. Poor Peggy; she'd never really wanted children. I rarely saw her when she wasn't dealing with Chad or marking schoolbooks, or harassed by laundry and shopping and frozen peas. I wondered how she might have been if she hadn't had all of us to deal with.

At dusk, she disappeared into our tent and stayed in there a long time. Eventually, I got up from the fire and ducked inside to see what was the matter.

She'd put on lipstick and a tight dress I'd never seen before.

'Alright,' she said, snapping her compact shut. 'I'm leaving. I'll see you in the morning. Don't tell Dad.'

I was gobsmacked. The whole trip had been a ruse to cover up some new affair. It wasn't difficult to work out it must be someone she'd met on her Croatian holiday. She would have been after someone new, because Barry was too vacuous and her headteacher lover had recently broken things off with her, leaving his unsuspecting wife at the same time. Unaware that I'd caught on to her affair, Peggy blithely told me she'd gone round 'to comfort the poor woman'.

I climbed into my sleeping bag and stared at the shadows moving on the side of the tent, my teeth gritted. One of the women popped her head in through the tent flap.

'Knock-knock, you okay? Where's Peggy?'

'Fucking someone's husband probably,' I whispered into my pillow. 'I hope the lesbians kill her tomorrow.'

Part Two

PsychoTheRapist

I don't know what I said to Marianne when she phoned, but it was enough to bring her across London to my door. She did her best; washing-up, plumping up my pillows, making tea, and, most helpfully of all, not freaking out. She contacted Dan and they agreed on a rota to make sure one of them checked in on me every day.

I dipped in and out of lucidity, hardly sleeping, not bothering to eat unless my friends coaxed me into it. Something was trying to come up; something I was wholly unprepared for. My mind continued cycling backwards. I was no more than two years old, a baby. *What was it?*

It was my birthday. I was the Messiah.

I wrote pages of nonsense, gobbledegook, until Marianne prised the notebook out of my hands. 'But look, look, Marianne, see how it's spelt? PsychoTheRapist! Oh God, oh God…'

I crawled on the floor, babbling, pulling all the sheets off my bed, while my courageous friend stayed with me. The phone rang and Marianne went into the front room to answer it. I followed her in.

'I'm sorry, she's not well. She can't talk to you just now. No, she can't.'

She looked shocked when she put down the phone. 'I've never in my whole life been spoken to like that!'

'Who was it?' I asked, lucid for a moment.

Of course, it was my mother.

After Marianne left, I rang Peggy back and got both my parents on the line. I thought I had it in me to sort this out. My mind hissed and crackled, the static poured out of my mouth. 'You broke me, you raped me, *you, you, you...*' I hardly knew what I was saying.

'Finley, love! Finley!' my father cried.

Then my mother chimed in, 'Finley! Finley!'

They didn't come; they didn't get help. They left me floundering in pain.

Late the next night, Dan turned up. I thought he'd brought a knife to kill me with.

'Get away from me!' I screamed, tearing at his shirt.

He wrapped his arms around me, trying to contain my terror. I struggled and bit him hard on the back of the hand before escaping out of the flat into the pub across the road. The bartender had just called time, but he let me have a tomato juice. Blood in a glass.

Dan came in, searching for me.

'Quick, quick, that man has a knife! Please!'

They cleared the pub and I ran back home while Dan stood with the bartender under a street lamp. How did he explain me? His hand was bleeding.

He called my old therapist and the following day she came to the flat. Dan talked to her while I wandered in and out of the room. Even in the state I was in, I could tell she was bowled over by my upper-class friend. I overheard her telling him that her sister had been psychotic and had never recovered.

After she left, Dan asked me how old I thought she was. I said she was ninety-two. He laughed, though there were tears in his eyes. Later, he drove me out to Epping Forest for some air. A woman who'd stung herself on a nettle approached us. I found her a dock leaf, placing it gently over her swollen hand. Moments of madness, moments of clarity. I couldn't tell. There's no true forgetting, and there's no moving on without awareness and love.

A young GP came to see me. She told me if I didn't start eating without help, I'd have to go into hospital.

'Okay!' I said, as though she'd invited me to a spa.

'Have you ever seen inside a psychiatric ward?'

I had once, when a young service user at the women's centre had been sectioned. I'd volunteered to visit her because I knew she had no family. The ward was an ugly, bleak place. I didn't want to go somewhere like that. It was a wise move from this young GP, to trust that there was a glimmer of lucidity still inside me somewhere.

I began to make myself rudimentary plates of food. The voices, the terrors, the extreme beliefs came and went, but over time I had more moments of respite, increasingly sustained periods when my system took me out of whatever hellish vortex it had plunged me into. Just once, when I was drowning in another fit of horror, I asked Marianne whether my parents might have known Fred and Rose West.

'It's possible,' she said, in her usual even tone, 'but unlikely.'

'I'm crazy, aren't I?' I said, a moment later. 'This feeling of having been sexually abused – I'm wrong, aren't I?'

'There's no smoke without fire,' my dear friend replied mildly. 'But here, have a couple of these for now, and I'll see you the day after tomorrow. Dan will be here in the morning.'

She handed me the bottle of sleeping pills the young GP had prescribed.

Rhubarb

My parents met at a peace rally in Liverpool. Peggy was three years Chad's senior and engaged to somebody else. I imagine my father charming her away with his rude humour and practical jokes, though Peggy said only that she had married a thin man who turned fat and jaundiced within the year.

She barely tolerated her new husband's addictions; firstly to sweets and cigarettes, then to the beer he consumed with his Hell's Angels friends. One time, he didn't come home for three nights, and after that they were barred from every pub in West Bradford. Other absences were accounted for by a short-lived obsession with golf, which my mother put a stop to by threatening to leave him unless he sold his clubs.

After that, marijuana kept Chad's demons soothed. Ours was the only greenhouse in the street that was whitewashed all year round, and when our neighbour enquired about the distinctive shapes he saw against the glass, Chad told him he was growing Mexican tomatoes. He harvested the leaves after dusk, hurrying inside to dry them out in the oven. The smell of a spliff still reminds me of a childhood in which my father is always rolling and puffing, rolling and puffing, trying to keep too much reality at bay.

When his mood was up, Chad behaved towards me and Charles like an overgrown, tyrannical child. He sat on us and grabbed our thighs, tickling until we were hysterical, or he pinned us to the floor and dribbled spit in our faces. Once, he clamped his hand so hard over my nose and mouth, I thought I was going to suffocate. I clawed at his fingers, thinking he didn't understand that a child needs to breathe.

'Don't, Chad,' my mother would say, without looking up from her newspaper.

This manhandling left me with a suppressed rage and the muscular tension of a boxer, but if I ever attempted to match my father's high spirits, if I tried to be funny or aggressively playful like him, Chad slammed me down hard. *Who d'you think you are, you bloody halfwit?* He had to be the only clown in the ring.

I don't know how old I was when he began beckoning me round to his side of the dining table. It was always after Peggy had left the room to make coffee or start on the washing-up. I did as I was told, quietly slipping off my chair to go and stand next to him so he could draw up my skirt and put his hand down the back of my knickers. He stroked my bare bottom round and round, exploring its fullness, while my brother sat opposite us, wary and silent.

This groping ended when my periods began and the thought of my father's fingers accidentally touching my sanitary towel produced a reflex of shame that made me pull away. He didn't insist and there's a photograph of me as a teenager nestled peacefully in his arms on the sofa.

Whenever my parents came home from Barry and Barb's in the early hours, Chad would come into my bedroom to talk drunken nonsense to me, stroking my head while I answered drowsily, half asleep. He loved to report back on my endearing responses in the morning. 'Mary, Mary, how does your garden grow, eh? *Cockle shells!*' he would lisp, pulling me close to kiss me on the lips while my mother looked on with a kind of knowing cruelty. She only occasionally went as far as to tell him to stop snogging with his daughter. She'd read the volumes of Freud that scared me so much, and informed me that every little girl wants to kill her mother and marry her father. In my case, she was only half right.

At weekends, miserable and hypervigilant behind my bedroom door, I would listen to them fighting in their room or, more rarely, giggling together over one of my father's ridiculous jokes. There was a brown stain on the wallpaper above their bed where Peggy had thrown a mug of coffee during one of their rows, and on one occasion I heard her cry out that my father's penis looked like a 'stick of bloody rhubarb!' There was a moment's silence, then my father howled with laughter. Then I, too, felt an unhinged euphoria – a moment of relief I knew wouldn't last.

Complaint

I have a vague memory of Dan arriving at noon and waking me up. I don't know how he knew I'd swallowed the whole bottle. He phoned the hospital and, no doubt due to his perfect articulation, they thought he was my doctor and put him straight through to a consultant. It was inconceivable that someone who sounded like Dan could be friends with someone behaving like me. The consultant said it was too late to make me vomit. I'd be okay, probably. Dan was to stay with me, to make sure I came round fully. *Came round.* I still thought he was trying to kill me.

I lay naked in bed while Dan fiddled with the radio. A children's story came on.

'Listen,' my old friend said. 'It's Clever Gretel!'

More gobbledegook. Why was he trying to make me follow so many words? I was sick and tired of being asked to listen. I tried to smile, to ignore the screams inside me.

'You're going to be okay,' Dan said.

A month later, I was out of the worst of the terror and back at work, still as thin as a rake and full of tremors. Whatever it was I'd been through remained a blur and I didn't want to talk about it. Fortunately, my manager didn't want to talk about it either. I thought she must be annoyed that I'd made a spectacle of myself in front of her psychotherapy friends; it didn't occur to me that she might be feeling responsible for inviting me in the first place.

I had other symptoms now, too. Every morning I woke in the early hours with my heart racing as though I'd run a marathon, though my body felt numb and paralysed. I waited, watching the clock, until I had to force myself to get out of bed to get dressed and get on my bike. I had sudden flashes of unreality as I cycled through Newham, fleeting paranoid thoughts, as though my brain still wanted to queer my pitch. But over time, as these moments of madness became less frequent, I felt a small, desperate sense of triumph.

I tried to return to my therapist. Since she'd been so impressed by Dan, I thought she might be more interested in me now. She offered me one session.

'You've lost your centre,' she said, shaking her head. 'This is beyond my remit.'

I responded by finding the thickest leather belt I owned – a gift from Filchie – with a heavy biker buckle, and attempted to hold myself together by strapping it as tightly as I could around my waist.

She passed me on to another therapist 'with more experience', an existentialist who told me the brain is a very delicate organ. She explained that I'd had a psychotic episode brought on by extreme stress and she told me to contact the Professional Abuse Network for Survivors, an organisation that helped people who'd experienced negligence at the hands of mental health professionals.

The woman at PANS said that since Mr Frame was a member of a counselling and psychotherapy association, I could make a formal complaint. I put together a letter describing just how badly things had gone wrong after my session with him. Spelling it all out felt like a revenge of sorts.

The reply came a month later. I hadn't indicated which part of their code of conduct Mr Frame had breached and I would have to do that to take my complaint forward. My new helper at

PANS was outraged. 'If you'd been raped, the police wouldn't ask you to tell them which part of the law had been broken!'

I wasn't about to be beaten. I went through the guidance booklet she gave me and the audio recording of my session, and wrote down all the moments where I thought Mr Frame had messed up. I spent a whole paragraph on the bit where he told me to carry on talking about my mother after I'd said I didn't feel safe. I typed up the transcript and marked that section with a highlighter pen, feeling secretly amused that Mr Frame had provided me with this perfect piece of evidence.

I was ahead of my time; trauma-informed therapy would be all over this in another twenty years.

This time, my complaint was accepted. Mr Frame would be asked to attend a tribunal where I'd get to present my case. Meantime, my PANS helper arranged for us both to meet with his assistant. She met us in her consulting room, clutching her walking stick, and told my helper that Peggy had tracked down Mr Frame and accused him of brainwashing me. In return, Mr Frame had concluded that my mother was the sort of person who couldn't bear to be in the wrong. That was about all she had to say, but before we left she reminded me that *she herself* had given me her attention in France, outside of my allotted group time. This had the intended effect; I felt tiresome and small.

Some weeks later, I received another letter from the counselling association saying that Mr Frame had failed to renew his membership, which meant they no longer had any jurisdiction over him and my case couldn't go forward. To double-check, I got Marianne to call him pretending to be looking for a therapist. She winked at me when he answered the phone and put on her best social worker voice.

'And are you a member of the CPA?'

'I'm currently completing the paperwork,' he said.

Liar. Pants on fire.

Asylum

At our next session, my new therapist picked up on my repressed rage. She invited me to stand up and said I could push against her if I wished. I stayed where I was, appraising her thin body. I knew she thought I'd pummel her a few times before collapsing and surrendering to a healing hug. I sat down again. If I'd let myself touch her, I would have beaten her to a pulp.

I held it together until September, when I was due to go to Brighton to celebrate my birthday with my current lover, a tattooed Mancunian with a passion for football and karaoke. She called me an hour before she was due to pick me up to let me know she'd drunk too much the night before, was still drunk and vomiting, and had to cancel.

Without that lifeline, I was facing four days at home alone.

My anxiety came in waves, increasing to a gut-wrenching dread that made my hands shake as I tried to fill the kettle. I stuffed the clothes I'd worn in France into the waste bin and set them on fire, then poured boiling water over them. I drew all the curtains, got into bed and pulled the duvet over my head. I felt as if I had no skin. By the time I emerged, I hadn't eaten or spoken to anyone for forty-eight hours. I hadn't been outside for days. The flat smelt acrid, and everything was hazy and out of place. I couldn't feel my arms.

I called Marianne, who was working in child protection in Fulham. I told her I couldn't go out, I was too scared. She was about to go on a home visit, but she promised to call the Newham mental health team for me. I waited for her to call back. My mouth was dry. I filled a glass with water and took it into the sitting room. As I sat down, it slipped out of my hand and broke on the arm of the chair. I picked up a shard of glass and stroked it along my forearm, watching the beads of blood appear. Blood dripped onto the carpet. I smiled – it was good the carpet was already red. I lay down and slept again.

A tap on the door woke me. I didn't move. There was another, louder, knock.

'Hello, hello?' Someone was speaking through the letterbox. 'My name's Angela, from the crisis team. Can you let me in?'

I don't know long she persisted before I undid the chain and opened the door. She ushered me back into the sitting room and sat on the edge of the sofa. I sat on the floor by the window and watched her through slitted eyes. Her shoes were yellow, her nails were polished. I liked her hair.

'Now, tell me what's going on. Your friend sounded very worried about you.'

I wondered if she'd still help me if I told her I didn't know. She noticed the gash on my arm, the broken glass in a neat pile on the carpet.

'Did you do that? Did you break a glass on purpose to cut yourself?'

A long sigh shuddered through me.

'You can't stay here alone, can you, if you feel like doing that? Would you be willing to come with me and we can find you a bed somewhere?'

I nodded, feeling my heart drop. At last, someone was going to help. Perhaps she would make it all go away, the terror, the exhaustion. The lifelong dread of not being able to cope.

She drove me to an outreach office and left me in the waiting room until a cab arrived to take me to St Benedict's hospital. The driver opened the door for me and slammed it shut without a word. I gazed at the back of his head as he fixed his seatbelt, wondering whether he'd had special training to deal with crazy people. What would he do if I tried to throw myself out of the car? What if I screamed at the lights to distract him and then jumped out and ran away? I sat meek and quiet on the back seat. He didn't speak to me even when he'd parked outside the hospital and we were waiting for a staff member to come and collect me. I wondered whether he had any curiosity at all about his shattered passenger.

I was taken up to the ward in a lift by another silent young man. Two sets of heavy doors locked automatically behind us and I realised what a dangerous position I'd put myself in. If I panicked and lashed out, they might try to section me, I could get myself on a downward spiral to lifelong incarceration. There was something intensely soothing about that idea.

I was shown to a small room with a single bed and a hatch in the door. I lay down with my face to the wall and stayed there until nightfall, when I got up briefly to close the curtains and strip down to my vest and boxer shorts before climbing back under the covers. Every hour, the hatch slid open and then closed again. At some point in the night, I began to masturbate. When the hatch opened, I jerked my hand away.

'Sorry,' a voice said.

I didn't know whether she was apologising for waking me or because she could tell what I was doing. I knew only that it wasn't right to feel sexually aroused in a place like this. On suicide watch.

In the morning, a nurse brought me two slices of white toast and a banana. 'After this, you come to the dining room. It isn't room service.' She swept out, leaving the door open.

Sometime in the afternoon, it occurred to me that since I'd come to the ward voluntarily, I ought to be able to leave if I wanted. The thought of going back to my flat filled me with a bleak terror, but I asked to be let out to buy a bar of chocolate.

A staff member came with me to make sure I didn't attack any pedestrians or throw myself into the river. We hurried across a courtyard to the newsagents and I bought a Turkish Delight and a packet of Polo mints and returned to the ward with them stashed under my jacket. I lay on my bed with my shoes on, worn out by my brief foray into the world. There was an old paperback on the windowsill. I imagined staying in this room forever, writing novels, studying philosophy. It wouldn't matter how mad I went; no one would know.

At lunchtime, I ate at a Formica table in the dining room, watching two patients playing ping pong and half a dozen more staring at a soundless television high up on the wall. I called Marianne from the payphone and told her not to visit, not to tell anyone where I was.

'When you feel better, we'll have a lovely holiday,' she said. 'We could go to Lesbos. You can take me to all the bars.'

I wondered why she sounded as though she might cry. Before she hung up, she wished me happy birthday. I realised I was thirty.

My keyworker appeared on the ward the following afternoon. We sat on my bed to chat while a woman in a nightdress floated up and down the corridor, poking her head into the room each time she passed.

I told her I was due back at work the following day. I wanted to go in; I thought I could handle it. Towards the end of my psychotic episode, I'd been invited to the theatre by an old flame, and afterwards we'd had a drink in the bar and chatted about mutual friends and the state of the world. She'd even tried to kiss me.

'Even back then, I was, you know, lucid enough,' I argued. I didn't mention that I hadn't followed a thing that happened on stage – they may as well have been speaking in tongues.

My mind floated back to my childhood, to Chad and my brother watching *Kojak* or *M*A*S*H*. I would try to tune in, staring at the television, but the words wouldn't make sense. The world wouldn't make sense. They thought I was just doing what they were doing; watching television.

'Finley? You were saying?'

'Sorry. If I don't go back to work tomorrow, I'm scared I'll...'

'You're scared you'll never make it,' my keyworker finished for me. 'But who goes to work from a psychiatric ward?'

If I'd been quicker off the mark, I could have named a handful of celebrities who were certifiable, but she had a point. In the end, she agreed I could go in if I really wanted to and come back to the ward at the end of the day. She couldn't really say no, since working was supposed to be a sign of recovery.

I got through a couple of days in the office, soothed by a backlog of typing. My manager was off with a sore throat and classes hadn't restarted yet. No one picked up that there was anything wrong; my co-workers were intent on making the most of the manager's absence and disappeared for most of the day with vague excuses about dental appointments and childcare. I ate my solitary lunches by the fire and tried not to wonder whether my life was always going to be this empty.

After another night on the ward, I'd had enough of the chilly bathrooms and the depressing food and shouting. I discharged myself, agreeing to return a month later for my case conference. I went back to my flat, threw away the pile of broken glass and sponged the spots of blood out of the carpet. I ran a hot bath and lay back in the steam. I'd saved a bit of money while I was in hospital; I'd get a takeaway moussaka later and perhaps a carton of Belgian cookies.

What on earth did I have to feel unhappy about?

Dirty Fingers

'Do you think you're clinically depressed?' the psychiatric team leader asked, leaning forwards in her chair. I could tell she was congratulating herself on her opener; *involve the patient, respect their view.* I shot a glance at the four sullen-looking professionals she'd brought in to observe me. One was still wearing his waterproof jacket, another had a brown mark on the front of her shirt. They clicked their ballpoint pens, waiting. I had no idea what the definition of clinical depression was.

'How can we help you without getting our fingers dirty?' she tried again.

I winced. What the hell was she trying to do?

'Your life has been very unpeopled.' Her smile was becoming fixed.

'I've had over twenty lovers in the last few years,' I snorted. 'That's hardly unpeopled.'

The rest of the interview did not go well. They decided I was, indeed, clinically depressed, with a generalised anxiety disorder into the bargain. I was put on the waiting list for psychoanalysis, and meantime I was referred to a woman with a grey bun and Birkenstock sandals, who was supposed to offer me short-term cognitive behavioural therapy. She seemed not in the least bit disconcerted by my state of mind and was keen to let me know she'd broken her little toe only the week before.

'That's how easily things can go wrong,' she said. 'That's how fragile we are.'

I didn't think so. I didn't bother going back. A few months later, the promised letter from the NHS arrived. As soon as a place became available, I would be offered two years of daily group psychoanalysis as a day patient at St Helen's Hospital in Edmonton. I was hanging on by a thread and, since nothing else seemed likely to help, I accepted.

Victory

It was another year before a place came up for me at the Oakham Unit at St Helen's. I'd long been clear that Dan hadn't been trying to kill me, there were no cameras in my lightbulbs and I wasn't the Messiah. I'd also discounted the possibility that I'd been sexually abused by anyone in my family. The whole thing, I'd concluded, had been the product of a disordered, deluded mind. It was just further evidence that I was more deficient than most people.

It was odd, then, that some part of me was still convinced something awful had happened to me. My session in France had awakened a deep sense of an early violation that I couldn't shift, even though I did my best not to pay attention to it. I was just holding on for the time when I could give up work and surrender to whatever Oakham had to offer.

'I've no idea what it'll be like; maybe I'll be spending my days basket-weaving,' I told Marianne over a cottage cheese salad in Last Out.

'That would be restful,' she said drily.

I laughed, feeling as though I was misbehaving, handing in my notice so I could mess around making collages and doing expressive dance all week. I glanced round at the tables of trendy coffee drinkers. I had enough money to do what they did, to look like them. Right now, there was nothing at all wrong with me, so why the hell wasn't I getting on with things? I felt again the familiar, harrowing sense of a double reality; coping and failing, failing and coping.

I'd learned some useful information about welfare rights at the women's centre and, while I waited for my hospital start date, I applied for disability benefits and a Freedom Pass so I could travel across London on public transport without paying. When the little green card arrived in the post, I stroked it all over my naked body; this, alone, was a prize worth going mad for.

One afternoon, Dan popped in to check up on me. He'd brought a book of poetry with him. 'It's an anthology,' he said, tapping the cover. 'I've got a couple in there. Have a look.'

I flicked through the pages, feeling piqued. I didn't want to know about his achievements. I found his name and read quickly down the page. He'd written about our visit to Epping, describing my state of mind with such plaintive clarity I couldn't stand it.

'*How could you*, Dan?'

'What? What's the matter?'

'How could you? Benefit from my breakdown, *publish* it?' I flung the book across the floor.

Dan bent down very slowly to pick it up, as though trying not to startle me into a further attack. 'I didn't know they'd choose that one. I sent them several.'

That was disingenuous. It was too much, his easy victory, when all my promise had come to nothing. I hated myself. I hated him.

'Go away, you're not a friend to me. Piss off.'

I listened to him leave, quietly pulling shut the door. I figured the only way to find any peace at all was not to let anyone in, ever. I certainly never wanted to read Dan's pretentious poetry again.

Top Marks

The psychiatric consultant introduced himself as Dr Bite and led the way down a dirty corridor. I inhaled his aftershave and admired the crispness of his pinstripe shirt as I trotted along behind. The leaflet that was included with my appointment details had said that the methodology at Oakham was to 'break down' patients' defences and then rebuild our personalities. From the look of him, Bite didn't seem likely to do anything half so aggressive.

He took me into his office and shut the door. 'You refused to complete my questionnaire, I believe.'

I said I'd completed it two weeks earlier and posted it back, first class. He found it in his desk drawer, cleared his throat while he refreshed his memory, and invited me to sit.

'How are you feeling today?' He kept his expression carefully neutral.

I tried to explain my depression, my racing heart and numbness. I tried, for once, to let the devastation in my heart show on my face, but I felt as though I was pretending. I came to a halt, hoping he'd help me to find better words. He shifted in his seat, changing gear. He had a mental list to get through.

'Did anyone close to you die when you were young?'

'Only my cat,' I said, for the sake of full disclosure. 'Fluffy.'

A bout of cat flu had finally finished off my tomcat a few

days after we'd shut him out of the house for the week while we went to Whitby. *It'll be fine*, Peggy had said. *It's only a cat.*

Bite's questions were too obvious, too wide of the mark. Did I come from a large family? Did we move about a lot? Did I think anything was odd about my appearance – for example, did I think my nose was too big? This landed badly, since one of Chad's favourite taunts had been that my nose looked like a squashed raspberry. He used to upbraid Peggy the same way, chanting hysterically: 'Big nose, big nose, you look just like your bloody mother!'

I shook off these thoughts. I knew Bite was trying to ask about body dysmorphia, which I didn't have. I told him I'd studied at Oxford, thinking this would make clear to him that although I wasn't managing very well just now, I wasn't an idiot.

'And how did you get on?'

I told him I got a first-class degree. Bite pointed out that he was trying to determine how I got on generally – did I enjoy student life and so forth – but he understood that getting 'top marks' was important to me. Feeling mildly humiliated, I replied that university was fine, that afterwards I'd lived in Salford for a while and since then I'd been working in a women's centre.

'So you've been under-functioning for a long time.'

I supposed I had, if going to Oxford meant I should by now be living in Chelsea and working for the BBC.

'We'll see you on Monday,' he said as he showed me out. 'You were very anxious when you came in.'

Thank you, I wanted to say, and you were very pompous.

Contact

I left my job on the Friday and cycled to St Helen's early on the Monday morning. The Oakham Unit was in a separate block from the rest of the hospital, next to the canteen. The staffroom was halfway down the dirty corridor, opposite Bite's office, and there were four other rooms for small group work, an art room with a potter's wheel and a back door leading out onto a grassy area. I found my way to the large dayroom with the stained carpet that stank of cigarette smoke. The walls were lined with sturdy upholstered chairs, and there was a little kitchen and a toilet off to one side.

There were already half a dozen patients in the room – women in their thirties to sixties – sitting as far apart from each other as they could get. Most of them were wearing jeans or tracksuit bottoms and loose T-shirts, with the exception of one very thin woman who was dressed from head to toe in white. I chose a chair not too close to anyone else and sat down.

A clock on the wall ticked steadily. No one spoke. The women looked at their feet or stared straight ahead. Bite had told me that most patients travelled in from home each day, and the rest came directly from the psychiatric ward and returned there after the sessions. I wondered which of these women were inpatients. It was impossible to tell.

After a time, a thick-set woman with short grey hair came

in. I felt the sudden tension in the room as she strode towards me. She stopped directly in front of me, hands on hips.

'That's my chair; can you please move?'

I got up and shifted a few seats away. The room shifted, too. A crisis had been averted and the women sank back into their private worlds.

Over the next twenty minutes, more patients arrived. There were a couple of pale-looking young men, a handful of obese women and one or two that looked half starved, including someone I was pretty sure I'd met on the scene. On the stroke of ten o'clock, four therapists trooped in and sat down. They seemed oblivious to the weird atmosphere, except for one guy with rosy cheeks and unruly hair who gazed at each of us in turn, grimacing at those who looked particularly shutdown. I later learned his name was Bill and that he was considered the grandaddy of Oakham because he once worked with Spike Milligan. Later, one of the women told me that for the whole of her first month, she'd thought he was the sickest patient in the room.

Bill's eyes fell on me and when I returned his gaze, he raised his brows. I was expecting some sort of welcome, an explanation of what we were supposed to be doing. His eyebrows fell and he moved on. The clock ticked. Ten minutes. Nothing. Then, slowly, a very white, almost bald woman with an intelligent face began to rock back and forth.

'Oh God, oh God...'

'Y'alright, Lynette?' the young woman sitting next to her asked.

'Yeah,' Lynette said, softly. 'It's just... oh God, I'm scared.'

'Was it the weekend? Did you see Ollie or sommat?'

'Sort of, I don't know. I just feel bad.'

Bill sighed, ruffling his hair. 'How hard it is to reconnect after the weekend. So much time alone. But now here we are and we can *think* about these difficult feelings...'

I wasn't convinced that would help; I'd been thinking hard since primary school. The session seemed never-ending, minutes of silence punctuated by a flurry of distressed exchanges and curt, careful remarks from the staff. None of the therapists spoke to me. I half thought I must be undergoing some sort of test. At noon, they got up abruptly and left, leaving the room inert.

At twelve thirty, Lynette gave me a ticket to get a free lunch and took me to the canteen. She'd found out I was supposed to join her small group for the afternoon, and once we'd eaten our vegetable stew and sponge pudding at opposite ends of a long table, she showed me to our room.

A circle of chairs had been set out and we sat down. The young woman who'd spoken to Lynette earlier came in and took a chair next to her friend. She told me her name was Alice. A little man in his fifties, who liked to be known as Irish Jack, also joined us and shortly afterwards two therapists came in. The male therapist, Antonio, was slim and dapper and reminded me of Sebastian Angel. The woman, whose name was Jules, had a cold manner and an accent I couldn't place. Lynette told me later she was the unit's doctor.

I tried to get comfortable, but the chair was too high for my short legs. I put down my bag to use as a footstool.

'I advise you to keep your feet on the ground in this group,' Antonio said, looking down his nose.

I picked up my bag. 'Actually, that reminds me, I'm supposed to give you details of my emergency contact person.'

I handed him a slip of paper with Marianne's phone number on it. He dropped it onto the windowsill behind him, staring at me in a way I supposed was meant to be meaningful.

'You want to make contact,' Jules said.

I repeated that I'd been asked to provide next of kin and that Marianne was the closest I had to family. They both continued to stare at me until I hung my head. I decided to keep my mouth shut until I got the hang of this.

Lynette began to rock back and forth. 'Oh God, oh God...'

Jules crossed her legs, smoothed her skirt. Antonio looked at his hands. He was wearing a thick gold ring.

'Oh *God*...'

Alice touched her friend's arm, making soothing noises. I wanted to help, but I was wary now. Irish Jack began to cry, stuffing tissues against his eyeballs and twisting them until they squeaked. He told us he'd had fits as a toddler and was put into the sink and drenched in cold water. I didn't feel sorry for him, I just wanted his snivelling and tissue-grinding to stop. Alice said she was due to finish the programme shortly. She'd been told by Dr Bite that she had a borderline personality disorder and would never recover, but she thought that couldn't be right.

'I mean, no one knows what's going to happen tomorrow, do they?' She looked from one of us to another, close to tears.

'No, they don't,' Lynette murmured.

'But we're here today,' Jules said. 'You can take advantage of what's on offer here to support you for the remainder of your time.'

'I know, I'm just worried about after...' Alice's voice became faint and her eyelids fluttered closed. She began to slide sideways. Her shoulder landed with a thump against Lynette's.

'Hey, hey, Alice!' Lynette took hold of her friend round the waist and tried to prop her up. I heard Antonio snigger. Irish Jack dug in his pocket and offered her a sweet. She blinked away the tears, coming back to life. Of course, low blood sugar.

The other patients carried on talking, the therapists' voices came and went, but they were all too far away, their words didn't land. I don't know much time passed before I heard Jules addressing me.

'Finley, where have you gone?'

I jumped and brought myself back.

At the end of the day, I cycled home with my mind whirring. I couldn't work out whether the staff had been callous on purpose, whether Antonio's smirk was supposed to trigger a backlash so they could work on our dysfunction. The alternative was that I'd seen what I'd seen; supposedly mentally ill people demonstrating tender emotional care and a therapist enjoying the spectacle of a young woman's loss of control. I lugged my bike up to my flat, ate a plate of pasta and slept for twelve hours.

Beetroot

The following day began with an art group in the dayroom. We helped ourselves to large pieces of sugar paper and paints, crayons or pencils, and used the first hour to draw whatever we wanted. At 11am, we laid our work out on the floor in front of our chairs for inspection. Antonio came in to run the group, closely followed by a guy in his early thirties with ginger hair and a goatee. He blushed and stifled a cough as he sat down.

'Hi everyone, I'm Rowan.'

I was dismayed; the hospital letter said he was my new keyworker.

Antonio fidgeted in his chair and clapped his hands, telling us all to wake up. He seemed freed up now the doctor wasn't around, and made us get out of our chairs and circle the room to look at each other's work. A woman wearing thick glasses remained huddled in one corner. She had a burn mark in the shape of an iron on her cheek. Earlier I'd seen her knock on the staffroom door and hold out her hand to Antonio so he could drop two painkillers from the packet straight into her palm without touching her. Health and safety. I took a furtive glance at her picture as I ambled past. She'd squirted poster paints all over a crumpled piece of paper and rubbed handfuls of mud and grit into the paint. She glared at her work through thick glasses and then at Antonio. Analyse *that*.

No one commented on anyone's picture. Once we were back in our seats, one of the men began to complain about something Antonio had said to him in his one-to-one session – something about him 'having trouble with his orifices'.

'You're trying to be the big man,' Antonio said, jabbing a finger at him. 'And it isn't working.'

The guy bit his lip and didn't speak again for the rest of the day.

'Is that you, Finley?' Alice asked gently, pointing at my picture.

I'd drawn a hunched, trembling figure with a frowning face, surrounded by disembodied noses.

'Yes and those are noses, I don't know why.'

'Perhaps you think people here will be nosy,' Rowan offered, turning beetroot.

If he'd made an interpretation like that at Oxford, he'd have been heading for a third-class degree, but I wasn't in a position to laugh. I tried to smile at him for trying. He lowered his eyes.

After another hour spent mostly in silence, the therapists collected up our pictures. The glaring-eyed woman's work shed a trail of grit across the carpet as Rowan carried it away, and the following day she cut herself so deeply Antonio had to take her into our small group room to bandage her arm. I caught sight of them through the open door, sitting knee to knee, Antonio's head bent in concentration. She'd taken off her glasses, her eyes were closed and she was smiling.

Poorly

Over the next few weeks, every time Jules saw my thousand-mile stare, she asked me where I'd gone and I would come back into my body. I was grateful to her for noticing, though she never showed any curiosity about what made me do it in the first place. After a while, she didn't need to prompt me anymore; I could bring myself back on my own. I'd had no idea I still slipped out of myself so often.

One morning after the large group session, the woman I thought I knew from the scene came over to sit next to me. She had on a pantsuit with complicated straps over the back and shoulders, her hair was done in shiny braids, and her lips and nails were painted blue. She said we'd met in Jezebel's a couple of times and I was so distracted by the memory of that first kiss with Filchie that it was a while before I realised she was still talking. She was telling me that she'd been raped in the school playground by two teenagers when she was twelve and that now she was having a clandestine relationship with her dentist.

'Bite is giving me one-to-one sessions for my bulimia, because my teeth are starting to fall out from all the acid. I think he's scared if the treatment doesn't work I might die, but I'm never going to tell him all this. Not unless he asks.'

She invited me back to her flat for a coffee. I was astonished at the curated beauty of the place; she'd painted her floor tiles gold, hung contemporary art on every wall, and draped white muslin curtains round her four-poster bed. She said she'd just been offered a job as a journalist and had decided to stop being a bulimic.

She showed me her biceps. She was going to start going to the gym and eating vegan. She hadn't vomited all day.

'I don't need Bite anymore,' she said. 'He doesn't understand a thing.'

A few days later, she and Alice both left the programme and a new patient joined our small group. He had curly hair and a sweet, sexy grin. He also had a court date looming with the threat of a prison sentence for arson. He and I were the first to arrive and we sat with our heads bowed like two awkward teenagers.

'I'm Paulie,' he said at last, tapping his chest with a translucent hand.

'I guess we're all a bit poorly,' I said.

He was quiet, sensitive and articulate, and we soon configured things so we always sat next to each other for our small group sessions. It occurred to me that I'd become territorial about my chair; at this point I would have smacked anyone who tried to take it.

Other patients came and went: a smiley Eritrean who was sex-obsessed; an older, fierce-looking woman from Essex whose daughter had died of an asthma attack; and a devout young Christian who dressed only in purple and stayed with her vicar at weekends. Paulie was told he didn't have to go to jail if he kept on coming to Oakham and he, Lynette and I became the stalwarts, the ones who were hanging in there for the duration. Or so I thought.

On Thursday afternoons, Bill (of the mobile face) ran a psychodrama session in the dayroom. It was the least dramatic event of the week; on any other day, there would be noisy confrontations, someone raging, someone sobbing, a chair thrown or a new cut or burn on display, but as soon as we were encouraged to act out, no one wanted to.

Bill forced us up out of our seats and slid the heavy chairs away from the walls, spinning them this way and that. He suggested positions for each of us, seated or standing, depending on what he thought the group dynamics were that week. Some patients refused to co-operate and left the room or lay down on the dirty carpet. Bill dragged two chairs close together, facing opposite ways, and invited Paulie and me to sit in them.

'We're going in opposite directions,' Paulie said sadly.

Bill's face fell. 'I was thinking more of a kissing seat.'

Paulie's interpretation proved closer to the mark. He left the programme a few weeks later and a short while afterwards his sister telephoned me to say he'd taken his own life.

I brought myself back.

A handful of us who'd been close to Paulie attended his funeral with Bill and we were invited back to his parents' house for tea afterwards. They gave me a smoke-damaged paperback that had belonged to their son; *The Tibetan Book of the Dead*. Sweet Paulie. I wondered what he'd been through to bring him to such a state.

His sister didn't come to the funeral because she'd converted to Islam and didn't want to be around any men, but a few weeks later, she invited me to go with her to bury Paulie's ashes in his favourite place in Alexandra Park. She said her prayers while two workmen dug a hole in a patch of grass between the trees. Once they'd left, she emptied the contents of the urn into the hole and dropped a white rose on top, though I thought her brother would have preferred a blow torch to burn the whole world down.

I brought myself back.

Faith

I still went clubbing now and then. I could just about afford it, with my disability benefit and the free hospital lunches. By some miracle, being at Oakham seemed to have rekindled my desire and I found myself a new relationship. Faith was a good-natured soft butch who cooked me hot dinners and blackberry crumble with custard, and made my lips swell so magnificently when we kissed that I slurred my words for days.

Whenever I met anyone I didn't much like, I enjoyed telling them I was having daily psychoanalysis at a hospital. It was as effective as saying I was on parole for manslaughter. But with Faith, I picked my words carefully, explaining it was a choice, that I'd left a full-time job to do it and I was confident I'd be back in work again within a year or so.

In return, Faith admitted she'd checked up on me before we slept together. Her mother knew the receptionist at the women's centre and Faith had rung up to ask what I was like. The elderly receptionist had said she'd been sorry when I left because I was a 'grafter' compared to the rest of the staff, who were 'complete slackers'. I'd rather she'd said I was clever or funny, but I knew it was my speedy touch-typing that had done the trick. She'd never had to run out on her arthritic hip to catch the last post, and if being a good secretary was what had convinced my new lover to go to bed with me, I wasn't going to complain. Being with Faith was one of the most intimate relationships I'd ever experienced. Not only did she make me fish pies from scratch, she hung in there even when the Oakham therapists managed to push me over the edge again.

I don't quite know how they managed it; they must have inadvertently stumbled too close to some home truths. Sitting in the dayroom one morning after small group, I felt the weirdness in my head coming on again. I knocked on the staffroom door to ask for a pre-emptive dose of anti-psychotics. It was a Friday and I didn't want to face the weekend going slowly out of my mind. I was told Jules would come to the dayroom to see me before five o'clock.

She didn't come. I decided she'd diagnosed me from behind the staffroom door and didn't think I needed medication. I got on my bike and cycled home, and within a couple of hours I'd completely lost the plot. I sang 'On Ilkley Moor Bah't 'at' down the phone to Faith and told her the worms were coming to get me. She called her best friend and by the time they arrived, I was floundering in a whirlpool of crazed wordplay. I thought my downstairs neighbour's blown-down fence was a broken boundary I should take personally, I wanted to bring down Marianne's fat cats and, left to my own devices, I would have got on the bus to Hackney Central in search of my lost centre.

Faith stayed the night, heaping me with blankets that acted as a kind of straitjacket, and trying her best to get me to sleep. In the morning, the emergency GP came with a prescription and by Monday I was so drugged up, I could hardly keep my eyes open.

Instead of dressing in my usual T-shirt and jeans, I put on my most extreme clubbing clothes: a pair of tartan bondage trousers festooned with zips and straps, a string vest and a fraying shirt with torn-off sleeves that I'd died a smeary black. Faith gave me a kiss before I set off for the unit and told me my breath stank. To her credit, even that wasn't enough to make her leave me.

As I swerved into the hospital entrance, one of the straps got caught in my chain and I almost came off my bike. I slunk into the dayroom, hands covered in oil, suddenly aware of how mad I looked. Now I'd have to wear my outrageous get-up all day and, on top of that, though I didn't quite have the Largactil shuffle, my legs weren't working as they should. I wobbled my way to the nearest chair and fell into it, praying no one had noticed how unhinged I was.

I needn't have worried. It turned out that one of the patients had contracted tuberculous and we were all sent off to radiology to have our chests X-rayed. I felt sorry for the nurses having to deal with two dozen lunatics wandering in, muttering about disclaimers and demanding tea and biscuits. When I returned to the small group, Antonio and Jules ignored my punk-dyke outfit. Either they thought it was beneath their notice or they couldn't work out how to psychoanalyse it.

'You seem to be somewhere else today,' Antonio said at last.

'Oh no, I'm right here,' I replied, smirking.

I'd just remembered I'd had a dream the night before about coming across him in a gay nightclub wearing a red thong. *The Full Monty* had just come out and since Antonio wouldn't let my remark go, I recounted my dream for the benefit of the group. Everyone sniggered and even Jules cracked a smile. I felt confident Antonio would be the laughing stock of the staffroom for the rest of the week.

Unfortunately, my embarrassment about my own outfit increased as the morning wore on and the drugs started to wear off. Just before lunch, in a sudden fit of frustration, I smashed some pieces of pottery against the tiles in the art room. I knew who'd made them and I knew she wouldn't care; her name was Maddison and she wrote *Mad* on all her work before smashing most of it herself. Bill, however, considered the pottery his special domain. He caught up with me coming back from the canteen.

'Finley, can you please clean up the mess you've made in the art room?'

'How about you lot clearing up the mess *you've* made?' I shot back.

He gave me a look before striding away. It was the one time in my life that the perfect retort had come to me at the right moment. Perhaps metaphors suited me in my madness, after all.

Towards the end of the day, Lynette wandered into the dayroom.

'I like your trousers,' she said, evenly.

She was the only person at Oakham who understood it was cool to look the way I did, at least on a Saturday night in Soho. Of everything that happened to me there, her comment was the only thing that ever really touched me.

I like your trousers. I loved her for that.

Prick

A round two thirds of the way through my time at the unit, I returned to my block of flats one afternoon to find Peggy outside.

'Hello, love, it's Mam!' she cried, as though she'd mistaken my frown for a lack of comprehension. 'Let me in, then.'

I stood motionless. 'No, you've turned up without any warning. We can go to the pub.'

'Oh, go on, let me in,' she wheedled, putting on a fake sweet voice. 'I'm dying for a pee.'

I wondered exactly how mad she thought I'd gone. I took her across the road to sit in a corner of the empty pub, the same place I'd cleared out when I told the bartender Dan had a knife.

'Are you alright? We thought you might have killed yourself.'

It had only taken her three years to come and find out.

'It depends what you mean by alright,' I said, knowing she didn't have the skills to unpack that. I knew, too, that she hadn't come all this way just to see me. There would be some nasty intrigue, some new southern lover.

'Does your brother contact you?'

'Do you wish he did?'

Peggy continued to throw out questions, which I deflected with all the skill I'd learned at Oakham. The conversation went on, with my mother becoming increasingly frantic and unpleasant, telling me I was very ill indeed. I was killing her. I felt myself shutting down and she left without having the supposedly urgent pee. I was pretty sure I wouldn't hear from her again.

At my case conference, Antonio stared out of the window, his legs twisted to one side. I wondered whether this was a last-minute show of solidarity, a pointed refusal to engage with the fishbowl situation I'd been put into, or whether he just had a bad case of empathy burnout. Dr Bite was concerned about the mehndi patterns on the backs of my hands.

'It's henna,' I explained. 'There was a Muslim celebration at the women's centre where I used to work.'

'You worked with the Asians?'

'I worked mainly with...' I wanted to say 'the Caucasians', but I bit my lip.

'And what made you do this?'

I realised he thought they were tattoos and was trying to find out if I'd done it as a form of self-harm.

'No, it comes in a tube and you just prick the end and use the paste.'

'You've pricked your skin?'

'No, the tube!' I hoped his staff were laughing up their sleeves.

The consensus was that since my brief psychotic episode, I'd 'settled down', which I understood to mean I'd become compliant and given myself over to the business of being analysed. I knew why Bite would think so. If I'd got myself thrown out, I would have been alone with my depression and despair. I couldn't handle that, so I'd learned the rules: don't ask a direct question, it'll only be thrown back at you; never say too much in one go because everything that comes out of your mouth will be analysed; and do not on any account criticise their method.

They decided I was well enough to work again and it didn't

take me long to find a job. Three days a week, I left the unit straight after lunch to help out at a training project in Homerton for unemployed young people, and a few months after that I was discharged. I wrote Antonio a story about a tightrope walker as a leaving present. I called it 'Keep Your Feet Off The Ground' and he was generous enough to pretend to like it. Rowan coughed and blushed his way through our final meeting, Jules almost cracked another smile as we shook hands, and I left Oakham feeling braver and less socially inept than when I'd arrived.

Marianne commented on how easily I joined in with the banter in the pub that evening. It was no wonder; nothing that happened on Bethnal Green Road on a Friday night was ever going to match the uproars I'd endured at the unit. But in spite of my new-found confidence, I'd also gained a renewed conviction that there was a fundamental flaw in me, something that could never be repaired. Now, it was simply up to me to hold it all together.

I thought I could do it.

It's Ava

Not long after I left Oakham, I made a mistake that was to triple my earnings. I had my terrible maths to thank for it. The young people's project had sent me on a speedy training so I'd be able to coach the apprentices and then go out and assess them on their work placements. There was more call for my services than I could handle on part-time hours and I suggested to my employers that I could cover the extra assessments as a freelancer – that way, their stats would look twice as impressive. They accepted my proposal and it was only afterwards that I realised I'd miscalculated and asked for three times the standard fee. They hadn't even blinked.

I was on my way to establishing a successful business and I was set to earn more in the next couple of years than I'd earned in the rest of my working life put together. If this was what Dr Bite had in mind by functioning, I was nailing it.

Except I wasn't nailing it, I was masking it. I kept trying to convince myself that Oakham was a blip, that I wasn't really the sort of person who should have a disability card. I'd just been off my game for a while. My anxiety and depression grumbled on, and my relationship with Faith fell apart because someone I'd once had a one-night stand with tried to get me into bed again and I'd been a bit too keen.

Having exhausted my capacity for short-term affairs with

London's butches, and since any other women I hadn't slept with were now under the impression I was certifiable, I decided to revisit relationships with men.

Mad had the perfect specimen in mind. When she wasn't being psychoanalysed, she sang at funerals for a living, and while we were leaning against a gravestone in Highgate Cemetery with a flask of whiskey, she told me her friend, Philip, thought he knew me and would be joining us shortly. I was intrigued. I'd spent the last few years surrounded by lunatics and lesbians so I couldn't imagine how Philip and I could have crossed paths, unless he'd had a breakdown or a sex change.

When he arrived, I still couldn't recall ever having met him. He was a smart, slim man with old-fashioned glasses and careful manners, and he seemed very taken with me. He grasped my hand and held on to it for several seconds. I wondered if I'd somehow acquired a stalker.

'Oxford,' he explained. 'I came to Charlotte College to talk to you all about joining the Liberal Democrats.'

I vaguely remembered this, though I'd only gone to the meeting because I wanted to sleep with one of the organisers. I hadn't listened to a word Philip said and I never would have recognised him again. I thought he must lead a very uneventful life to be able to remember me.

He said he was living in Bristol these days and was editor of an interfaith magazine. It was evident that he was excited to be conversing not just with an ex-psychiatric patient, but one who was also, to all intents and purposes, a failed lesbian. Once I'd taken in that he had the requisite curly hair and was unlikely to be a serial killer, I began to return his attentions. I'd given up any attempt to make sense of myself; it would have to do that Philip made an obvious sort of sense to us both.

Mad left us to it with the excuse that she had to go and sing 'Ave Maria' to some rich people, and Philip and I went to a café and ordered a large slice of lemon cheesecake with two forks, please. A couple of weeks and several stilted phone calls later, I caught the bus to Bristol.

Having just spent two years at an institution, I thought Philip's little house was heaven. He had parquet floors, bookshelves lined with titles like *Enjoying God,* and a sunny garden full of passion flowers. He also had the Egyptian cotton sheets I'd come to expect of his type. He blanched when I threw off my top.

'Oh goodness, I've never met a woman who didn't shave her underarms.'

I wondered what he was going to make of my hairy nipples. On my side, it was quite a thing to see and touch a penis again after all these years, and even more of a thing to realise that while I'd been swimming in a sea of lesbian sex, straight men hadn't made much progress. Philip was clueless about my clitoris and perfectly happy to orgasm twice without making any attempt to figure out what might make me come. I'd never been in this situation before and Philip looked petulant when I put it to him that sex wasn't finished until everyone had finished. It occurred to me that he might have been expecting some sort of feminine artifice, but orgasms were the one thing in my life I'd never had to fake. In the end, I began to sort myself out, though he looked so uncomfortable I thought he might leave the room.

Nevertheless, within six months, we'd agreed I would sublet my flat and move in with him until we figured out what we wanted to do in the longer term. Apart from telling me his mother thought I'd be less neurotic if I had a baby, he seemed willing to more or less ignore my bouts of anxiety, and it helped that I would be hopping on the bus to London every couple of weeks for work.

'If we end up moving to the big city, I'll rent this place out,' he said.

'What about all this?' I waved a hand at his bookshelves. 'Storage?'

'Nobody would ever steal a book!'

I chuckled. It was nice to be in polite society again.

We went to barbecues with Philip's upper-class friends, spent the evenings reading on his leather sofa, and went to bed early. I knew a couple of dykes in Bristol who I could hang out with when it all got too much, and while Philip was at work I swam in the river and sat in cafes trying to write about Saint Hild, the founding Abbess of Whitby monastery.

This wasn't because Philip's religious proclivities had rubbed off on me. In between my periods of depression, I'd continued to write and I was simply casting about for a new topic. After the *Gin and Ginger Cake* story that had impressed Dan so much, I'd written a novel called *Chips with Wendy* about a young woman in foster care who went out with a lad called Charlie before dumping him in favour of his sister. Then there was *Gillingham Spit*, which had a slightly less virile version of Filchie as the protagonist and earned me an agent but no publishing deal, then *Walking on Pins* with a narrator who sounded a lot like Jay, but which proved too vulgar for my agent's sensibilities, and finally *Goddess,* about a woman who had a breakdown and killed her parents. My agent didn't like that one either.

But I was still holding out hope, especially now I had Philip's financial support and time on my hands. He was encouraging and gave me advice on finding another agent. And since I hadn't shown any signs of incipient mania and I was now working hard on something he considered virtuous, he decided I was ready to be introduced to his relatives.

First up was his mother in Hampstead. She was a tense little woman whose eyes darted everywhere. While she took Philip into the house to help with the tea things, I was left on a fold-up chair in her manicured garden. I heard her shrill voice coming through the open window.

'I didn't think she'd turn up in boots!'

I looked down at my DMs with the bouncing soles, perfect footwear for walking on the heath. I'd spent so long out of the straight world, it hadn't occurred to me that I was supposed to come to lunch in heels and a frock.

'Have you had many boyfriends?' Philip's mother asked as she offered me a scone.

'No, I've had a lot of girlfriends. How about you?'

She looked unsettled only for a moment before embarking on a long story about her gay gentleman friend who worked in the opera. We left just before *Gardener's Question Time* with the remaining scones packed carefully into Tupperware: four for me and Philip, and six for his married brother who we were due to meet for dinner.

I hoped for better things from this brother, especially when I saw we were both wearing the same waistcoat. We spent a subdued evening with him and his silent wife at their gloomy house on Clapham Common, surrounded by weird oil paintings in gilt frames. In the centre of the dining table was a large ornament depicting Jonah disappearing inside the whale.

Philip had mentioned to me that his brother worked as a psychiatrist at Morton Hospital, and so to rescue the evening I put on my most charming manner to lure him into a heated debate about just how far psychoanalysis had lost its way. He answered in polite monosyllables before turning to Philip to discuss whether he'd be interested in writing an article about his book on mentalisation. I stifled a giggle. Dr Bite was becoming a proponent of this method, too; at least they'd be hitting the brick wall together. On the phone afterwards, Philip's brother told him I 'wasn't his kind of person'. In a fit of barely suppressed rage, Philip told me I'd antagonised everyone.

'And I'm sick and tired of your *fucking* anxiety!'

This time I laughed out loud. I'd made him say fucking.

Once we'd watched all the decent box sets WH Smiths had

to offer, we booked a week's holiday to Corfu. I was touched by the sight of my lover's bony white shoulders as he picked his way across the pebbles and into the sea for a paddle. The rest of the time he avoided having too much to do with me by getting stuck into the large pile of reading material he'd brought with him. I spent equal amounts of time practising yoga and sunbathing, with the result that Philip came home with extra frown lines and I came home with long hamstrings and a tan. We did, though, manage one standout conversation on the plane back.

'Why are you not interested in God?' Philip asked.

'Why are you bothering with God?' I replied.

Philip's mother had volunteered to stay in the house while we were away so she could water the garden. On our return, I discovered she'd packed up all my belongings, going as far as to retrieve my underwear from the laundry basket and stuffing all the tampons I'd left in a convenient bowl on the bathroom shelf back into their box. The passport-sized photograph of me in Philip's study had evidently given her some difficulty, since strictly speaking it belonged to her son. She'd solved this by taking my picture out of its frame, lying it flat on the mantelpiece and placing a pebble over my face.

She'd also left Philip a letter, which made clear she thought I'd broken up with him. It was full of barely concealed glee and ended with a confession that she would have liked to 'bash me up', but that I'd no doubt gone back to London and my bisexual ways. I was mystified and I wasn't going to let this go. I made Philip give me her phone number so I could call her straightaway.

'I want to understand why you thought I was leaving Philip,' I said with fake calm.

'What else was I to think after you left such a horrible voicemail on his answering machine?'

This was even more mystifying. 'What voicemail?'

'You said, *It's Finley, it's over, you're not there so I'm sending you a letter!*'

For a split second, I thought she, too, must have delusional moments. I had an image of me and Philip's mother sharing a cigarette in the dayroom at Oakham, me in my DMs and her in an oversized nightie and a pair of pink slippers. In another moment, the penny dropped. While Philip and I were away, the facilitator of a London writer's group had left me a voice message: '*Finley, it's Ava. You're not there, I'll send you a letter.*'

Stifling my triumph, I carefully explained this to Philip's mother. 'So can we draw a line under this now?'

She was silent for a moment and then she rallied. 'Alright, but I must mention one last thing.' I could sense her physically drawing herself up. 'The house was *very* dusty.'

I was cut to the quick.

Over the next few weeks, it began to dawn on me that I was as deluded to believe I could make a life with an upper-class Christian as I had been to try and do it with an old bulldagger from Luton. It was exhausting having to pretend I wasn't a hairy, bloody, screwed-up mess all the time. Philip didn't even try to hide his relief when I told him I was leaving. I went back to London and my bisexual ways, and a couple of years later I heard that Philip had published his first book, *Why Bother with God?*

Touché.

Bodies

Back in my flat, without Philip's mother to annoy me, and with the news that my agent had yet again failed to find me a publisher, I felt lost and low. I tried to track down Dan, hoping I'd be forgiven for being a piece of work, only to discover he'd married his Spanish girlfriend and they'd gone off to do good deeds in the rainforest.

Marianne was also married. She'd found herself a gay Canadian so she could go and live in Ontario for a year while he went wild in Soho. She was just about to leave when I returned and made me promise to send her regular updates about what was happening in *The Archers*. This development worried me more than the idea of her being dipped in honey and thrown to the Americans.

The edge was taken off my unhappiness when I accepted a contract to deliver training at a little project for mental health service users in Finsbury Park. The finance worker had underspent on the annual budget and they needed to throw some money around before the new financial year, with the result that I was offered an excellent fee. The rest of the team were rowdy African and Caribbean women, who sat in each other's laps while they wrote up their case notes and told bawdy stories about their sex lives. 'We did it five times last night!' one of them exclaimed while she slapped me on the arse. 'Do you want to see the photos?'

Nobody minded working overtime because they knew that the boss, a Puerto Rican with a laissez-faire management style, would be ordering in pizza and cupcakes. He also took us to the local spa to make up for the rats that lived behind the office skirting boards. We could hear him laughing in the chillout room while a Turkish woman threw buckets of cold water at us in the sauna.

He gave me free rein with my expenses and in a further effort to reduce the surplus money before it got clawed back, he contracted a Harley Street consultant to run a series of workshops on positive psychology. I loved this guy. He was obsessed with Tesco's Finest choc chip cookies and I'd never seen anyone look as positive as he did when he opened up a fresh new packet. The plan was that he would train me up as his assistant so we could work together at his fancy office. In the first session, we endured an hour of uninterrupted negativity from the group and he could scarcely believe how serene I was.

These sessions were a great addition to my CV and I got a lot out of them while pretending to know what I was doing. The group really did seem more positive by the end of the afternoon, though I couldn't help noticing that by the time they returned the following week they'd gone back to their habitual moroseness. Apparently, even a high-profile psychologist operating out of a prestigious address and charging £300 an hour wasn't in possession of the silver bullet, but what he taught me expanded my freelance repertoire no end. Before long, I was getting contracts to run workshops on mental health awareness all across London, while holding tightly to the mantra 'Insight through experience' to convince myself I was a fit person for the job.

Meantime, I also decided to train in remedial massage. My freelance associates regarded this as a bizarre decision, like a mathematician suddenly deciding to become a hairdresser, but I was set on it. I'd slept with enough folks to be aware of the wide variety of sensitivities and ranges of motion we enjoy, and I'd spent so long unsuccessfully trying to sort my head out that I wanted to see if I could fix up some muscles instead.

The massage school was a fresh hell I was wholly unprepared for. The owner and principal teacher had set himself up in competition with another school whose name sounded suspiciously similar, and he'd poached a couple of their tutors into the bargain, presumably because they were willing to treat him as a god. He was, by turns, charming and domineering, and ran the whole operation as a well-oiled money-making business.

Most of the tutors were working class, and one or two of them were clearly enjoying a power they'd never before experienced. One, in particular, had all the gleeful disregard for facts that you'd expect from someone who didn't trust anything that wasn't shouted at them from the tabloids. He took a special dislike to me and if he paid me any attention at all, it was to jump on my slightest error.

'*Do not* drape your towel like that, Finley. If I see that again, you will fail.'

I was under no illusion; it was payback time for the Oxford graduate who'd dared to poke a nose into their empire.

I became sceptical about what we were learning pretty early on, but I wasn't going to say anything because I needed the qualification to get insurance to practise. It didn't make sense to me to believe you could change a muscle by pushing and prodding at it; after all, if it was that easy, we'd all have flat bottoms from sitting down. Nevertheless, we were introduced to more and more complicated techniques for 'tissue release', and everyone else seemed convinced that the tissue had indeed been set free. Once I understood that I was being too clever by half, I decided to approach my monthly anatomy and physiology submissions the same way I approached fiction writing, with the result that my marks greatly improved and I scraped into the distinction category, though the school never admitted to it. It wouldn't be an overstatement to say I worked harder to pass my diploma in remedial massage than I did to acquire my degree and I was more relieved to get away from the place than I was to leave psychiatric hospital.

I set up my bodywork business in my front room, with my collection of lesbian erotica shoved under the sofa and the television hidden under an ethnic cloth. I worked like a dog to establish myself, spending half the week elbowing the aching backs of stressed-out desk workers and runners. I was well cut out for this energetic sideline; I was never hung over at the start of the week, and thanks to all the yoga and cycling, I had the stamina of an ostrich.

It was an added bonus that in the years since I'd first moved into my Elizabeth Park flat, the local demographic had changed beyond recognition. There was a new sourdough bakery on the corner, wood-fired pizza was available in the pub, and an influx of weekend warriors all wanted my attention. Since my overheads were low and I had no family or drug habit to support, the money rolled in and stayed. There was only the occasional scare.

'Any health issues I should know about?' I asked a pale-lipped young man, pen poised.

'No, no, all good,' he said.

It was only when I'd finished slathering him in oil that he mentioned he'd just come out of a coma.

There was also the woman who wanted a super-deep abdominal massage, whose excess of wind later turned out to be a three-month old foetus she definitely *didn't* want to expel, and the medical student who asked me to stand on his neck 'just to see what would happen'. Fortunately, I had the sense to just say no.

Now the massage school no longer had its claws in me, I could study as widely as I liked. Being a nerd helped and I began to introduce techniques and ways of working that my fellow massage students would have found unintelligible. I discovered the work of Peter Levine, Bessel Van der Kolk and Stephen Porges, who introduced the world to polyvagal theory and normalised the dissociation I'd experienced all my life. I couldn't get enough of these guys. At last it seemed like there might be the beginnings of some answers. I began to understand the weird and wonderful things a nervous system can do when it decides a person is under threat, and my clients appreciated my efforts to find real strategies for their distress. I made it a point of honour never to suck my teeth and blame it all on muscle knots.

A local young woman soon set herself up as my rival in the holistic massage stakes. She did me the favour of pinching snippets from my website, undercutting every discount offer I made, and putting up posters three times the size of mine in the local newsagents. At last I had a stalker worthy of the name. I got furious and upped my game. Within two months of her arrival on my radar, I had eighty five-star Google reviews.

The result of all this aggressive marketing was that my website shot up the ranking and became so visible my brother managed to find me from Italy. Perhaps he also felt more comfortable re-engaging with me now he thought I was doing something unassuming for a living, rather than delivering workshops for the insane and dispossessed. He called me to say he was flying into London and would like to see me before he travelled on to Bradford. I couldn't help feeling curious, so I said yes please.

Old

I chose a bar in Islington that I thought would have some straight people in it and Charles turned up in a well-fitting shiny suit and a pale pink tie. He parked his suitcase between the bar stools, collapsing the handle in the practised manner of a seasoned traveller. I noticed his hair was thick again and his forehead didn't move a muscle.

'Dew I look old?' he asked, running a hand through his fringe. His accent was now a bizarre blend of Yorkshire and Italian.

'No,' I lied.

He launched in straightaway. He was still very upset about my sex abuse accusations to Chad and Peggy, and wanted a full apology.

'Yew don't know wot it did ter Mam and Dad, yew sayin all that.'

'Okay, I'm sorry,' I said. 'I didn't mean to hurt anyone. I was in a psychosis. I know how hard it must have been for you all. I've spent a good few years since then trying to support people with mental health problems.'

'This breakdown you say you 'ad,' he persevered, 'yew don't know the half of what it did tew us.'

I contemplated mentioning one or two of the less palatable things it had done to me, but thought better of it.

'I accept something must 'ave 'appened tew yew. I don't know what, mebbe at skewl. But it wasn't Mam or Dad, that's for sure. We know yew better than anybody else dus.'

'Okay.' It reminded me of the time when, as a teenager, he'd told me he believed there *was* someone who once did the things Jesus was supposed to have done, but that person wasn't the son of God and he definitely wasn't called Jesus.

Not long after this, presumably because my brother had reported that I was contrite, Chad called me. Peggy had caught a rare virus and was dangerously ill in hospital. He said there were three types of medication they could try and after that, there wouldn't be much hope. He sounded like a scandalised little boy.

I thanked my lucky stars I wasn't in a position to drop everything and rush up to Bradford to hold his hand. I made the right noises, asked to be kept updated and we ended the call without too much damage. Peggy recovered before they gave her the second drug and this ushered in the beginning of a new phase in my relationship with my parents. I was right-thinking, winsome and acceptable again.

Gordon

In the wake of this family reconciliation, I met Gordon. I'd signed up for a one-day Indian head massage course in the suburbs, mainly because I fancied a trip out of London and the brochure showed a picture of a country house with students eating sandwiches by a pond.

Gordon and I were paired up to work together for the day because we were the same height. He greeted this proposition with a smile on the widest mouth I've ever seen, accompanied by a riot of lisping and squinting. He had a bouncy strawberry-blonde ponytail I couldn't wait to get my hands into and we got on like a house on fire. Perhaps because of something the massage did to my head, before the day was over, I'd asked him out on a date.

We met in a café near his office in South London where he worked for the tax office. He arrived right on time and he must have changed at work because he was dressed in an oversized beige sweatshirt covered in hieroglyphs, a pair of cargo pants, walking socks, sandals and a cravat. Either he was having the kind of identity crisis I could relate to or something had gone horribly wrong with his wardrobe.

He told me that although he was a civil servant by day, he was also very much interested in 'personal development', which explained the head massage course. In his free time, he cared for his elderly mother, who'd been diagnosed with heart disease.

She sounded like a sensible woman who was taking a pragmatic approach to death and paperwork.

'So, are you looking for a relationship?' I asked. I'd decided it was time I made a proper commitment to someone and since Gordon was solvent, functioning and funny, he seemed like a prime candidate.

He waved around his slice of cheese on toast. 'I don't want to get married, but I do love to cook. And I'd like to share a pet and ironing and things like that.'

He sounded ideal.

After our date, Gordon left me a series of maudlin text messages that made me laugh like a drain. I wasn't deterred even when I found out he'd meant every word. His lisp, his harmlessness and his conventional job were all so far removed from where I'd been that I fancied I was bound to end up halfway decent if I hitched myself to him for the rest of my life.

The following week, we met up again and caught the train back to Gordon's house in Penge. While he was taking off his shoes and socks in the hallway, I wandered into the sitting room. The walls were covered in maps of London, and inside a glass cabinet was a large sculpture of an obese earth goddess with pendulous breasts. This was more on my level than Philip had ever been; less god and more body.

Gordon padded in behind me and grabbed me round the waist. Just as one would expect from a civil servant about to get naked, his toenails were painted all the colours of the rainbow.

'Big love,' he whispered, spitting lightly into my ear.

We tried, in a desultory sort of way, to have sex. It was nowhere near my usual standard – a state of affairs I ought to have anticipated. Gordon was approaching fifty and had already admitted that he'd been celibate for almost twenty years. We may as well have been from different species, since by this time I'd been shagging my way around London and beyond for well over a decade. But what his penis lacked in inspiration, he made up for in enthusiasm. I'd never felt so comfortable with a lover and he looked adorable when I tickled him.

'I don't see any reason why this won't work,' I told Marianne over the phone when we finally managed to get the time difference right.

'He sounds as camp as a row of tents,' she said, cautiously.

No matter; this was an improvement on the last time I'd wanted her approval, when she'd informed me that my one-night stand sounded like a psychopath.

Not very many weeks had gone by when Gordon climbed into my bed one evening, tucked himself in and settled down for a good night's sleep without so much as a peck on my cheek. I lay staring at the ceiling, naked and wet, and muttered, 'Shit,' under my breath.

In spite of my new lover's abstemiousness, and in spite of catching him doing yoga in my front room in nothing but a pair of baggy Y-fronts, I was undeterred. Gordon was going to be the one; Gordon meant that my madness was truly over. He moved into my place and to seal his commitment to me, he put his house on the market, which really put the willies up me. I dreamt that my floors had exploded under the weight of Gordon's shoes. This seemed almost prescient when he called me from work a few days later to say he had to stay late because of someone called Richard Reid.

Very soon we were sleeping separately, one in the living room and one in the bedroom, depending on who turned in first for the night. I didn't mind; his chocolate puddings were divine. Things perked up when Gordon confided in me that he wanted to become a woman, an idea I could wholeheartedly embrace. I loved watching him drop his briefcase on the bed, take off his socks to reveal his prettily painted toenails and sashay into the cupboard to choose a dress for the evening.

I taught him how to shave his legs and helped him to find silky but supportive underwear, so I could admire my new-found sister as she sat in our best armchair, feet tucked elegantly to one side. It was all so much better than the underpants and it didn't occur to me for a moment that we were a complete car crash.

In return for my unconditional support for this transition, she – for there was no doubt that Gordon was now the feminine presence in our home – bought me a ginger kitten. We named him Princess Michael Happiness and competed to see who could spoil him the most. Gordon won when she insisted our new fluffball 'needed' to sleep with her each night, because the thought of all that cuteness shut away downstairs was too much to bear.

My flat became a playground for softies. The three of us romped from room to room trailing feathers and ribbons and trying on each other's clothes. Princess Michael looked particularly fetching in a lace mitten Gordon tied around his neck like a Victorian ruffle, and I loved Gordon's discarded boxer shorts with the toucans on them. Once everyone was ready, Gordon would pull up her sequinned blouse and chase me round the kitchen, shaking her little pot belly and growling, 'The belleee, the bellleee!' in a far from menacing way while I screamed in delight.

These antics were the most benign imaginable replay of Chad's teasing, and whenever I'd had a particularly gloomy day, I would sit near the front door, waiting for the rattle of Gordon's key. The sight of her smiling, squinting face and the thought of the delightful transformation that was about to happen never failed to cheer me up.

Bliss

Now that Gordon was settled, her mother was able to go ahead and die and leave us her bungalow. This generosity seemed to me a tad unfair because Gordon had an older sister with a family, but Gordon had been their mother's main caretaker and, knowing her son as she did and having met me a couple of times, she probably thought we needed all the help we could get. Fortunately, Gordon was as careful with money as I was. Neither of us owned a car or went on extravagant holidays, and it soon became evident we could afford to buy a house.

'We must be clear we're doing this as friends, not partners,' I said, sternly.

Gordon nodded, looking only a little intransigent.

I found the perfect place just up the road; an ex-council property, sturdy, spacious, with a little garden at the back. The drug dealer living next door was charming and we could move most of our stuff ourselves, with a bit of help with the heavy stuff from an old butch and her three-legged dog.

We immediately entered into domestic bliss. When we weren't prancing about like five-year-olds or cuddled up on Gordon's bed like two lost souls clinging to a life raft, we behaved like an eccentric suburban couple transplanted into the bowels of Newham. At weekends, Gordon went on shopping trips to Waitrose and cooked like Nigella, and through the rest of the week I kept house in between thumping and slapping massage clients in the spare room.

My new sister comforted me through my various breakups with women and men, and whenever the frights overwhelmed me in the night, I could pop myself into Gordon's bed, where she cuddled me like a teddy bear. I tried several times to discuss the ambivalence of our relationship, but this always resulted in such an adorable attack of incoherent lisping and squinting that I was disarmed for days.

Any stress at all was bad for Gordon. She suffered from what she'd been told was Crohn's disease, and every few months, she spent a couple of days lying uncomplaining on the sofa, getting up only for explosive sessions on the toilet. During these periods of incapacity, I took over the cooking duties, producing as much comfort food as I could muster: boiled eggs with marmite soldiers, leek and potato soup, and bread and butter pudding with a smiley face made out of cherries on top.

Thanks to a speedy bit of research, I was able to conclude that Gordon didn't have Crohn's disease after all, just terrible bouts of irritable bowel syndrome. The biggest testimony to how much she trusted me was that I was in charge of our toilet roll purchases, and in all the years we lived together, I ensured we never had fewer than fourteen replacement rolls on hand. In my book, that was a sign of true love.

Witnessing my sex hair on a regular basis eventually rubbed off on Gordon, and she developed an interest in getting some for herself. In our third year of living together, she repeated the one-day Indian head massage experience and this time it worked like a dream. She found herself a fellow civil servant, an enormous woman with thighs and breasts not unlike those of the goddess sculpture, and an impressive repertoire of songs from *Joseph*. Incredibly, this goddess liked Gordon back. I regularly heard them shagging and farting away in bed, which was more than I'd ever been able to do for Gordon.

I couldn't quite understand what this rather ordinary woman saw in my colourful housemate, but as long as their relations didn't disrupt my perfect life, I was fine with it. Over time, it transpired that the goddess was a practising Catholic and that Gordon, unbeknownst to me, had once embarked on a quest to become a vicar. Apparently, she'd been told she was 'strong on heresy' and had failed her vicar exams, but there must have been just enough residue of piety left in her to satisfy her conquest. To further humour the plus-sized goddess, the dresses and nail polish went back in the closet, and Gordon returned to masculine pronouns. The please-everyone-but-yourself civil servant was back on a full-time contract.

The Big C

There were two incentives for me to go to Bradford: it was Christmas and Peggy had cancer.

She'd been complaining of tiredness on and off for a couple of years, but she'd put that down to the after effects of the life-threatening virus. It was only when she began to lose weight that the doctor – no longer the dour Scot, but a young woman Chad had recruited to take over my role of soothing and attending to him – sent Peggy for tests. A large tumour was discovered at the top of her bowel. The consultant was amazed she'd had no pain. I wasn't amazed. My mother had always been incapable of feeling much discomfort of any kind.

'Have you caught cancer again?' she used to mock, whenever my father complained about his health. Chad had a history of jaundice, recurrent disc herniations that had him off work for months, psoriasis and gallstones, but Peggy still thought he was a hypochondriac. My brother succumbed to childhood pneumonia and occasional bedwetting, and I caught every cold going, but the Wilson family story was that we did not get ill, nor did we struggle with money problems, addiction or dysfunction of any kind – all that was for losers.

Peggy herself really did seem to be immune. Just once, at the height of their card-playing days, she developed a sore shoulder that was painful enough to send her to the doctor, who told her she had bursitis. My mother found this idiotic and never mentioned it again. Getting diagnosed, now, with a potentially terminal illness must have come as an almighty blow.

Her surgery was due to happen shortly after Christmas, and Charles and I were summoned to spend a few days with her beforehand, which made me think she was frightened she might die on the operating table. We booked ourselves into separate hotels, taking care not to co-ordinate. No one, it appeared, wanted to spend too much time together. Nonetheless, I wanted this to be good. Now that my brother and I were both earning well, we could make this a Christmas worth remembering. I imagined welcoming embraces in front of an open fire, Chad's jokes tempered by a new-found sensitivity, and a wry recognition of everything we'd put each other through over the years. We would be a proper, loving family at last.

I went into a frenzy of present buying, finding Chad an enormous pair of navy-blue luxury bath towels in John Lewis and a matching pair in pink for Gordon, who would be spending the festive season with the goddess. I had no idea what my brother and his partner would like, so I went for consumables: Harrods' duck pate, wine from Berry Bros. and Grenadian chocolates from an obscure little shop in Piccadilly. Peggy got a cashmere bed jacket and, in a final burst of enthusiasm, I bought Chad an eye-wateringly expensive roll of handmade artist's paper. There was barely room left in my luggage for a change of clothes and some pyjamas.

I brushed off a niggling unease as to why, when I didn't even like my parents, I was trying so hard to be good.

Fraud

I said I'd get a taxi from the station to Chad and Peggy's new
house, which I hadn't yet seen, but Peggy insisted she'd come
and pick me up. I was pleased about this; the drive would give us
twenty minutes alone together to talk about how she was feeling,
which fitted in well with my plan to discover a heart-warming
new connection between us.

I spotted the car turning into the parking bay and hurried
over. I threw my rucksack onto the back seat and got in next to
my mother.

'Hello, love,' she said.

I smiled, nodding.

As Peggy pulled out of the station, my smile froze. It was
as though someone had thrown a bucket of glue over me. I felt
stuck, shutdown, appalled. I didn't know what was happening,
but I couldn't stop it. The car smelt vaguely of shit; my mother
must be wearing some sort of incontinence pad, but it wasn't
that. Here I was, being weird again, unable to provide the kind
of attentiveness towards my elderly mother that any normal
daughter would have found perfectly straightforward. I hated
myself and I'd gone off so fast even Peggy noticed.

'What's the matter?' she said, sharply, keeping her eyes on
the road.

'Nothing,' I muttered. I could have said I felt horrible, but I
didn't want her to touch me.

She ignored me for a while, then as we turned onto the A58, she pointed out the bunches of dead flowers at the side of the road.

'See just there? That's where our neighbour's grandson was killed by a lorry. I was giving her a lift into town when she got the news. I had to stop the car. I tried to give her a hug, but she just wanted to get out. She wouldn't even talk to me!'

She shook her head, affronted, and I shuddered. Had she really thought she could contain that kind of grief? I recalled a time in my late teens when she'd announced that one of the girls she worked with was being sexually abused. My mother had given her a hug and taken her under her wing. She took the girl shopping for new clothes; they went to watch the fireworks on the moor together; and the girl was invited round to play Monopoly with Chad. Even back then, I'd thought there was something off about it. Had the girl understood she could say no?

We turned into a cul-de-sac and Peggy parked outside a row of identical new-build houses with glossy black front doors and rose-gold knockers. My father opened the door to us, red-faced, panting.

'I was expecting you ten minutes ago. Peg?'

Peggy waved a hand, distracted. 'Traffic was bad.'

She shooed us into the lounge and ran upstairs to the bathroom. I heard water spattering into the sink.

'I don't know how to cheer her up,' Chad said helplessly.

I wondered whether cheering up was what she needed. My brother had emailed the day before to inform us that she must fight back, that she must win this battle. I couldn't help sniggering at his cliches.

While Chad boiled potatoes, Peggy took me upstairs to the spare room that she used as a study. On the desk was a photograph of my mother I hadn't seen before; it must have been taken after I'd left for university. She was in her late forties and she had on one of my old mini dresses, a black choker and a gash of lipstick. I felt a pang of pity.

Peggy pulled open a drawer in the filing cabinet and began flicking through the files. She slapped a pile of papers down on the desk. 'Now, pay attention.'

'Still the boss, eh?' I said softly. She didn't hear me.

'These are all our outgoings.' She handed me a list of bank account numbers and associated bills, tapping the page with her fingernail. 'Cancel that one straightaway and that one, but leave him the Sky Sports. Your father will be useless with money if I'm not here.'

'But—'

'Now, look.' She handed me a separate sheet of paper with the details of a different bank account, a different bank. 'Take everything out of this account and close it. If I die.'

'That would be fraud, Mam, jeez!'

She looked at me wide-eyed for a moment, then her face fell. I'd just scuppered her hope of ensuring that Chad would never find out she had a secret stash of money.

'My mother would be dead and I'd be in jail!' I elaborated.

Her expression softened and we chuckled, her common sense meeting mine.

Christmas day was got through. Charles arrived with his girlfriend, whose hair was now peroxide blonde and set in stiff waves. She took off her hot pink jacket to shake my hand. My brother and father shouted together about the football until Charles cut Chad off to answer his phone. He sauntered over to the window, still talking too loudly, unaware of his posturing or our father's petulant expression. I'd gleaned from my parents that my brother had sky-high blood pressure these days and was being checked out for pains in his chest. Later, he gave me the same information himself in a tone of bemused helplessness. I wondered how much anxiety my brother was suppressing.

Charles' girlfriend's English hadn't improved. My mother did her best with her evening class Italian, leaving me and Chad to sit looking at the television for most of the day, which suited us both. I was still feeling very odd; nauseous and foggy. I kept congratulating myself for booking a hotel room; I wasn't sure how long I could handle this feeling of suffocation. Around seven in the evening, I made the excuse that I had work to do and went to get my coat. Charles and his girlfriend had already said the same thing and the three of us left with promises to return straight after breakfast the following day.

On Boxing Day, we went for a walk on a scrubby patch of ground next to the estate, pretending not to hear the hum of motorway traffic in the background. Chad strode on ahead while Peggy wandered off to look for late blackberries. Charles dawdled behind with his girlfriend, who was trying to keep her stilettos from sinking into the mud. I caught up with Chad and offered to continue on to Great Acre Park with him – a round trip I calculated would take us the best part of three hours, and which we completed mostly in a sort of distressed, companionable silence. At one point, Chad said I looked well. Tears pricked my eyes. Sometimes, just sometimes, my father noticed I was a person.

After lunch, my parents and Charles played cards, while I read a book and Charles' partner sat with her phone. Peggy and Chad had an afternoon nap, and my brother managed not to say another word to me until it was time to say goodbye, when he lunged at me to do two European air kisses. My cheeks trembled with amusement and distaste.

Haven

I was glad to get home, to see Gordon's open, smiling face again and to sit in our kitchen among familiar smells while Princess Michael wound himself round my legs. My wife stirred a pot of curry and I ordered a hamper of junk food for Chad to get through while Peggy was in hospital and couldn't keep tabs on what he ate. He told me it made him cry when it arrived and I wondered how long it was since she'd let him have a samosa.

I bought a black dress and walked round Elizabeth Park learning by heart a poem Peggy had once exclaimed over, long ago, when she was scouring a textbook for something to teach to her class. 'Oof, how wonderful,' she'd said. 'I want that at my funeral!'

When she left the room, I'd had a look at the book. I was only twelve at the time, but I was amazed to discover that my cold, unsentimental mother had been reading *Heaven Haven* by Gerard Manley Hopkins. It was as though she'd inadvertently let slip that she had a soul. I copied down the title and kept hold of it.

When I told him I still had it, even Gordon was shocked at the tenacity of my forward planning.

As it turned out, Peggy didn't die in theatre. She was told she had the heart of a spring chicken and that the operation was as successful as it could possibly have been. She had a few nodules on her lungs, but they were so tiny no one thought them worth worrying about. She'd be able to go home as soon as she'd had a successful bowel movement. A couple of days later, she rang me from her hospital bed, sounding tearful and constipated.

'I don't know where your father is. He should have been here an hour ago. Can you call him?'

Chad didn't answer the phone. I tried over and over for an hour, while my mother sent me increasingly frantic text messages. Finally, I called their next-door neighbour, a body builder who was eager to break down the front door. He was just about to go at it when Peggy texted me again to say Chad was with her. He'd got to the hospital early and had been watching cartoons on the television in the waiting room, expecting a nurse to summon him once they were done with Peggy. Typically, my father had missed all the drama – but at least Peggy was on the mend.

'The food is absolute muck,' she texted me. 'Rubbery muck.'

Then Chad texted, 'She's done a little fart, so that's good.'

For once, he wasn't being facetious.

Then, my mother again. 'Don't tell Dad, I dropped a poo on the floor. I can come home.'

Chad sent me thirteen texts and four emails the day Peggy left hospital, and for the first time in my life I really wanted to tell my father to fuck off.

A Fool at Forty

All of a sudden, I was turning forty. Feminine Gordon was loaned out to me by the goddess the week before, and together we embarked on a frenzy of chopping, whisking, whipping and marinading in order to produce enough food for the forty people I'd invited to my party. Since Peggy had made a full recovery and relations between my brother and I had improved to the extent of the air kisses, I invited them all to join us.

As well as the mountains of food Gordon and I were preparing, I'd booked a scary lesbian with a keyboard. She looked like a Gothic version of Amy Winehouse, and had a wider vocal range and even better lyrics. She was the idea whose time had come, she loved her Briar Rose, and there was one song with a chorus that sounded to me like 'Finley is mighty kingly', although Gordon said he didn't think so.

My parents and Charles and his partner were the first guests to arrive. They huddled together in the spare room for a couple of hours before escaping back to their Canary Wharf hotel so as not to accidentally meet any of my friends. I didn't mind; according to my bellicose singer, we had sin in the front, sin in the back and sin on the roof rack. The women from the Finsbury Park project came and added decibels to the proceedings, some Oakham patients arrived bearing white lilies and a packet of crisps, and there were enough butches standing in the corners of all the rooms to satisfy anyone who wanted one. Princess Michael Happiness, in best ruffle and tail bow, watched the comings and goings from the top of the kitchen cupboards, his eyes as big as saucers.

I was only sad that Marianne didn't make it. Ever since she'd conquered the heart of an Ontarian lesbian and committed herself to a long-distance relationship, we'd seen very little of each other. She always seemed to be on the verge of yet another adventure; trekking in the Karakoram mountains, scuba diving in Egypt, or feeding giraffes in the Serengeti. I couldn't keep up. I found it stressful enough to have to go to Leyton.

When the last of the party people had departed, Gordon helped me with the clearing up. He was in a funny mood, a little too shrill, and he kept clattering plates into the sink without any of his usual care. At three in the morning, when I was just about ready to drop, he insisted on teaching me how to empty the vacuum cleaner. I made sure to make a pig's ear of it so he wouldn't ask me to do it again, and Princess Michael helped by dashing into the dust cloud and emerging with a hairball crown. Time for bed at last.

The following evening, Gordon didn't come home. He usually spent Sundays with the goddess, but in all the time we'd lived together, he'd never not returned by 7pm on a school night, and he never left me in the dark even if he was running just a few minutes late. I called his phone. I called the goddess's phone. I found the goddess's landline number on our phone bill and called that. No reply. I called a couple of their friends. Nobody knew a thing.

When Gordon left that morning, I'd shouted goodbye to him from the living room instead of going into the hallway for our usual hug. I'd been too busy eating leftover party cake and reading the thank you messages on my new mobile phone to bother getting up. It was the kind of thing people regretted after someone died, I thought, beginning to panic.

I roamed around the house wondering what to do. I got hold of Marianne in the Bay Area. She told me it was way too early to worry, and to try and stay positive. After another day with no news, I called Gordon's sister, who told me in no uncertain terms to call the police.

A few hours later, a young officer came by and took away a photograph of Gordon for identification purposes and, more worryingly, his toothbrush. I took myself to bed, pulled the covers over my face and tried to will myself to sleep. At midnight, I heard the back door being unlocked. I ran downstairs to find Gordon in the kitchen, looking shattered.

'Oh my God, I'm so glad you're home. What the hell's been going on?' I tried to give him a hug.

'No!' he whisper-shouted, as though admonishing an unruly kitten. 'It's not appropriate!'

I stepped back, hurt. 'What's the matter? What's going on? Let me make you a drink while you tell me.'

He said no thank you, looking as grimly determined as his multiple squints would allow. It turned out Gordon was never going to let me make him anything again. He told me he was moving in with the goddess and that, according to our contract, I had three months to get used to the idea before the house must be put up for sale. With that, he turned on his heel and disappeared upstairs.

This was a shocking development; I couldn't quite take it in. On the advice of our more cynical friends, we'd had a legal agreement written up when we bought the house, but like any besotted spouse going through the motions of a prenup, I'd never for a moment imagined we'd need it. Since Gordon had contributed the lion's share to our deposit, I owned only thirty per cent of the property, and given London prices I knew I couldn't afford to buy him out. If I wasn't careful, I was about to lose my home as well as my ridiculous, wonderful wife.

I ran up the stairs after him, hoping I'd be able to persuade him out of it. He was moving quickly between his bedroom and the bathroom, thrusting things into a holdall, lips pressed tightly together.

'So, you're just going to be whatever she wants you to be for the rest of your life, are you?' I said, dodging to one side as he reached for his comb. 'You're going to hide everything away again?'

I indicated the silk slippers he kept stepping over and caught the flicker of anguish on his face, but it was too late, the goddess had coached him too well. I knew his conventional side ached, for weekend trips to IKEA and church on Sundays, and this woman would give him all of that. I couldn't bring myself to push the argument any further, I might break him.

Within an hour, he was gone. I collapsed onto the sofa, gazing at our abruptly abandoned life; the tin of fairy cakes we'd baked as an afterthought for my birthday guests, Michael's robot mouse, Gordon's magnificent amaryllis. I'd shagged and loved and lost here, upped my yoga practice no end, and laughed more than I ever thought I would. It struck me that this situation must have been brewing for quite a while, and was the reason Gordon had wanted to make sure I learned how to use the vacuum cleaner. He hadn't been able to face leaving while I still had insufficient cleaning skills.

When I found the energy, I called the goddess's landline one more time. She told me if I ever phoned there again, she'd call the police. It was a ridiculous threat, but I was dismayed to realise she was that scared of me. I blinked away tears of self-pity and tried to coax Princess Michael into my lap for a cuddle. He didn't want to talk about it either.

Over the next few days, I pieced together what had happened.

Gordon and the goddess had gone on a little road trip to discuss the nature of their relationship and the disagreeable fact of my presence in Gordon's home. At the end of this trip, the goddess had issued Gordon an ultimatum: he must drop me and move in with her, or she'd finish the whole thing. Poor Gordon wasn't equipped to stand up to such assertiveness. No doubt the goddess had also convinced him of the deviant nature of our relationship and the prospect of eternal damnation if he continued to make me buckwheat pancakes. Like any good HMRC boss, she had frightened him into compliance.

Cobwebs

Chad and Peggy were still at their hotel, after spending a couple of days with Charles before he and his partner flew back to Italy. My father, too, had acquired a mobile phone, which he was very adept with. He answered on the first ring. I told him what was going on. He'd forgotten to put in his hearing aids, which always made him shout.

'I'm coming over! If the little shit comes back, I'll have something to say to him and he won't like it! *No one* gets away with hurting my daughter!'

You did, I wanted to say. But when he came and sat like a bulldog at the kitchen table, guarding the back door, I'd never loved him more.

Peggy arrived mid-morning with his hearing aids and a feather duster she'd bought in the corner shop. She picked the price sticker off the handle, tutting at how much she'd paid, and began chasing cobwebs round the window frames. Gordon's squinty eyes clearly hadn't spotted them.

'You can't sell the place in this state,' she said, hopping onto a chair to do a better job. 'And you're going to need all the money you can get.'

Here we were, my mother finally dusting cobwebs for me just as I turned forty. Perhaps things were going to turn out alright after all.

After a couple of mugs of tea, Chad decided I needed a lock on my bedroom door, otherwise Gordon would be stealing stuff as soon as my back was turned. It didn't seem like a bad idea, though I was thinking more about what I could steal of Gordon's. I had my eye on the bread maker and a couple of his cashmere scarves. Chad went off to make arrangements with the locksmiths down the road and I boiled the kettle again.

Peggy began rattling on about a friend of hers, whose daughter had just given birth to two little boys who were in delicate health.

'They're so sensitive,' she said, shaking her head. 'And Cynthia is so good with them! When I think how I treated you...'

I turned to look at her. Her head was down. I couldn't see her face.

'I damaged you. I'm sorry.'

My head swam. I couldn't take this in. I was too busy thinking of all the practical things I had to deal with.

'It's okay,' I said at last, since I didn't quite know which of all the horrible things she was talking about.

'No, it's not,' Peggy said harshly, and left the room.

Trapped

Even though I'd found us a reputable solicitor, Gordon appointed one of his own. After that, all our communications were done through expensive legal channels. At one point, no doubt in a ploy to save Gordon money, his sister telephoned me to offer to 'mediate'. I told her coldly that would be about as helpful as getting the cat to do it.

Living alone in the house didn't serve me well. I had too much time on my hands; I couldn't stop ruminating about where the hell I was going to live and who would get custody of Princess Michael. It wasn't a fair playing field because I wouldn't be able to afford a garden. As my distress increased, my ability to think straight deteriorated. I paced round the kitchen, clutching the breadknife and seething. Gordon had made a fool of me by keeping me in the dark, and after all we'd been through together, he was abandoning me without a backwards glance. I found myself prostrated on the floor, howling like an actor in a Shakespearean tragedy.

I was interrupted by a ping from my phone. Gordon had texted to say he was coming to pick up a letter that hadn't been diverted. The idea of laying a trap came to me in a moment, fully formed. I threw his letter in the bin, put an identical-looking envelope on the kitchen table and locked the door that led from the kitchen into the hallway. I knew he'd come up through the garden and straight in through the back door.

I hid in the corner, half concealed by the fridge, fully aware that Gordon had zero peripheral vision and only half aware that I was losing it again.

He was bang on time. I watched him mince over to the table, his squinty eyes unaware of me lying in wait. Just as he picked up the empty envelope and turned to leave, I stepped out. He jumped and gasped, eyes agog. I eyeballed him back.

'Why are you doing this to me? Why?!'

He tried to steer me out of the way. I stood my ground, telling him he couldn't take away our home like this – it was hurting all of us – and even if he didn't care about me anymore, he should think about what it was doing to Princess Michael.

Gordon didn't say a word. Since he couldn't get past me, he tried to escape into the hallway. He yanked hard at the handle before realising the door was locked. He turned and fluttered his hands in my face in a kind of silent consternation. I barred his way to the back door and as we stumbled against each other, I sank my teeth into his cheek. I staggered backwards immediately. I hadn't left a mark, but I'd definitely tried to bite him. It was Dan-gate all over again.

While I tried to recover from the shock, Gordon fled out the back door and down the garden path, banging the gate shut behind him. Princess Michael eyed me from his chair, inscrutable.

A day later, two policemen turned up to arrest me. I was so distressed I didn't hear what the charge was. I supposed it was assault and I knew exactly who'd set this in motion. The goddess must be loving it. They let me phone Marianne before taking me away and said they wouldn't use the handcuffs on this occasion.

I sobbed in the back of the police van while we moved slowly through the traffic. I couldn't see out and I had no idea where they were taking me. I tried to remember the instructions for arrest I'd learned from the student direct action group. Say nothing, admit nothing. I felt a terrible urge to confess.

At the station, the officer on the front desk took my details before leaning in to his colleagues to ask if it had really been necessary to bring me in. They both looked at their shoes, while another couple of officers searched my wallet. They sniggered over my 37p and carefully examined my Tesco Clubcard before asking me who 'P M Happiness' might be.

'My housemate did it as a joke for our cat,' I said, tearfully. 'Because he eats so much.'

A policewoman took me to a cell and locked me in 'to think things over' while they waited for the duty solicitor. I didn't think about anything, I only shook and cried.

I was let out briefly for fingerprints and a mugshot. Distressed by my streaming face, the young police officer tried to get me to smile. 'Otherwise you won't look nice for your photo.'

Silly bugger.

A doctor arrived and, after taking details of my history of mental illness, he was about to give me a tranquilliser, when the duty solicitor knocked on the door. She told me her job was to get me out as quickly as possible and the simplest way to make that happen was to answer 'No comment' to every question.

'Okay,' I said, quietly. 'I can do that.' I didn't even care about her curly hair.

The interviewing officer had a report that said I'd bitten Gordon on the chest. It was typical of Gordon not to let the truth get in the way of a good story; either that or the officer couldn't quite read his own handwriting. I looked suitably shocked and the officer rolled his eyes and said, 'I know.' It was clear he didn't believe it of me either. I realised I was in a strong position; none of these guys would take well to Gordon and his lisp.

Once the charges were dropped and I was free to leave, the

duty solicitor told me I could make a counter claim against Gordon if I wished.

'No thanks, I never want to set eyes on him again.'

'Way to go!' She gave me a fist bump and left me in the lobby to wait for Marianne, who'd not long landed at Heathrow and had offered to come straight to the station to pick me up.

'The little fucker,' she said as she led me to her snazzy new car, her eyes swollen with fatigue. 'Who would've believed it.'

I shook my head, though privately I could have believed anything of Gordon and me.

As Marianne drove me home, it occurred to me that although she was being supportive, she might well be getting fed up of me and my crises. I felt like an annoying little sister who kept having to be rescued. These days, Marianne had people who could meet her in the Cotswolds or the Sahara at a moment's notice, instead of in the car park of a dodgy East London police station. She didn't need me anymore.

'But tell me, how are you, hon?' I asked, trying to keep the desperation out of my voice. 'Don't worry about me, I want to hear all your news.'

'I sent a letter to my uncle,' she said, hesitantly. 'I said I know what he did to me.'

'Oh, wow, what – what happened?'

'He collapsed. My cousin had to drive him to hospital – she thought he was having a stroke, but they said it was just a panic attack.'

'I guess that's an admission in a way, no?'

Marianne shook her head, keeping her eyes on the road.

'Nope. A few weeks later, he went on a radio programme to talk about false memory syndrome.'

'Oh Christ, I'm so sorry.'

She drew in a breath. 'It's okay.'

I couldn't make out her expression. I had no idea how she

was coping and I didn't have the right to ask anymore. She gave me a kiss before I got out of the car.

'I won't come in.'

I felt even more wretched as she drove away.

A few days later, a booklet from Victim Support arrived for me in the post. The police clearly had no idea whether it was me or Gordon who was really to blame and I didn't know either. We'd both proved ourselves incapable of managing adult life with any dignity at all.

Marianne and I saw less and less of each other over the next few months, and eventually I lost track of her altogether. I missed her effortless cool, her dry wit and the unspoken understanding that had bound us together. She'd always been a foil to my chaos, but there was nothing to be done. I'd messed things up again.

I found a buyer for the house and began to pack up my things. The same estate agent I'd appointed to sell the house told me he was also selling a tiny flat just up the road. It was beyond my budget, but I wanted it with all my heart. There was even a little patio for Princess Michael and it wouldn't be so much of a wrench if I could stay on the same patch of Lizzie Park that I'd inhabited for most of my adult life.

I was in with a chance, only because there'd be a speedy double commission for the agent if both purchases went through at the same time, and it didn't hurt that he'd taken a fancy to me. When he asked if I was 'courting', I slyly made myself seem available. It was the only time in my life I'd flirted without any intention of following through, but the flat was worth a little injury to my dignity. The minute I'd exchanged contracts, he found the door shut in his face.

On the day Gordon was due to remove the last of his belongings, we agreed through our solicitors that I'd vacate the house for eight hours. Neither of us wanted to be in any danger of remembering how much we used to like each other.

I moved everything I owned, plus a few things Gordon owned, into my bedroom and locked the door. Since I couldn't get my armchair up the stairs, I stuck a large notice on it that read: DO NOT REMOVE – LEGAL PROPERTY OF F. WILSON. I hoped Gordon would find this both poignant and terrifying. I also debated whether to leave out a sign I'd unearthed showing a frenetic-looking woman underneath the caption, '*Better to have lost and loved than live with the psycho for the rest of your life*', but then I had a better idea. I was confident that Gordon's IBS would be playing up big time on this special day, so I scoured the house for every toilet roll, paper towel and scrap of tissue I could find and locked them all in my room.

I enjoyed that, I really did.

Writerly Duties

For the second time in my life, my mother didn't die, and I completed on the basement flat.

Chad and his mate with a van stood outside with me in the drizzle while we waited for the key. Princess Michael yowled in his cat box and a cheerful-looking woman in her seventies lifted her net curtain to peer out at us. Five minutes later, she appeared with a teapot and three mugs on a tray. She told me she'd lived in her house all her life and her father had lived there from the age of two until he died. He'd survived the bomb blast that accounted for my 1960s block wedged in between the grand Victorian houses.

'Come in a minute and see,' she said, beckoning me up her front steps.

I admired her 1950s wallpaper, her Bakelite radio, and the crocheted antimacassars all over the place. Her house felt so comfortable and safe, it made me want to weep.

Chad's mate installed a cat flap in my back door and between them they put up three sets of shelves, cursing like troopers as they wore down all their drill bits on the concrete walls. They figured out that the underfloor heating system was so out of date it would take a day to warm up, but I hardly cared. Before they left, I gave Chad's mate a wad of cash that would see them both hit the pub the minute they got back to Bradford and flopped onto my bed, feeling almost content.

The next day, I got up early, fed Princess Michael, admired the light from the street lamp falling through the slatted blinds onto my newly varnished wooden floors and did ten sun salutations before breakfast.

Although I'd only moved ten minutes' walk up the road, this was a different demographic altogether. Instead of a view of social housing and late-night fights, I had the fulsome leaves of Elizabeth Park to look at. From my little kitchenette, I could watch various neighbours getting into cars to stock up at the deli or walking to the newsagents, and I could listen to them chatting on the pavement. The upstairs ones invited me round for tea and Dutch biscuits, and asked if I wanted to share their cleaner or their organic veg box delivery. It looked like I'd arrived.

Since I was now so sane and respectable, I decided it was time to discover the formula that would finally get me a publisher. While I was at Philip's, I'd turned my *Gin and Ginger Cake* story into a novella, which was eventually accepted by an obscure indie press. They'd just wanted a few changes because they thought the character I'd called Nish was a little stereotypical, living above his parents' corner shop and being into chemistry and all. I was scared and annoyed in equal measure, and in a fit of petulance, I'd withdrawn the manuscript. But it had given me hope.

I decided to enrol on a two-year part-time MA in creative writing. I was flattered when they gave me Blake Morrison as my personal tutor, even though I hadn't quite forgiven him for writing *The Ballad of the Yorkshire Ripper*. Any northern feminist worth her salt knew that if you must speak of that man at all, you had to call him boring Peter Sutcliffe.

'I don't think there's anything wrong with writing as a form of therapy or confession, as well as writing for publication,' Blake said.

I ignored this and embarked on *A Breath of Light,* which I considered my tribute to yoga and the ultimate escape from my worthless life. It was set in India 5,000 years BC and one editor suggested it could become a cult hit, but just like all my other attempts it fell short of getting me a contract. It was always: 'This is an interesting writer', 'I'll be keen to see what they write next' or 'Not a good fit for us but I trust this will find a home'. These responses never failed to crucify me, but nonetheless, after each handful of rejections, I licked my wounds for a few weeks and then doggedly started over again.

My final thesis was entitled 'How Novelists Tell the Truth'. The markers weren't entirely complimentary: *In this section the candidate has disregarded all their writerly duties*' was one of the more blistering comments. But Blake caught me in the forecourt a couple of days before the end of term and told me quietly that he'd enjoyed my work very much. I flushed with pride. Submissions were supposed to be anonymous – he'd recognised my style.

After the MA, I kept on writing, though with less and less enthusiasm. Sitting alone in front of a laptop for hours on end made me feel like a head on a stick – something I hadn't experienced since my university days. My characters seemed increasingly two-dimensional, my narrative drive insufficiently driven. I kept thinking there ought to be a depth charge in me somewhere that would blow all these failed attempts out of the water. But if there was, I couldn't get to it.

When the service charges on my flat increased and I had to take on more clients to cover the bills, I finally gave up writing altogether. My half dozen stillborn novels were put away in the closet, buried under jumpers I didn't like and never wore. Life suddenly felt easier, lighter; just as it might without a heart.

Oily

Without a novel on the go, I discovered reserves of energy I hadn't known I possessed. I might not have made it as a writer, but I was confident I had untapped potential as a bodyworker. I tracked down a pain specialist who could help me dive deeper into the mysterious world of the nervous system and, armed with a covert hope that he might also help me sort out my own ongoing dread and dissociation, I made an appointment to see him at his pad in leafy Richmond.

My new teacher suited me down to the ground. He was a materialist, an atheist and a total nerd, which made him about as far removed as he could be from the alternative therapists I'd tried in the past. I tied back my hair to show off my serious forehead, wore my new reading glasses and my best waistcoat, and hoped he'd be as impressed by the acuity of my questions as he was by the stylishness of my leather-bound notebook. I was ready to lap up everything he had.

'What exactly do you mean when you say the term 'nerve pain' is inefficient?' I asked.

'It's a polite way of saying it's wrong,' he replied.

It was fortunate for both of us that he was married and had no hair.

We revisited Peter Levine's technique for running away from paper tigers and explored a deceptively simple method for feeling more embodied. My guru also believed he had a process that would sort out my anxiety once and for all. It involved performing a series of simple yoga-type exercises, something I excelled at, and then having a lie-down while trembling like a mouse on acid. I was very good at this, too, and I felt a whole lot better for it. For a while, I thought I'd found if not the Holy Grail, at least something that wasn't a crock of shit.

This shamanic-like shaking was a bit of a niche market, so, in the spirit of throwing lots of mud at the wall to see what would stick, I decided to further increase my smorgasbord of offerings by learning Chavutti Thirumal. This was a highly vigorous form of massage which involved getting the receiver to lie on a thin mat on the floor, legs and arms splayed, so that the practitioner could cover them in copious amounts of hot oil before proceeding to skate up and down their naked body with their bare feet while hanging onto a rope suspended from the ceiling. It sounded right up my street.

The only person I could find who might teach me was a guy called Dave who ran a rather shabby massage school in East London. When I looked him up, one reviewer had dubbed him 'the hooligan of bodywork'. Intrigued, I sent him an email. I reassured him that I understood I'd have to be 'undraped' in order to learn and I was okay with that. I'd danced topless in enough gay nightclubs not to be self-conscious, I only hoped Dave would manage to hold himself together at the sight of my enormous nipples.

He was up for it, especially if I'd bring £600 in cash for two days' training, and we arranged to meet at his house in Essex where he offered 'retreatments' in a shepherd's hut in the middle of a field. He said for a small additional fee he could put me up in it for the night to save on travel time, but I pretended I needed to get back to feed Princess Michael. The prospect of staying over after we'd just spent the day half naked and covered in oil together struck me as being a little too auspicious.

Dave met me at the station in a greasy old van.

'Hi, Finners, hop in,' he said, slapping the passenger seat.

He was older and greasier than his photograph, his hair was longer and turned out to be curly. For a moment, I regretted saying no to the hut.

He parked outside a lovely cottage at the end of a country lane and showed me into the front room, where he'd laid out a double futon mat covered in plastic. There was a five-litre bottle of grapeseed oil on the windowsill and a copper pouring jug on a little stand above a candle. Two thick pieces of rope hung from a ring screwed into the ceiling. It was difficult to say whether the set-up would have worked better for kinky sex or a joint suicide.

Chavutti Thirumal requires the receiver to wear a thong and naturally Dave didn't possess such an item.

'I got these online,' he said, showing me a pair of paper pants. 'Only I tried them on and they're definitely for a woman. Do you want them?'

I said I was okay, thanks. I'd come prepared, with carefully shaved legs and the edges of my pubes trimmed back so that nothing sexual would escape from my own thong, which I possessed only because when you're the oldest massage practitioner on the block, you don't want to add VPLs to that.

Dave lit the open fire and some candles, and disappeared into another room to change while I undressed and wrapped a cotton scarf round my hips. Although I wasn't bothered about him seeing my breasts, it suddenly occurred to me that my underarm hair might be as much of a shock to straight Dave as it had been to pious Philip. It was too late to worry about that now. Dave returned wearing a short sarong and a pleased expression, and while he looked over his notes, I examined the illustrations he'd given me. These had been laminated to withstand the amount of oil we were about to use, but even so they were suspiciously clean. I got the feeling Dave had never actually taught Chavutti to anyone before.

He showed me how to lie face up on the plastic, with my hips directly underneath the rope and my arms and legs stretched out, and the fun began. I yelped as he poured hot oil over my stomach. Dave laughed and dribbled it down my legs.

'Keep your eyes open!' he barked, grabbing the ropes in both hands as his sarong swung open over my face.

I tried to concentrate, squinting modestly as an oily foot ran up and down my arm and his naked crotch came and went from my eyeline. Clearly he hadn't found a substitute for the paper knickers. The whole thing was mesmerising.

Dave was over six feet tall to my five two and hardly had to swing on the ropes to complete a full stroke. He'd done a good job of memorising the fiendishly complex sequence and performed a series of swift, circular foot strokes that started at my right hand and progressed across my torso down to my opposite foot. At one point, his foot slid over my breast. 'Oops, made a booboo,' he said. We snickered and whatever boundaries I thought I possessed slithered quietly away.

After that, we relaxed into it. He completed his demonstration of the supine sequence and suggested a break for brunch, offering to make me poached eggs from his own hens. I did the washing-up and we sat on stools in his kitchen and chatted about bodywork and awkward clients and how to earn more money by pretending distance healing was a thing. When he got up to make us some tea, his cock slipped out between the folds of his sarong and nodded hello. We could have been husband and wife.

Next, it was my turn. It was going to be much more of a challenge for me, with my short legs and gorilla-length arms. Dave splayed himself out on the mat and I covered him in oil.

I hung onto the rope for dear life, skidding about while he gazed up at me like a smitten concubine. At one point, I almost had to do the splits to complete a move and on the recovery I accidentally swiped off his sarong.

'Oh God, sorry!' I tried to nudge it back over his groin with my toe.

'No worries,' he said, momentarily closing his eyes. I didn't tell him the postman had just seen us through the window.

The following day, we finished the rest of the sequence, and I went home with instructions to memorise it, practise on ten different people and record the results. Then, I had to contact him to book an assessment. The jammy sod – he'd wangled himself a free treatment as well as all that cash.

But I was super happy with what I'd learned, particularly when a number of butches let me slither all over them in the name of revision. The only problem was that spending two days half naked in front of an open fire with a man with curly hair had just about done for me. I hadn't felt this horny for the opposite sex since I got grabbed in the woods at the Christian barbecue when I was thirteen. I completed even more rounds of wanking than I had back then, surrendering to the sex hormones that were drenching me as thoroughly as Dave's hot oil.

I nailed my assessment and it crossed my mind to ask Dave whether I should miss my train home, though I couldn't quite imagine the logistics of sex between a short arse like me and someone my mother would have called a great long streak of piss. I resisted the urge and I've never felt so proud of myself as when Dave dropped me off at the station and we waved a cheery goodbye. I was a qualified Chavutti practitioner and I hadn't even shagged my teacher.

The builder who attached the rope to my ceiling tugged quizzically on it a couple of times. 'What on earth are you going to get up to with this?'

'Oh,' I tried to sound serious and profound. 'I do an Indian form of massage with my feet. It's very good for backache.'

After receiving a cut price session for himself, the builder started sending me all his mates. I spent the next three months sliding over grateful scaffolders, electricians, cabbies and unemployed bouncers. It was only when one of them complained that my heels were 'a bit on the rough side' that I thought of seeing the local podiatrist. She was more dismayed by my ragged toenails than what I did for a living and wanted to know if I picked at them.

'Actually, I sometimes bite them.' I tried not to sound smug. Not many people could still do that at my age.

'Oh well, good for you. I tell all my new mums to bite their baby's toenails. It's the safest way. Hang on, though…' She was examining the sole of my foot with a large magnifying glass. 'You've got a verruca. Technically, you shouldn't work with your feet again until it's gone.'

I was gutted. My reputation as the most eccentric bodyworker in East London was thwarted almost before it had begun. No matter. I'd caught the learning bug and trauma was becoming a buzzword. The Americans were onto it and a guy called Richard Schwartz was blowing everyone away with his radical approach to working with crazies like me.

Our minds, I was soon to discover, are even more jaw-dropping than our bodies.

Dhal

The problem with dating a former Buddhist monk is they tend not to have any money, unless it's the one who founded the digital mindfulness company that became worth millions. My one wasn't that one.

I'd slept with a couple of Buddhists before, but neither had lived up to expectations. The first, a psychoanalyst with a high-powered practice in central London, turned out to have an eating disorder that meant I couldn't risk turning up a moment too early in case I caught him in the throes of cake. He used to coach the directors of Newman Brothers, a global financial services firm that went bust in the 2008 crash. I couldn't entirely put that down to trying to have your cake and eat it, but it did make me wonder. The other was a yoga teacher with a predilection for getting me into unpronounceable postures and then trying to have sex with me. The less said about that, the better.

I'd found them both through the Buddhist HQ, which was a short bus ride from my flat and offered free meditation for beginners. I'd rarely felt quite so demoralised as I did when I walked through their doors only to be greeted by two dissociated young men and a plate of stale digestive biscuits. I later discovered that their founder, Dennis, was a sexual predator. I won't dignify him with his anointed name, suffice to say it sounded something like Shangrilarachipshop. No wonder they were miserable.

I was still full of rage at what Gordon had done. I kept telling myself my ex-wife was only as messed up as I was, no better or worse, and that the whole disaster had been inevitable. But no matter how hard I tried to let it go, Gordon had made me feel out of control in a way I found unforgivable, and I was beginning to lose hope that there was anyone who could help me. The Buddhists wanted me to experience loving kindness, which was about as likely as experiencing the backs of my eyeballs, and the lesbians were falling for traditional psychotherapy, which was falling short in ways I didn't have the heart to explain. Everyone else seemed to be dealing with their problems either by drinking too much or telling lies on social media.

In a last-ditch attempt to get a handle on my Gordon fury, I signed up for a weekend course on conflict resolution. The training was held in a large meeting room in a South London community centre that promised to deliver mung bean stew and Barleycrap on tap. It was like being back at Sam and Robbie's, only cleaner.

The trainer, whose name I misheard as Dhal, was almost as good as me at working with groups, and he had a level of patience I had no hope of ever achieving. Plus, he had the delicate, ethereal looks you'd expect for someone who really had spent a huge amount of time meditating up a mountain.

He told us the key to resolving disagreements was 'a genuine wish to communicate from the heart'. I was disappointed; I'd fallen at the first hurdle. I didn't want to connect with Gordon from the heart, I wanted to stab him in it. Nevertheless, I was impressed with Dahl's training skills, and at the end of the workshop, I wrote him a gushing evaluation and left without a word. I felt certain he must have a partner and, besides, I was far too nervous to consider approaching such a healthy human being.

On the tube home, I couldn't help feeling annoyed with myself. It was looking as though I'd end up living in my basement flat with Princess Michael and no central heating for the rest of my life. The only consolation was that Elizabeth Park was getting more gentrified by the minute, which meant I'd be able to eat smashed avocado on sourdough every day while I grew old and lonely.

A few weeks later, I had a spare half hour before going to run a men's health workshop at the old Finsbury Park Project. They'd messed up with their budget again and offered me some end-of-year panic contracting. As I got ready to leave, I couldn't help looking forward to the fresh round of sex anecdotes I'd be treated to by my old colleagues. Winter was coming and I had no lover of my own to keep me warm. On a sudden whim, I logged in on my laptop and scrolled down a couple of pages of an online dating website, glancing even-handedly at profiles of women and men. I checked my watch, I had a few more minutes. I clicked on a third page.

I couldn't believe my eyes – there was Dhal, the workshop guy! Even better, since I already had his phone number, I didn't have to pay the subscription fee. I punched in a text. 'Hey, what are you doing on Soulmates??! Want to meet up, we could talk about our work?'

I wasn't being coy, I genuinely wanted to find out whether some of his saintlike patience might rub off on me, even if nothing else did. Later that night, I was cruising down the hill on my bike after persuading a roomful of working-class men to get their prostates checked, when my phone pinged. I screeched to a stop by the kerb. It was Dhal.

'Let's meet!'

This was terrible timing; I was going to Bangkok the following week to brush up on my Thai massage skills. But it occurred to me that if I mentioned this fact, it would make me sound much more interesting than I was. I asked him if he'd like to get together when I got back.

'Before!' came the reply.

Cool.

.

Presents

We met up for a walk in the park and we liked it. Dhal hadn't long relinquished his Buddhist name and had his own story of fallen gurus to tell. He also admitted to being in a tonne of debt as a result of all the time he'd spent up various mountains, but I didn't mind. I was still raking in the pounds from my bodywork, minus the fancy footwork. It only remained to find out whether he would respond to my oily capabilities as well as everyone else had. We met up again and he took away my underwear to remind him of me while I was in Thailand. Enough said.

Dhal was a keeper and I was in keeping mood. They say that we're attracted to people who feel familiar – that it's a question of finding someone just like horrible mummy or feckless daddy and thinking, 'This time I'll get them to love me'. But Dhal was everything my parents weren't. He was tolerant, emotionally intelligent and willing to bear with my occasional meltdowns. It was beyond my wildest dreams that he'd want to commit to me.

Inexplicably, he did.

We couldn't afford anywhere in London that would be big enough for us both to work from, so as a compromise Dhal rented a room in my beloved Lizzie Park. This meant we could see each other every day, even when we didn't want to. Every once in a while, we fought and I stormed off, initiating a quickfire round of childish text messages.

'I'm absolutely NOT going on holiday with you now!!!'

'Fine, I can get some work done instead.'

'That place looks amazing, I'm going to go on my own!!'

'No you're bloody well not, I'm coming with you!!!'

It was a point of pride that I could tip even an ex-monk into occasional raging exasperation. But we were doing it – doing it in a way I'd thought would be forever beyond me.

There were milestone moments; the time my Dhal was able to hug me and I almost relaxed, and the time he offered to be my demo body for the advanced Thai massage exams, which meant letting me twist him into shapes his body was never intended to make while my instructor helped out by kneeing him in the groin.

When Princess Michael began vomiting on a daily basis, Dhal took turns with me to clean up, and he was with me when the vet's fees became exorbitant and I decided it was time my princess went to pet heaven. I wanted to end his life at home and so a young locum vet was booked to do the deed. Afterwards, I sent him a photograph of Princess Michael's body lying in a basket surrounded by roses and he sent me a link to The Communards' pop anthem, 'Don't Leave Me This Way'.

Dhal and I drove Princess Michael's body to the pet crematorium in Dhal's hairdryer, a clapped-out old Skoda that never let us down. On the way, I taught him the tune to 'The cat crept in, crapped and crept out again' and we sang at the tops of our voices all the way to East Grinstead. In the Farewell Room, the pet crem attendant talked us through the procedure in hushed tones and then turned to me conspiratorially. 'You take as much time as you like with him, Princess, then I'll take very good care of your Dhal.'

He didn't join in with our sniggers.

We came home with a cardboard tube full of ashes. I was pleased I'd opted for the individual cremation rather than the communal one, which would only have secured us a small pouch of pet mix.

Dahl supported me through my bereavement, and encouraged me to take on more training, more holidays, more intimacy than I'd ever intended to. He'd endured enough spiritual woo-woo to last a lifetime, so instead of celebrating Christmas like ordinary folk, we made alternatively merry on winter solstice with a walk in Epping Forest, which had until now been off limits as the site of my lunacy and Dan's poetic poaching. We followed up with a vegan feast of roast beetroot and Dhal's coconut dhal, and festooned everything in my flat with handfuls of holly and ivy. Princess Michael's cardboard urn took pride of place, decorated with one small concession to conventional Christmas frippery: a wreath of pink tinsel.

It was three years before Dhal managed to persuade me to buy him a present. I thought it would make us too much like a family, but once I'd started, I really got into it. My numerous offerings of alpaca socks and silver pens and jars of wild honey and hazelnut coffee were the most aggressively authentic gestures of love I'd ever made. And after some initial glitches, our holidays were successful too. We had a favourite place on the Sussex coast – a cottage owned by two gay men who left us blingy little welcome gifts and, eventually, after I left them an enthusiastic review about rainbows and honeypots, issued us with an invitation to join them for a foursome. We missed our annual visit that year because I didn't want to disappoint them by not having a penis.

As an alternative, Dhal suggested we should look for our own home by the sea, somewhere within commuting distance of London. My tiny flat had almost doubled in value since I bought it and so we began to tour the coast, searching for the right area and the cheapest not-ugly house where we might start our committed life together.

We found the perfect place when I was as close to drunk as I'd ever been. The process of looking round horrible houses with horrible estate agents had got me so stressed I'd started bringing along a hip flask, and I'd just taken a large swig from it when we arrived outside our final viewing of the day, a little Georgian affair perched on top of a hill above the pretty Tastings Old Town. The open sea greeted us to the east and Morrisons superstore twinkled down below in the west. It was literally head and shoulders above everything else.

Full of rum and alarm, I hardly knew what I was looking at, but I opened a tiny cupboard under the stairs and thought how handy it would be for umbrellas, and I loved the back path down the hillside, which was covered in nettles that could be made into soup. I left Dhal to count up the number of rooms and work out whether we could live there together without a police incident. I thought separate bedrooms should do the trick.

The elderly owner was a social activist who'd once travelled across Bangladesh in a camper van. I think she fell in love with the idea of selling her house to a drunken dyke and her wraithlike partner, and so, after a second visit – during which she almost threw herself off the back steps as she was pointing out the view and I caught her in my capable arms – she accepted my offer.

On the drive home, Dhal did mental arithmetic about our finances, while I panicked quietly inside.

Part Three

Tastings

We moved to Tastings in September 2019. We moved to the seaside to be happy. It's a mercy we can't see what's coming; most of us would want to hold our heads and howl.

At first, we were euphoric. Each evening, we sat on our little back patio to watch the golden September sunsets, and in the mornings we walked on the hill in the autumn sunshine, gazing in disbelief at the sparkling sea. I loved the seaside tack; the crazy golf and the stalls laden with sticks of rock and trays of fudge, and the silly handwritten signs: 'The Bottle of Tastings', 'Harold's Opticians', 'The Cod Father'. In the antiques yard, the portly, bearded owner listed all the upcoming festivals, the pram race, the welly race, the pirate day and the one I most liked the sound of, Jack in the Box. 'Just join in, join in with everything!' he said, spreading his arms wide. It was evident that the inhabitants of Tastings were a little bit touched, in the nicest possible way.

Winter arrived and a gas leak in our basement kitchen alerted me to the fact that the foundations of my house were rotting. We got the floorboards taken up by a tattooed biker builder and the three of us stared in awe at the bright green copper pipes hissing quietly on the damp earth. Our builder kicked at a joist and a chunk of wood crumbled to nothing.

'Those stairs likely goin'a cave in shortly,' he said in his soft West Country accent. 'Every piece'a timber needs to be replaced.'

Plus, he said, there was a possible infestation of beetles eating the upper floors, and a hole in the roof so large it looked like someone had been living in it. He was about to become our new best friend.

Three months of hell and expense followed. While Dhal was up in London bringing in the bacon, I lay on my bed with my hat over my ears to try and block out the sound of hammering. Occasionally, I was called on to go down into the bowels of the house to help shift the fridge, the units or the cooker while our solitary builder told me how many corners had been cut on materials last time round. He showed me a couple of bits from a church pew that had been used as a cross beam.

'No doubt they stole 'em, then they did a terrible job, so at leas' you can be sure they wont'a gone to heaven.'

Then he discovered that the general sewage pipe ran directly under our house. If the manhole cover in the downstairs cupboard turned out not to have been properly sealed, there was a danger of flooding, which would contaminate the thousands of pounds' worth of new timber he'd just installed. On hearing this news, I fled to the shopping mall to escape from the scandalous wreck I'd bought. I sobbed into my mittens on a bench and, for the first time in my life, I really, really wanted someone, anyone, to ask if I was alright.

Later that day, I thought of something that might help. Jay and I had once stayed in a caravan with a couple of women who'd taken themselves off-grid and spent their time foraging for food. They took us to the mouth of a river to collect mussels from a ruined wall that was falling into the water. When we got there, it was high tide and the mussels were submerged. We stared silently at the river, then I abruptly stripped off my clothes and jumped in. My skin was lightening-struck. I emerged feeling reborn, ecstatically clutching two handfuls of shells while Jay glared at me for being attention-seeking. I wanted to be saved like that again.

A few days later, I walked along the Tastings seafront with my new wetsuit chafing under my clothes. The Bluebuoy Sea Swimmers, three men heading for their eighties, greeted me like one of their own. It was only as we started to undress that I realised I still didn't have the right gear. The pebbles were unforgiving underfoot and the wind seemed to have sucked the heat out of my head.

The guys lent me an orange neoprene hat and some neoprene socks, and we staggered down to the water's edge. I plunged into a miracle of icy water and sea spray, swallowing salt air and spume and battling the waves with everything I had. One of the old men bobbed past me in his pink bobble hat, singing at the top of his voice: 'Steak and kidney pie, cocoa, apple-crumble-custard!'

Afterwards, we huddled by a portable radiator in the café, shrunk into our coats, hollowed out, blue-fingered and happy. The owner brought us mugs of tea and a pile of blankets and patted me on the back. For a few minutes, we were a tribe, sitting knee to knee and trembling in a sort of chaotic Mexican wave. One of the men told me that, years ago, when his mother became ill, he'd bought a dilapidated building and turned it into a fifteen-bed care home. After she died, he sold it for half a million and then lost the whole lot in a scam. The sea had saved him from despair.

I understood. My first cold swim with these ancients was worth all the trouble my rotten old house had given me, and once I was properly kitted out with a boyleg swimsuit, neoprene booties and oversized thermal gloves, I felt like an undersized wrestler heading out to grapple the sea into submission.

Three days before Christmas, I helped our builder to put the cooker back into its corner, gave him a wad of thank you cash and the rest of the Hobnobs, and hoped never to set eyes on him again. To save on heating, Dhal and I shuffled round the house in our solstice socks and sheepskin slippers, and in January, when fifty-mile-an-hour winds tore across our seaside hill, shattering roof tiles and sending refuse bins skidding into the road, we were well prepared. We snuggled up together in our fleecy joggers and bathrobes, hoods up, clutching our hot drinks and smooching like a pair of naughty monks.

The storm was still raging when my first Tastings client turned up for a Thai massage dressed in three sweaters and a trapper hat. I tried to dissuade him, explaining that the power was off, it was arctic in my treatment room, and the neighbours' kids' trampoline had just lifted itself out of their garden and landed on the roundabout.

'It's all good clean fun,' he said, undeterred.

I covered him in blankets and walked up and down his arms and legs while the house shook on its foundations and the chimney vent slammed open, blowing a blast of cold air across the room.

'Heavy duty, you're a little powerhouse,' he laughed.

He gave me a big tip and moments after he'd stepped outside, next door's front window blew out, sending shards of glass hurtling up the street. It was the closest I'd come to killing a client.

Our builder returned with the Hobnobs to mend the roof again and then Covid hit London. Since Dhal was still commuting to his Liverpool Street office, it was inevitable we were going to catch it, but apart from a nagging exhaustion we didn't suffer too much. Dhal was proud of his Covid toe, which, he read, was a sign of a brisk immune response and more common in teenagers. I had Covid eye and, predictably, headaches that shot through my skull like lightning bolts. Then, my tinnitus started; a low rumbling and high whistling, which, coupled with the growing deafness I'd inherited from my father, put an end to any possibility of following a telephone conversation ever again.

There was a silver lining: no more attempts to meditate; I didn't have to phone Chad and Peggy anymore; and they couldn't come to visit.

Trauma Town

I passed the first lockdown sealing the gaps between our newly laid floorboards while Dhal moved all his clients and workshops online. Before the second lockdown arrived, I'd found a new place to swim, closer to home and inside the harbour arm. I met Ashley on the fishing beach, a bonny young woman from South Shields with a withered leg, a dirty laugh and a chain-smoking habit. She told me stories of a youth spent living on travellers' sites, of a year riding horses bareback in Mongolia, and a mother with dementia.

'She mainly likes ironing sweet wrappers,' she told me. 'And putting the dog in the bin.'

Soon, I had platonic loves at a two-metre distance all over town, including a cadaverous-looking funeral director called Jeremy, a beautiful bangle-bedecked Trinidadian who lived on our street, and all the lesbians my heart desired. At the same time, Tastings was rapidly turning into trauma town. Almost everyone Dhal and I came across seemed either to want to kill themselves or someone else, or there was someone who wanted to kill them. To meet this pressing need, we began to learn more about the trauma healing method developed by Richard Schwartz – the American I'd come across not long before we met. I knew he'd taken on murderers, sex abusers and plenty of psychotics and potential suicides. It seemed there was hope for us all.

Schwartzy was pushing seventy at this point, and he was both brilliant and humble. Online, I thought he looked like an ageing yogi bear and, during the comfort breaks, he wasn't averse to dancing round his living room in his sandals. He showed us a video of his twelve minutes of fame addressing the Dalai Lama, who spent the whole time sweating and yawning. Schwartzy took it in his stride and the following day he made the headlines.

During a hilltop walk to admire the view of Beachy Head, Dhal and I went over some of his teachings.

'I love that he says our minds are naturally multiple,' I said. 'It's obvious when you think about it.'

'True,' Dhal said. 'Part of me always thinks Norwich are going to win and part of me knows they're scum compared to the All Blacks.'

I stumbled to a halt. 'Oh, shit.'

'What's up?' Dhal drew his eyes away from the horizon.

'My fucking zip has broken.'

I hopped over to a bench and sat fiddling with my boot and cursing until Dhal suggested a trip to Timpson's for a repair. I looked at him as though he'd just told me to go top myself.

'Oh *really*? You really think that's going to fix this, do you, Dhal? Is Timpson's even allowed to open at the moment? Do you really, really think it's going to be that easy to sort this out? I don't fucking think so!'

I continued to rant on about how far I'd absolutely, totally fucking had it. It was an incoherent meltdown, the likes of which I hadn't experienced since the Oakham days, and when I'd finally finished, my long-suffering Dhal led home a limping, sulky child with one sodden sock and a face like a gargoyle. I needed Schwartzy's method.

By a stroke of luck, Dhal had a colleague who might be able to take me on. I'd met Clara briefly when we bumped into her in Tastings Old Town shortly before the pandemic. She and

Dhal had exchanged a few words and she'd seemed grounded, straightforward and friendly. Plus she didn't trigger my usual dislike of anyone too put together, too straight. Even her beautiful blonde hair hadn't put me off and knowing my nervous system accepted her was more than good enough for me. We exchanged messages and, although her waiting list was officially full, she agreed to give me a one-off appointment as a favour to Dhal.

I wonder if she was ready for me.

Broken

Clara lived in Lovebroken, a sleepy village halfway between London and Tastings. I caught a train to the nearest town and then a taxi to the village high street. I didn't want to be dropped off right outside her house; I'd planned on being pathologically early so I could get my story straight before I had to face her.

We drove between hedges and fields and up a winding, tree-lined hill until we emerged to a view of the village nestling in a little valley below. As we descended, my driver pointed out the farm shop and the church.

'They love Christmas in this place!' he yelled from behind his mask. 'Every year, the streets are lit up like Las Vagas! I always gotta bring the wife and kids to see it or I don't get no peace at all. It's marvellous!'

I gazed at his chunky shoulders and the picture of a grinning toddler covered in birthday cake that was sellotaped to his dashboard, and wondered what it must be like to be part of a family that were so easily pleased. He dropped me off at one end of the high street and I wandered along the little row of shops, already regretting my decision. If attachment theory was to be believed, I was doomed to ruin my relationships over and over again unless I found a therapist who could be a parent figure and provide me with the right sort of corrective experience. Given

261

the failure of any of them to correct me so far, that prospect seemed remote. Besides, I didn't want to be told I needed a stranger's love to heal, because who in their right mind would love the disaster inside me?

I pushed open the door of a place selling twee pottery cats and jewellery made out of seashells. The doorbell tinkled, I inhaled the smell of perfume and a woman with light pink hair looked at me over her spectacles. I hurried out again, feeling like a coward. If I couldn't even face the owner of the village shop, how the hell was I going to manage Clara?

I bought a cheese and onion pastie in the bakery and sat on the damp grass at the edge of a field. I was shaking and, suddenly, intensely hungry. I'd met students at Oxford who came from wealthy villages like this. They used up their trust funds pretending to be New Age seekers and talked about 'energy' with a spaced-out look in their eyes, before knuckling down to careers in the stock market. It was the kind of spiritual bypass that would never have worked for me. I was too much the northern atheist; I knew perfectly well that nature doesn't have a conscience and God doesn't have a beard. I finished off the pastie and stood up to brush away the crumbs, hoping Clara wouldn't give me any of that crap.

She welcomed me with a warm smile, opening her door wide and showing me into her therapy room. The window was letting in a breeze that blew my hair straight into my mouth. I spat it out, feeling a little deranged already.

Clara fixed her mask and offered me the sofa while she took an armchair with a rug folded over the back. There was a rug for me too and a box of tissues on a side table next to a line of individually wrapped mints. I thought of Persephone and the pomegranate seeds. I had no intention of consuming anything; I didn't want to end up trapped in hell.

'I just want to go through my policies with you,' Clara said, 'in case you decide to pursue regular therapy with me once a slot opens up.'

I hoped she'd be quick – this was costing me more than a pound a minute. She gave me an opening spiel about her cancellation policy, payment terms, the limits of confidentiality and what she'd do if I became a risk to myself or others. I listened impatiently; all that depressive stuff was in the past. I was better now, living the good life; I simply wanted to know why I'd had a meltdown on the hill when Dhal said I should go to Timpson's to get my boot mended. One session should sort it. Two, at the max.

'This is a body-based process,' Clara was saying.

I was sceptical. It was clear to me that I was going to stay firmly on the sofa while she sat on the opposite side of the room. I was too far away even to kick her ankles, so how body-based could it be? I really wanted to keep an open mind, but, as the saying goes, I didn't want it to be so open that my brain fell out. She asked if I'd like to give her any background and I said no, let's just dive in.

We began to untangle the knot of feelings I carried, teasing apart all the intensity. I saw how my new-found fury protected me from an unendurable feeling of helplessness, an almost annihilating sense that I was out of control.

Within twenty minutes, instead of talking about my meltdown on the cliff with Dhal, I found myself in touch with an inner version of myself – a child who lived in abject terror. For as long as I could remember, I'd had dreams of babies dying, dreams in which I tried to save them, to feed them, only to see them wither away to nothing, leaving me empty and hopeless. Towards the end of session, inside my mind, this frightened child stood up and spoke.

'I don't like my mammy.'

'Well, there must be a reason,' Clara said gently.

'I was interfered with,' came the answer.

Clara asked how I felt towards this young version of myself and what she was saying.

'I don't care,' another inner voice said.

I thought that was the end of it. Then I felt my nose drip. Blood spattered onto the back of my hand. I stared at it, feeling suddenly chilled to the bone.

Clara broke her safe distancing rule to hand me the box of tissues. I stuffed the corner of a tissue up my nostril, and while we waited for the bleeding to stop, I told myself that correlation isn't causation and not to be a fool.

'I'll have a regular space for you at the beginning of next year if you'd like to take it,' Clara said as I touched my debit card to her machine.

Four months away. My guts churned. I didn't want to do it.

I knew I had to.

A Little C

On New Year's Day, I found a lump in my breast. Using my best palpation skills, I made out that it was a cyst and most probably a benign one. I wasn't worried. The local GP sent me to the hospital to get it aspirated, which involved having a jovial consultant stick a needle in my tit and draw out a good two inches of pale yellow fluid. He presented the syringe to me for inspection as though offering me a bottle of wine, which I politely waved away.

Once I was dressed, he suggested I start taking evening primrose oil, drink less caffeine and return in a couple of weeks for a mammogram. Since I didn't like coffee and a quick internet search confirmed that evening primrose oil did nothing for cysts, I simply returned for the mammogram. I wasn't worried when they asked me to wait while they double-checked the results. I still wasn't worried when they said they were going to send me to Brighton for further pictures and a biopsy, though I wasn't keen to learn that the Brighton crowd would also shoot a metal pin into my tit.

In Brighton, they nuked me for over an hour before figuring out they could get a better picture if they got me to lie down. I tried not to panic when they left me trapped by the breast in the machine while they whispered about the X-rays behind my back.

'Might I need a lumpectomy?' I asked the one who seemed to be in charge.

'Don't think ahead!' she cried. 'It could just be pills!'

'I'd prefer to know what the worst outcome would be,' I said, trying to sound calm. 'So could you please tell me?'

'Don't think ahead!' she cried again.

As soon as they'd unsquashed me, I caught the train home and thought ahead.

I was called back to the Tastings hospital a week later. After an hour's wait, the same consultant who'd sorted out my cyst called me into his room and mumbled not quite so jovially into his face mask that I had extensive abnormal cells and would need a mastectomy. My work with Clara was going to stall almost before it had begun.

I told him I didn't want reconstruction. My chest was small and I figured the less messing, the better.

'I understand,' he said. 'Some women hate their breasts.'

'No, I think mine are quite cute. But I can manage with just the one if I have to.'

He laughed awkwardly and booked me in for a surgery in a fortnight's time. I was handed over to a poker-faced MacMillan nurse who sat me down in a cubicle and began throwing leaflets at me one after another, delivering information in a tone that implied I'd done something very bad indeed.

'You will moisturise your arm,' she said, making aggressive stroking motions. 'You won't give blood or have any needles in it, and you will use insect repellent and sunscreen.'

I was bewildered. 'Wait, what? Insect repellent?'

'And sunscreen,' she said.

'But why must I—'

'Because of the lymph. You probably won't need a drain, because he uses glue, but bring a gift bag with you in case you do have to have a drain.'

She seemed to have gone a little insane. It almost didn't surprise me when she added that after the surgery I should expect to look blue in the face 'from the dye'.

'And you'll need a prosthetic bra,' she went on, slapping down another glossy booklet with a picture of a smiling, big-breasted woman on the cover.

I owned two bras. I wore them only if I was seeing a new client and it was very cold, because otherwise my over-large nipples stood out like bullets. 'A prosthetic – why?'

'Because you won't be symmetrical.'

'I'm not bothered.'

'But people will notice!'

'I don't care!' I almost shouted. If I was going be left with a blue face, the prospect of someone noticing I had one tiny tit and one non-existent one was the least of my worries.

'Okay,' she said, finally remembering her manners. 'It's your choice.'

I couldn't wait to get away. Dhal was outside in the car. I got into the passenger seat and took a breath. 'It's not good news, it's cancer.'

Something shifted as I said it. I swung out of my body for a moment and returned with an identity that no one in the Wilson family would have recognised. I hardly recognised myself. I felt scared, vulnerable and, with Dhal at my side, most magnificently human.

Dhal held onto my hand as we drove home and later he had a little cry. We reminded ourselves how much we loved each other, how precious every moment was, and how much we wanted to go to the new Turkish restaurant on the seafront that did a vegetarian mezze.

Once we'd stuffed ourselves with dolma and hummus, we strolled hand in hand back up the hill to our little house, nodding at the elderly dog walkers and the drug addicts. I remembered how, at seventeen, just before my A Levels, my breasts had started to tingle and I'd thought I was going to die. The dour Scot checked me over before asking if I was worried about anything. She must have been thinking I might be pregnant.

'Only exams in three weeks,' I'd replied.

She yelped and decided that was reason enough for my symptoms. Sure enough, the tingling went away soon afterwards, though the underlying terror did not.

'We're all a bit patched-up round here,' Dhal said softly as we reached the top of the hill. I looked back towards the sea, appreciating the tender acceptance in his words, his quiet sense of impending old age. I made plans to sew myself a sex sash that would cover my forthcoming wound and make me look like a geriatric beauty queen.

The Tastings massif left allotment veggies on the doorstep and handed me candles, cards and potions on the beach. I was given a couple of hardy, damp embraces by my old men swimmers, who swore that saltwater killed the Covid virus, if not cancer cells. I wasn't complaining, I could use all the hugs I could get.

I tracked down Anish, who I hadn't been in touch with for years, and who had since turned into a Professor of Biochemistry at the university. Even more incredibly, he and his team had just found a way to manipulate an enzyme to trigger cancer-killer cells. I felt certain, given my news, that he'd become the brother I never had and manipulate my enzymes too, but when I tried to pursue this idea he swerved, frustrating all my attempts to meet up, and eventually ignoring my messages altogether. I wondered whether I ought to have had more sex with him all those years ago. Or possibly less.

My new friend Ashley, who was in a bubble with us, rushed over to see me as soon as I texted her my news. I started to blub the moment she came through the door. It was something to do with her bonny face and her general air of pluck.

'You should do a goodbye ritual for your boob,' she said, pulling a screwed-up tissue out of her sleeve to give to me.

'That's a really good idea,' I sniffed. 'But what?'

She shrugged. While I was making us tea, I had an idea. I gave Ashley a couple of felt-tipped pens and we sat in the front room while she drew a heart shape round my doomed breast, and wrote *Gone But Not Forgotten* above it.

'There's history in that nipple,' I said as we gazed at my pert appendage.

Ashley nodded gravely and took a couple of pictures. She didn't know the half of it.

Nasty

While we waited for my surgery date to arrive, Dhal bought me a plush toy seal I named Sanguine and a stuffed seagull he named Seagull. They quickly developed minds of their own. Seagull was Dhal's alter ego, a loud, demanding character who talked a hundred miles a minute and squawked obscenities all around the house, while Sanguine was the version of me I'd like to have been: unruffled and optimistic, with an aptitude for not entirely tuneless singing.

Dhal was also reading me various histories of Tastings. He'd discovered there used to be a local fisherman called Nasty Bumstead and Nasty became a permanent feature in Dhal's stories, which were rapidly going off-piste. Nasty morphed through the centuries from fishing and smuggling to becoming head chef at The Priory, and, finally, once the abbot had discredited him for stealing the coveted custard skin, he became the jovial host and proprietor of the 'Swan In'.

We invented a best friend for him, a non-binary healer called Jezebel Snickerwitch who lived in a hut on the edge of a cliff, surrounded by various creatures. They included a hedgehog employed as a boot scraper, a redundant spider named Bob, and Jeremy the gentleman ghost, styled on the funeral director I'd become friends with. Jezebel and Nasty also acquired human friends called Timbo Imbumbo and Singsong Hilo from Africa and Asia respectively, though they were rapidly dispatched back home due to their tendency to incite political incorrectness in the narrator.

Every story ended with Seagull shitting profusely on the villain of the piece, usually one of my new Tastings acquaintances depending on who happened to have pissed me off that day. Now that I had a relatable cancer, I was ready to open up about it to anyone who would listen. It was so, so much easier to say 'I'm having my breast chopped off' than it would have been to say 'I've begun to suspect my mother molested me'. So much easier. Even so, it proved a great opportunity for everyone to put their foot in it. Dhal and I developed a formula called 'Shit and Chips', the number of shits correlating to the level of insensitivity in the responses I got, and the chips reserved for the brave few who came up to scratch. Standout awards were as follows:

Ashley: *Cool, you're gonna look like an Amazon!* 95 chips.

Dog walker: *I'm a cancer victim myself. It's a vile journey.* 42 shits.

Old man swimmer: *Ah, that don't matter, I'd still chase you round the block!* 25 chips, 25 shits.

Next-door neighbour: *Get well soon because I can't carry on being this nice for much longer.* Lifetime supply of chips.

It was mayhem, and in my over-hydrated pre-surgery state, I nearly pissed myself laughing in Dhal's bed.

We spent the last few days before my operation self-isolating and dancing round the house in our slippers to the tune of Stayin' Alive. I knew all there was to know about wound healing and stocked up on protein-rich tofu, eggs, cheese, smoked salmon, Greek yoghurt and nuts. I didn't tell anyone how much I was looking forward to stuffing myself after the op.

On the morning I was due at the hospital, I snuck out at 6.30am and had a solitary swim in a milky sea. If nothing else, my immune system was going to be in good shape for this. I'd already googled my surgeon. He'd almost taken his own life the year before due to the stress of working for the NHS, but he was off the anti-depressants now, and I figured if he was well enough to write an article about it for the local paper, he was probably well enough to hack off my breast.

Dhal dropped me off at the hospital and a polite young man buzzed me into the ward. He showed me to my bed, pointing out the toilets on the way, and wheeled over a machine to take my blood pressure. He omitted to tell me I shouldn't actually use the toilet. I returned to find a nurse waiting to take a urine sample. My blood pressure shot up as I wailed that I'd just been for a pee and to please not hold up my operation just for that. The fact that I was menopausal and Dhal had had a vasectomy carried no weight at all – apparently, I might still be pregnant.

While I was willing my bladder to fill up even though I wasn't allowed to drink anything, the surgeon came by to say hello. He was wearing a comedy head wrap, which was cheering, though I couldn't help hoping he was also going to put his beard into one of those hairnets they wear in food-processing factories. I didn't want his whiskers in my stitches.

'Thanks for doing this,' I said, breaking Covid protocol to squeeze his hand. I imagined he didn't get much in the way of gratitude.

'Don't be silly,' he said.

I hoped he was better with his scalpel than he was with his words. Over the next couple of hours, half a dozen nurses and junior doctors came in relays to ask if I was diabetic, did I know why I was there, and which breast they were taking, until I started to wonder if anyone had the slightest idea what was supposed to be happening. The nurse in charge of post-op recovery studied her clipboard carefully before telling me I should take maximum doses of ibuprofen and paracetamol for the next five days, starting today.

'But what if I don't have any pain?' As a body nerd, I had every reason to think that was a possibility.

'We advise you to take them anyway.'

Since she was nice, I didn't like to tell her she was being absurd.

'Now, let's get you a prosthetic.' She unzipped a bag and presented me with a cloth breast the size of my head. I wondered if I was supposed to be flattered.

'Have you got anything smaller?'

She dug around in the bag again, offering me various other plump articles. In the end, to put her out of her misery, I accepted the smallest breast she had, which was about twice the size of mine. I thought it would make a handy pin cushion.

I forced out a dribble of urine just in time to keep my place as first in line for the op, and I was awake and out of theatre less than an hour later. I patted my bulging dressing and staggered to the toilet to look in the mirror. No sign of a blue face, which was disappointing. A couple of hours later, I was given a tuna sandwich and a cheery wave from my surgeon, and after another barrage of tests and a couple of suspicious looks when I insisted I had no pain, I was let go.

By three thirty in the afternoon, Dhal and I were walking slowly round our hill. I was delighted to find I could move my right arm enough to ensure I wouldn't have to endure his cooking for the next few days. All my yoga and bodywork began to pay off; I completed my prescribed exercises, and three weeks later I was doing push-ups and headstands again. My backbend was still hopeless, but I could carry heavy shopping and hang upside down from my Iyengar yoga ropes, so all was well.

Within five weeks, the sex sash was made, sex was had and I was back to arguing with Dhal like there were plenty more tomorrows to come. Given my miraculous recovery and everything I knew about the healing potential of bodies, it was hard not to imagine my tit was going to grow back, too.

A few weeks later, I saw yet another doctor at the hospital, who told me the cancer had been high grade but that, as far as it was possible to tell, they got all of it and my lymph nodes were clear. Also, I had one of the best healed scars the nurse had ever seen. The upshot seemed to be that I could either celebrate or take hormone treatment for the rest of my life in a bid to protect my other breast. I decided to celebrate.

Buds

There's nothing quite like a quick bout of cancer to put a rocket up you. In spring, as soon as the little independent cinema reopened, I booked all forty-eight seats to show 'the worst film ever made': *Plan 9 From Outer Space*. I sent invitations to the patched-up people of Tastings, baked fifty severed fingers with almond fingernails and red pesto gore, and hid a single severed breast at the bottom of the tin.

A raucous time was had by all, with only a hazelnut nipple left to show for it. No one ever admitted to eating the breast. I suspected Ashley, but I didn't want to spoil her guilty secret.

Ruby, who I hadn't seen for fifteen years, came for the event. Now a chief nursing officer, she'd turned into a matronly figure with two grown children and an ex-husband living at a convenient distance. She sweated up the hill, becoming very quiet when she entered our scruffy house that had no proper chairs, jars of yoghurt and kombucha fermenting in the bathroom, and no sugar for her tea. I wondered whether she was lost for words or just out of breath.

She seemed to relax once she'd taken over our kitchen and started cooking the kind of salty, fatty food we wouldn't normally touch. She'd brought all her own ingredients and the house was soon filled with the smell of thyme and pimento.

'I told my mam I was coming to see you,' she said, once we'd settled down with our fried fish.

'What did she say?' I wondered whether her mother remembered the time I'd slapped Ruby because she couldn't pronounce 'electricity'.

'She used to worry about you. She said you always looked like you needed a hug and a hot meal.'

I wiped my mouth with a napkin to conceal my surprise. I thought of Ruby's mother answering the door to me in her housecoat – a bony woman with a kind face and tired eyes.

'Oh my, no hat, no gloves, no scarf, you gonna freeze to death!'

I'd always ignored her concern because it cast doubt on my capacity to handle myself. Now, I felt stricken. Ruby's mother had seen something, understood something. But if it was so obvious I was in trouble, why hadn't she helped?

Ruby did the washing-up and we went for a walk round the hill. My dear friend tucked my arm into hers, fending off a yappy dog like the mother hen she was. When she began to struggle with the slope, we sat on a bench to watch the sunset. Now that she didn't have to look me in the eye, she told me something I hadn't known: her own breasts never developed.

'They're still, you know, buds,' she said uncomfortably. 'I've never told anyone this before.'

In the morning, I took her to TK Maxx so we could pinch the padding out of the sports bras – some for her and some for me – giggling like we used to in the olden days. Ruby's was the first of many breast-related conversations. Over the next few months, my clients treated me to stories of breasts made bigger, smaller, chopped off, redesigned, tattooed, flattened under binders or bolstered with chicken fillets. And best of all, my magnificent scar gained me access to a breastless queer community I hadn't known existed. Finding my flat friends, I felt I'd come home.

I waved Ruby off on the train, wishing my life was as uncomplicated as hers, knowing that it would bore me senseless if it was. With my cancer under control, it only remained to contact Clara again, to try one more time to see if I could sort out what was really the matter with me.

Clear

I wish someone had told me we ignore our inner lives at our peril before I spent all those years trying to cure myself through yoga and deep breathing. Even the weird shaking method my bodywork guru had taught me hadn't quite done the trick. It made me calm on the outside, while the old dread was shoved deeper down inside. I determined to work with Clara for as long as it took to heal my ongoing terror and feelings of worthlessness.

By this time, Dhal and I were into all the latest trauma research. Dhal focused on the psychology, while I got to grips with the physiology, and his good-natured credulity coupled with my northern scepticism kept us on track. At this stage, we might have been one of the UK's best-informed couples when it came to trauma, and all the while my subconscious was humming away in the background, checking for safety, checking for credibility.

When Clara and I met again on Zoom, the thread of what I'd experienced in the last session picked up where it had left off. In the safety of her compassion, I listened to what my mind and body were telling me, what they'd been screaming at me to hear long before I'd had the resources to listen. The shame in my gut knew it, the terror and fury in my heart knew it, and the insistence of my mind was now telling me the same thing over and over; my mother had sexually abused me when I was very young. With this new certitude, my world turned 180 degrees.

You're not grinning, you're not grinning, you're not grinning anymore!

Everything was unrecognisable and everything fell into place. I was devastated, heartbroken and, suddenly, unexpectedly whole. I began to get in touch with a body that held a secret history, a mind that knew how much outrage and overwhelm it carried, how hard it worked every moment of the day to repress what it knew and what it had endured. This, I knew, was what the textbooks called 'ontological security'; without meaning, it's impossible to heal.

For the next three weeks, the details of my life rained down around me, creating new, shimmering reservoirs of understanding. The undercurrents of helplessness, the dissociation and hyperarousal, the terrible fear, all made sense at last. So did my pattern of loving hard then pushing people away. All my life I'd been desperate for connection, while at the same time being compelled not to let anyone get too close. I thought of something Bill had said to Paulie more than once during our time at Oakham: *You can't live with people and you can't live without them.* Yes, Bill, but why the hell didn't you ever help him to discover why?

I'd lived with a sort of amnesia and coming round was appalling, agonising and potent. I fell into myself. I'd never felt so gutted and I'd never felt so real. I sobbed on the beach; I sobbed in Dhal's arms. By turns, I was drowning in pain and uplifted by possibility.

You're not grrrinnnning anny morrre!

I zoomed Ruby. At first, she didn't understand. Also, her laptop screen wouldn't stay put and she sank slowly out of view until I could only see the top of her head.

'Oh, that's horrible, Fin. I feel sorry for your mam, too, though. It's ignorance,' she said from somewhere off camera.

I was startled for a moment, then the penny dropped. She thought it was a bit like genital mutilation; something mothers were coerced into. She didn't understand Peggy's need for control over me or that for someone with so little sense of themself, the power to hurt can be gratifying. But bless her, Ruby was quick to grasp what I took pains to explain. She wanted to support me and her kindness soothed my hurting soul.

I longed to reach out to Marianne, too. More than anyone, I thought she would understand. But I didn't know how to find her and though I ached for her with all my heart, I only had myself to blame for letting our friendship fail.

Multiplying

The sessions with Clara continued and I began to see that if I'd had more sense, I wouldn't have kept asking what was wrong with me all those years, but what the hell happened to me? It had taken over half a century to uncover the source of the pain that had reverberated through my life and now all the disappeared children that lived inside me began to show themselves. They were dim and amorphous at first, but over time I got to know them; their distress, the patterns of their suffering, their shame and terror. There are multiple ways of accessing memories and only a fraction of them are verbal.

After one session that left me particularly raw, I met Dhal coming down the stairs. My legs folded under me and we sat huddled together on the bottom step, his hand squeezing mine. He leaned into me with soft concern as I told him more of the dismal backdrop to my life.

'Remember how I told you I talked about my mother on that psychotherapy retreat and I went into a psychosis? The thing that kept coming to me was that someone raped me with their finger when I was really, really small. But everything went so crazy after that, I don't know if she really did...'

'Perhaps she did,' Dhal said with calm neutrality.

The moment he admitted to this possibility, it was out. Something inside me tore and I wailed out loud as an agony of grief stiffened my body. Such complete knowledge cannot be simulated; such distress cannot be faked. Over and over, my mind and body let me know. Yes, yes, yes. *This.* This was what I had been waiting to have heard and known and understood all these years; this was what I had been terrified of knowing, of letting anyone know. My mother – my cold, unboundaried mother – always desperate to know more than anyone else, desperate to have her child be the object of her control, had done this unspeakable thing.

Dhal held me until the waves subsided and I resurfaced, tear-stained, absolved, shattered and renewed. I recalled the strange fear I'd always felt when Peggy whispered to me from *Goldilocks and the Three Bears*, trying to get me to me sleep. The sickening sense of dread when her body breathed close to mine. Was this bad mummy or not? Even my confusion had to be repressed.

In an attempt to keep something ordinary in my days, I continued to meet with my swimming friends on the beach, listening to their conversations about family Zoom meetings, longed-for holidays and recipes for soup. They worried about my blue fingers, my cold water shivering. Not for the first time, people were attending to my scratches while I bled quietly from my soul.

How does anyone say: I've just remembered what happened to me over half a century ago; I've just understood who my mother is, who I am and I'm appalled. I'd set up a whole bodywork business on the assumption that I was well enough to be helping others. I was good at what I did; better than good. But now this. I had a secret I didn't want.

I tried to share what was going on with one or two of my more sensitive friends. I came to anticipate the moments of confusion, the eyes moving rapidly side to side, the attempts to connect. There was the knee-jerk: 'That's very rare', to the desire for things not to be as they were: 'It will change; you will reconcile'. Every so often, someone would tell me there must have been *something* good, some kindly aunt or cousin who made a difference to my childhood. But no, there was only my immature, narcissistic father and my unfeeling, disconnected mother. And Charles, who hardly counted.

One clever, bespectacled friend asked me, point-blank, 'Why on earth would she do that?' I said nothing, though what I wanted to say was, 'You want to ask a baby girl why her mother raped her? Actually, if you really want to do that, go ahead. My inner child will tell you. But – do you *really* want to know?'

I couldn't wait to see Ashley. I knew she wouldn't dodge this; she was too tough, too worldly. We sat on the grassy hill in our coats and her priceless response was out of her mouth before she could stop it.

'The dirty bitch – she needs a slap in the cunt herself!'

We rolled on our backs, laughing until our faces ached. I told her I wanted to google terrible things: 'Can you break a baby with your fingers?' or 'Do *all* survivors hurt in the genitals when they see something bad?'

And I thought again of Jennifer Jane, my mirror image, my soul sister in pain. Where are you now, poor, masochistic, messed-up Jennifer Jane?

Spades

Clara, luminous in her clarity and her willingness to sit hour after hour with unbounded agony, did me proud. She was there when I screamed and sobbed; she was there when I doubted. She was there when I sat in a crisis of self-reproach about my discovery and the potential consequences. The tectonic plates of my psyche were moving, attempting, this time, a reconfiguration without fracture. It was a lot.

The difficulty wasn't only that I understood myself, now, to be a survivor, but that I'd got to this realisation with an approach my sceptical part couldn't countenance. It wanted hard evidence. I'd inherited the belief that a spade is only ever a spade – you've got to be able to pick it up and dig with it to know it's real. And even as I came out of denial, I was trapped in a matrix of conflicting realities: my ordinarily dysfunctional family, and the wretched, disordered consequences of an atrocity beyond belief. *This* was what could lead to the asylum.

Thank God for Van der Kolk, for Schwartz, for Levine, Porges, Fisher, Rothschild, Siegel and all the others. Thank God we evolve and can find the courage to heal. With Clara, I went safely to the memory that had been surfacing all that time ago in France, that had surfaced again when Dhal held me on the stairs. She witnessed my processing of the rape and, with it, the sudden, startling recollection that my mother had put a pillow over the side of my face to stifle my screams.

'Oh God, Clara! Oh God…'

You're not grinning anymore…!

I was clear Peggy hadn't been trying to suffocate me; she'd wanted only to prevent my protest from reaching the neighbours' ears. That my system knew this, knew the precise energy of her action, convinced me I wasn't wrong. I didn't for a moment try to elaborate on it, to make her act even more monstrous than it was.

I saw, too, that my breast cancer had been an accident waiting to happen. On this point, the research coincided with what trauma specialists had long understood; adverse childhood experiences are a risk factor for disease. I came to see my scar as a badge of honour, my war wound, a token of my violated body and my will to survive.

I continued to respond to Peggy's emails and text messages as though nothing had changed. She was unlikely to notice the subtle shift in my replies: a new caution, a new distance, and keeping her in the dark felt like the kindest option. And now, with the lifting of lockdown measures, she had a birthday coming up. Months earlier, before I woke from my trance, Dhal and I had booked a flat round the corner for my parents to stay in for a couple of nights. I'd planned flowers, gifts, elaborate meals; something for them to look forward to. They were due to arrive in three weeks' time.

It's not every day a mother turns eighty.

Wreck

What kind of daughter lets down her ageing parents when they're looking forward to their first holiday in two years, after a pandemic that's kept them isolated at home? I couldn't do it. Besides, Peggy wasn't the woman she used to be. These past ten years, she'd given me proper money on my birthday, sewn me cushion covers and knitted jumpers that Dhal actually wore. She'd found a sense of humour, sending me text messages every so often that only ever said, 'ARE YOU THERE??!!!' Plus, she'd faced her own mortality twice and that, and a general surrendering to old age, had softened her.

Dhal and I had a strategy: he was to sit between me and her at all times; he was to walk with her while I managed Chad; and if I looked at my phone and said, 'Oh, this client might be better off seeing you, Dhal,' it was code for 'Get my mother away from me now.' Besides that, there would be bracing walks, a fish lunch and ample time for them both to take long afternoon naps back at their apartment. A couple of early northern teas and very early bedtimes would be encouraged. We were going to be such considerate hosts.

It was raining as Chad's BMW pulled up on the side of the hill just beyond our house. I was standing on the front step, looking out for them, and I caught sight of Peggy's profile through the driver's window. My stomach turned over. There. My abuser.

She threw open the door and hopped out, her short white hair lifting in the breeze. Smaller than me, these days. The passenger door opened more slowly and Chad struggled out wearing his usual harried expression. I could hear him trying to prevail upon his ungovernable wife.

'Peg. Peg! It's a double yellow line!'

'Oh, give over, we'll only be a minute.'

Chad, easily defeated, was already at the car boot, unloading the boxes of crap Peggy had brought down for me. She grinned, arms open wide, when she saw me coming. Old Peggy wanted to hug her daughter.

I shuddered and grabbed hold of a box. 'Let's get all this inside before it gets wet.'

'I'll guard the car,' Chad said. 'Don't be long.'

Peggy came tripping after me with the Singer sewing machine she wanted me to have. She thumped it down in the hallway.

'Ooh, love – get me a plaster, will you? I've banged myself.'

She sat down on the bottom stair and pulled up her trouser leg. There was a crusted, oozing growth the size of an orange on her shin. I felt a lurch of disgust, then a shiver of annoyance that she'd tricked me into looking at it by pretending it was a scrape. I ducked into the bathroom and rummaged about for something big enough to cover the thing. My heart was thumping. Was it a sign her bowel cancer had metastasised? Was this her way of telling me she was dying for certain this time?

In the hallway, her phone was ringing. I knew it would be Chad, furious at being left outside in the wet while we took our time indoors.

'Mam, your phone!'

She was retying her shoelace, either too deaf to hear or taking no notice – a strategy she often used to manage Chad. I threw a plaster at her and ran outside. Chad was standing by the boot of the car. He'd already put on a mask, but even with his face half-covered I saw the familiar look of angry hurt.

'Where's Mam?' he said, indignantly. The pair of them had managed to create a situation before I'd even put the kettle on.

'Sorry, she needed something from the bathroom.'

'Oh, well,' he slumped a little, suddenly contrite. He detested blundering into women's issues.

I lifted the last of the boxes out of the boot. I'd like to be able to say I slammed the lid shut and strode off. I did not. I was trying to dodge bullets, to navigate the mirage of ordinary family life that this visit was supposed to represent. I'd been well taught that acquiescence was the way to avoid my parents' furious disdain.

Chad and I got the rest of the stuff indoors and dumped it in the hallway. On top of the boxes was a stained old quilt, probably a relic from my grandparents' house. It looked as though Peggy had been having a good clear out, getting ready to die. I could hear her downstairs in our basement kitchen, talking to Dhal.

'Take your mask off, love. There's absolutely no need.'

I ran down to solve Dhal's dilemma. We'd discussed being careful for the sake of Chad, who had a chronic lung disease.

'Mam, we ought to wear our masks for Dad. If you catch Covid, he'll catch it, too.'

Peggy ignored me and it crossed my mind she might have an unconscious urge to kill her husband. Chad was already at the open window, taking noisy gasps of air. To be fair, I had a hidden agenda, too. I'd been looking forward to covering up; that way, I wouldn't have to struggle to hide my discomfort at Peggy's intrusive glares. My mother's perfume wafted towards me and my face trembled; the cracks were showing already. I pulled a mask over my face. It was intensely relaxing. Chad sprayed his chair with the anti-viral spray I'd given him, and Peggy began to detail the horrors of the traffic and the queues at the service station, the foulness of the coffee.

Fortunately, these days my parents liked their food. I left Dhal to entertain them while I clattered about in the kitchen. Since we didn't own a dining table, Dhal unfolded a couple of small tables to put at my parents' knees. I brought in bowls of Greek salad and lentils and herbs, the rye bread and blue cheese Chad liked, the avocado and tiger prawns Peggy had developed a taste for, spinach soup, posh butter, the baguettes they'd got used to on their holidays in France. I kept it coming. A pot of tea and black chocolate for Chad, coffee and Medjool dates for Peggy.

My parents were appreciative and grateful. My heart softened and wept. Why couldn't it always have been like this? Why couldn't we have always liked each other, been respectful and appropriate? Why couldn't Peggy see me as an adult with my own inner world, my own ideas. I had some depth to offer, some understanding, if only she would take it.

If only she hadn't fucked me.

We got through the rest of the afternoon with a box of old photographs Peggy wanted to show Dhal and a long bout of clearing up. Then, it was afternoon nap time. They went off to the apartment and I flaked out on my bed. Dhal gave me a hug, silently aware of the enormity of it all.

In the early evening, we dropped round to their apartment. Another bite to eat, one game of Scrabble, some wildlife on the telly and we were done for the day. I was almost pleased. I'd handled myself and my parents were oblivious to my state of mind. So far, so good.

The following morning, we picked them up in Dhal's hairdryer and took them to the beach Dhal called Pets' Heaven, because of all the dogs. The outdoors was Chad's territory; since retirement, he'd become a dedicated walker, as long as the walk ended with a good pub and a couple of beers. He veered off to talk to some people fishing. We took photographs of the weathered groynes, the flat grey-green sea and the shingle set against a magnificent sky. Peggy in the fresh air was easier, mollified by the views and the exercise.

We drove straight on to a fish restaurant for an early lunch. I knew they'd like the place; it had white tablecloths and a good wine list, and the food was fresh. I hadn't anticipated the elderly camp waiter, who spent so long fussing over the silverware that Chad looked apoplectic. Peggy touched the waiter's hand, speaking brightly. She thought he was flirting.

Chad and I paid the bill and I hoped that was it – we'd go our separate ways for another afternoon nap. But no, Peggy wanted to visit the Shipwreck Museum across the road. The piles of old coins, anchors, bottles and bits of rope were laid out in cabinets along dimly lit passageways. Chad went out back to look at a boat and Dhal lingered on behind, paying more attention to each display than the rest of us put together.

I hid from my mother, keeping track of her whereabouts and scurrying on ahead whenever I saw she was catching up with me. Under the bright lights of the restaurant, we'd looked like an average family having Sunday lunch together, with only the average undertones of frustration. Peggy had even called Dhal 'my son-in-law' to the waiter. Now, in the shadowy corridors of the museum, we were separate, mute, but still pretending all was well. Once, when I took an evasive corner, I glimpsed my mother through the glass, small and alone, and my heart sickened.

Behind her cold armour, Peggy was always alone.

When I couldn't bear it any longer, I went outside to wait, my face in the sunlight suddenly stiff with panic. I was exhausted and the awareness of what Peggy had done to me was surging up again, another shockwave of disgust, terror and howling rage. I needed this to be over.

Dhal came out to find me. 'You okay?'

'I need to get home. As fast as we can.'

We marched my parents up the hill, Dhal slowing down now and then for the sake of Chad's lungs. Peggy, indomitable, was unfazed by my pace and tried to catch me up as I powered up the steps. After all these years, I thought. After all these years, *now* she wants to give me her attention. Perhaps she sensed something.

We left them at the end of our street and I got myself indoors and collapsed, retching, on my knees in the hallway. My brain was on fire. Dhal crouched next to me, a hand on my back.

'How the hell am I meant to do this?' I wailed, clutching my head as my mind tore at itself. 'She's *old*; she's not the person she was fifty years ago. She's even trying to be kind! But I'm fucking dealing with all of this stuff now. How big am I meant to be?' I looked at Dhal, my face streaming. 'How? How am I meant to do this?'

'I don't know,' he whispered.

My hands stiffened and I retched again as an almighty headache crushed me. Dhal couldn't help me navigate this. It was my burden alone and it was overwhelming.

Later, he called Chad and told him I had a client crisis to deal with, but that we'd pick them up in the morning and take them to Fairfield as arranged. I thought I could pull myself together by then.

It was a good car drive, followed by another blustery walk. I strode along the beach path shoulder to shoulder with Chad, who had his hood up against the wind and wasn't inclined to talk. Dhal, like the gentleman he was, attended to my mother. She seemed frailer today. I knew she hadn't slept well.

We dropped them off and Dahl and I went back to the house to collect up the leftovers, and took them round to the apartment for a buffet lunch. We left as soon as we decently could, supposedly for another long afternoon nap. After that, there was a trip down to the sea to watch the sunset and, apart from the goodbyes to get through the following morning, we were done.

I was so shattered it made no difference to me how I went through the motions of seeing them off. As their car drove away, our Trini neighbour waved to us from his upstairs window. He drew down the sash.

'You okay, Finley?'

I leaned into Dhal, my face crumpling. No. No, I was not okay.

That evening, as though he knew it was time, as though I'd never forfeited my right to his friendship, Dan emailed me a copy of the Epping Forest poem I'd thrown back at him almost thirty years ago.

Storm Eyes

You are naked at the door.
Empty eyed.
You've taken ten temazepams and forgotten.
I phone the hospital.
They think I'm your doctor.
You are borderline.
We wait on the bed holding on to each other.
You make me lip-read your confusion,
touch your bruises,
answer the door and phone your friends,
make tea.
We listen to the story of Clever Gretel
and as you try to work out the thread
I can feel your mind ravelling off from the pain.

And it is half past three when we make it
out into the sunshine
and drive through a windy London summer Saturday
to a secret garden high on a hill,
where we eat sandwiches, crisps and chewing gum,
feed squirrels out of the palms of our hands.
And as we pick blackberries through brambles and nettles
 Your eyes are two distant footsteps
That come clattering back only when a stranger asks for help.
'I've stung myself,' she says 'Is this a dock leaf?'

And two days later you are staring like a five-year-old
knock-kneed,
rushing fingers through your hair
with smiles like darting fish on your lips,
looking as thin as your mother,
breathing fire in the middle of your sentences,
cracking like an egg on my shoulder,
searching my eyes like an animal.

I am out of my depth.
Surviving with you day to day.
Then as days pass – hour to hour.
And then as hours pass – minute for minute.
And when the day starts going backwards
your eyes grow small as thorns,
looking at me through brambles of sounds.
And you are fragile and wiry,
chattering a poetry of confusion,
crawling the floor,
radiating power –
til a tide inside you turns
in the middle of the night.
You flop like a leaf budded with cold rain.
And your eyes are closed.

And now you are pushing that collapsed tin of time
Into new shapes around you.
It's sharp and cold
Living for days and weeks and months again.
And there are new kinds of electricity in your dreams.
Metal in your words.
Your eyes in the morning have a cloudy desperation,
At night a stormy calm.
  DT, March 1993

Stockholm

Clara was concerned I'd had a major setback, or at least that I'd taken a detour by allowing the visit from my parents. I was confused, lost, despairing and, for a while, the trauma we'd been so delicately, painstakingly addressing took a back seat while I tried to figure out how to handle an impossible situation. Before she left, Peggy had made it clear that she expected me and Dhal to visit Bradford soon.

'Come for a few days,' she'd instructed. 'We've got plenty of room. We'll take you to York and the Pennines.' Turning to Dhal, 'You don't know the Pennines, do you?'

I began to register that it wasn't just the one visit I had to get through, it was all the visits for the rest of my parents' lives.

'I can't do it,' I told Clara. 'Every part of me is saying no. I don't even want to go to their house. I can't.'

At first, I'd thought that my memory of the rape was going to heal everything. I hadn't understood that it was the punctum in a field of dysfunction, that I'd lived all my life in subtle thrall to my mother. And even still, there were parts of me that wanted to insist that all was well in our family, that it was me who had messed everything up like the wicked child I was.

Weeks passed and Chad bombarded me with his usual banter and photographs of his paintings and drawings. Sometimes I was expected to follow the whole process, from sketch to marking out the canvas and on until the final struggle over a tree or a barn door. It made me want to weep, this little boy grasping for approval. 'Hahaha, that's a good one,' I replied over and over to the jokes, though I wasn't in a laughing mood; 'Beautiful, I love the light in it,' to yet another painting; 'Well done, amazing,' if he told me his blood pressure had gone down. As long as I always responded quickly and always lied, Chad was placated. But if I missed a single message, he would email, voicemail, WhatsApp and text me until he got what he wanted. *Yes, Dad, you're great. I'm still here for you. There, there.*

Dhal had always hated my father's demands and the tightrope I walked so as never to upset him. 'How do you do it? You always know what he wants to hear and you never get pissed off.'

I shrugged. 'It's easy. I was brought up to service him.'

Eventually, I told Chad I had a lot going on and could he please tell Mam that, too, and not to worry if they didn't hear from me for a while. Since my father found any glimmer of psychological depth disturbing, I knew he'd let himself think I meant only that I was bombarded with work and he'd back off. But even this small pretence became too much. I was leading a double life, still wearing my mask, and now it was suffocating me.

The more I began to understand how much my parents had done to dump their burdens of pain onto me, the more I saw how coerced I'd been. There was so much I'd swallowed to be a good girl. I was filled with a new fury and a massive dose of resentment. And yet... and yet.

'What chance did she ever have?' I said to Clara. 'She's a mother – it's the last taboo. She must have been abused herself; she was probably re-enacting that in some way. That's *double* what I'm dealing with.'

'We don't actually know if she's suffering,' Clara said.

This landed like a gut punch. It hadn't occurred to me that Peggy might be so switched off, so good at letting me feel everything instead of her, it was possible she felt nothing at all. Nonetheless, I tried to think of a way to keep a thread of connection with her that wouldn't involve saying anything. Go to Bradford, but stay in a hotel on the grounds that I had confidential work to do? Only ever see them over Zoom? It wouldn't wash; I couldn't make excuses forever.

Some years earlier, Peggy had mentioned that if Chad died first, she'd pay me to go and look after her. It was another of her fantasies; she seemed to think that whatever she had left over from her pension would be enough for her spineless daughter to live on, and she ignored the fact that I had a life of my own, a job I liked, a mortgage, a partner. And yet, a small part of me held the unwavering conviction that if I didn't do Peggy's bidding, I wouldn't survive. Clara mentioned Stockholm Syndrome and I experienced a shiver of relief as my compulsion to be obedient was given a name.

It was time to face my terror and come clean. If I told my mother I was aware of what she did, she'd understand there was no possibility of my caring for her towards the end of her life, and she'd stop asking us to go to Bradford. Neither Dhal nor I subscribed to the idea that you had to confront anyone as part of the healing process – I knew only too well how that had worked out for Marianne. But since any other option would mean continuing to live with debilitating inner conflict, I decided to take the plunge.

Over the winter break, I composed a careful email to my mother: *I know you sexually abused me when I was very young, and I want some time and space to heal. I hope you can hold onto the small moments of connection we've had. I'm not going to look after you when you're older, so please use any money you have to buy whatever care you need. I'm on my feet these days, I don't need to inherit anything. Look after yourselves and each other.'*

The good girl in me made sure I texted Chad to let him know I was sending Peggy an email she'd find difficult to read and could he please be there to support her. Not that I thought he'd be much use; he'd never in a million years be able to handle this. But I was ludicrously hopeful that my mother might respond with some contrition, some acknowledgement. I recalled her past gestures towards confession, the fragments of self-awareness that had made my head spin. *Be careful or I'll tell you something in a minute. I damaged you, I'm sorry.*

Perhaps now we'd be able to have it out, because an apology by itself wasn't going to be enough. If someone breaks your back and says they're sorry, you still have a broken back. I took a breath and pressed send.

Within twenty minutes, I had a reply.

Total shock and disbelief. I have only ever given you love and care. I thought I had a daughter I got on with. My heart bleeds for you. You're killing me.

Shit. I shouted for Dhal and he read Peggy's email while I sat drowning in a flood of doubt. Time ticked on. My infuriatingly slow partner. Catch me, for God's sake, catch me!

'Could it have been someone else?' he said at last.

The bottom dropped out of my world. My Dhal, my closest ally who'd witnessed me time after time after my sessions with Clara, had been thrown into doubt, too. All the world seemed to be telling me I was wrong, that there was something deeply wrong with me. Again.

Before long, Dhal's dear, slow, meticulous brain began firing again. 'All the things you've told me about how she treated you, though – it all fits.'

'I know,' I said, beginning to sob. '*I know.*'

I sent Peggy's email to Clara. She threw me a lifeline, reassuring me that she believed me and she couldn't imagine how I must be feeling to have received such a response. I could hardly imagine it myself. I understood the terrible strength of Peggy's position and the vulnerability of mine. It was many months before I saw the fragility in my mother's rebuttal: she would say that, wouldn't she? Why on earth would *I* say such a thing.

Scream

I needed a break. I booked an Airbnb back in my old Lizzie Park stomping ground. The village had completed its gentrification and I was longing for Sri Lankan lunches overlooking the lake, strolls between the old plane trees and the downward doggers, and an old Thai woman to walk all over me and thump me to oblivion in the spa.

The Elizabeth Park demographic was even younger than I remembered, and since the pandemic, they'd taken on fifty per cent more dogs. In the morning, stepping carefully between the piles of poo, I bumped into the local osteopath outside the bakery. He was a genial, overworked guy with attractive blue eyes and a happy bedside manner. We used to study together sometimes, arguing about the latest craze for fascia or foam rolling.

We got our hot drinks and bowls of porridge and sat in the courtyard under a gas heater, and he told me that two months ago he'd been about to sell his business and move to Cornwall when his buyer slipped getting on a train and had to have a metal plate put in his skull. He clutched his paper cup, coffee-crazed, defeated. I didn't tell him that since we last met, I'd had a breast removed and remembered some serious child sex abuse. I didn't want to spoil his breakfast.

When I got back to Tastings, Dhal came and picked me up

in the hairdryer. He looked strained. We parked on the hill and he took my hand in his.

'Your mother emailed me while you were away.'

I tensed. 'What did she say?'

He brought the email up on his phone and passed it over. Peggy had tried, one last time, to gain the upper hand. She wrote that he didn't know I'd been mentally ill before he met me, that I'd made similar accusations back then. It was clear I was ill again now, that I had false memory syndrome. She hoped he could cope with me.

I felt a surge of indignation. She might have been able to indoctrinate me all these years, but she wasn't going to get away with doing that to my Dhal. I would sure as hell let her know he was off bounds. Also, I felt a small impulse to laugh.

'Shit, how could she – how dare she? Doesn't she have any idea what we both do for a living, how much we understand? As if I wouldn't already have told you about my breakdown!'

'I know,' Dhal said. 'I want to respond to this.'

The more I thought about it, the more reckless Peggy's email seemed. Even though she'd never tuned in to what I did for a living, I thought she had some idea of Dahl's work, his status. In our new incarnation as trauma specialists, she'd badly underestimated us.

Unfortunately, Dhal wasn't in any hurry to reply. I should have been prepared for this; he was a forceps delivery. I'm speedy, always early, always finished first, whether it's a meal or an orgasm, whereas Dhal needs a helping hand to have any chance at all of getting out of the house on time. Plus, he was three times busier than me. I was going to have to wait. It was like waiting for a gun to go off.

Over the next few days, in between bouts of work, Dhal told me some of the things he wanted to say. He knew about the neglect I'd suffered as a child, which had always pained him.

And the giants in the field of trauma had described all too well how our bodies remember our histories. He drafted a reply, but he wasn't yet ready to send it. He wanted to tweak it, to make sure it was right.

I waited. We'd already agreed how he would end his message: *Please don't contact either of us again with claims that Finley is deluded or unwell.* This time, Chad would be copied in, too, so there could be no doubt in his mind about what had been said. There would be no going back and I was in an agony of anticipation. Sending Dhal's email would destroy any last vestiges of our collusion with the story my family had worked so hard all my life to maintain: that I was a deficient cog in an otherwise well-functioning machine.

Dhal didn't get it. He took his time. Finally, on the fourth morning, he heard me on the stairs and called me into his room, where he was sitting at his laptop.

'I've just sent the email to Peggy.'

A reflex reaction doubled me up, my fists crashed onto the bed. Then I heard it. The most guttural scream I've ever known. And again. And again. Three screams came out of me, yet they weren't willed by me. Every moment of anguish I'd been holding all my life was in them.

I uncurled my body, stunned, relieved. At last, at long last, I heard the howling of wolves, calling me home. Thank God Dhal was so calm.

It still wasn't over. In the coming weeks and months, I experienced fresh waves of crippling guilt and frightened murmurs of doubt, egged on by parts of me that wanted to return to the family paradigm, to become again the acceptably flawed daughter, the daughter who, for a short time, had looked as though she might make something of herself, about whom people would say: she must be forgiven for failing, for being feeble after all. Never mind, poor thing. That couldn't be any worse than accepting that my mother would do anything, say anything, to save her own skin, including turning her own daughter suicidal and mad.

I had a choice. I could stay in my own sweet version of Stockholm Syndrome, helplessly appeasing my parents, or I could come to terms with my tragedy. My psyche had already chosen. It was shifting and I was coming out of the trance. It was painful, slow and bloody brilliant.

I began to understand that my dissociation hadn't only arisen to throw me out of harm's way in those early days; it had become a strategy to manage my ongoing fragmentation. I was the little girl who wanted nothing more than to please her mammy, who knew her life depended on maintaining that connection. And I was the little girl who knew her mother might, at any time, turn again into the terrifying person who molested her. When I wasn't living semi-paralysed with fear, I was numbed into a foggy bleakness that was close to death.

More insights came tumbling in the early hours. Years ago, I'd read *An Evil Cradling* by Brian Keenan. Among the countless incidents of obscene torture, there was one that had struck me and stayed with me more than anything I'd ever read. Brian is being beaten over and over by his captors, and eventually he hears coming from himself a noise he never wants to hear again: '*that one awful, anguished scream.*' Had I screamed my own anguish any sooner, the sound would have broken me. Now I knew what it was to let it out at last.

Next, the rage came in thunderous clouds. Inside my mind, with Clara's blessing, I slaughtered Chad, I slashed up Peggy, Charles was dispatched with a carving knife. My mother lay in a bloody mess while I stomped on her with my wellies and mashed her to a pulp. The great thing was I could resuscitate the three of them and do it all again.

There is no set order to these things. Suddenly, my suicidal urge returned. It was triggered by my hermit lover mooching round our house the whole darn day. Dhal had no need to go anywhere; *his* mind was a balmy place to be. I, on the other hand, needed time alone to process all my devastation, and with my contented partner always in the house it wasn't going to happen. I wanted boundaries of steel. I couldn't get them and the violated child in me couldn't stand it anymore.

Finley, a voice inside me said. *I can save you, Finley, my love. You and her, the little girl. Come to Beachy Head with drugs. We'll make a day of it.*

I checked the trains and whether anyone patrolled up there midweek.

Clara looked a little fazed, but only while I said I wouldn't fucking talk about it. Then, I cried and talked. There wasn't any anger in my wish to take my life, there was no desire for revenge. It would be a dreadful act of love, a way out of the pain. I made a deal with that loving voice. Give me a month to find another way and, if I can't, you can come and take me out.

Dhal went to a B&B while Clara got me through. I loved him even more when he came back. Then, walking round Morrisons one gloomy Monday morning with a rucksack full of vegetables, I felt a quiver of happiness. As quickly as it arose, it was gone again. I wondered if I'd ever get it back.

Truth

I'd gone to Clara with the intention of having a couple of sessions to get to the bottom of a tantrum about a broken zip. My incredible unconscious got me to her, knowing full well that something much older was broken, something that was capable of mending. It took me two more years to bring my system towards the beginnings of some harmony. Two years of a process of transformation beyond anything I'd ever thought possible, though I'd longed for it all my life.

I hardly thought of Chad through all of this; he'd not once tried to contact me. I thought more often of my brother. I veered between fear of Charles' hostility and fear *for* him, for his shutdown life, his shame, his ailing heart. Out of the blue, he WhatsApp'd me a picture of him and his partner holding drinks. It said, 'Sherry Christmas!' underneath. It was February.

I asked if he'd like to zoom and I was shocked when he said yes. I thought of a time when we were young, when Chad and Peggy had gone out. I'd tried to get my anorak down from the heavy cupboard in the hallway, but the hook was too high for me to reach. I stepped up into the cupboard to tug on a sleeve. The whole thing began to teeter, then it toppled, crashing down on top of me. As I crouched, panting among the coats, I heard my brother's wail. *Finleeey!* It was a miracle to me to know my brother didn't want me dead. I wondered if he had that in him still.

In the Zoom room, he'd chosen a stark background of the moon. He was wearing glasses with yellow frames. He asked if I was working, did I have any friends, who was supposed to be helping me, and were they any good at all.

'Charles, it feels like you have an agenda with these questions,' I said.

'I 'ave absolutely no agenda whatsoever. If yew only want tew 'ear the sound of yer own voice, please go ahead.'

'Of course that's not what I want. I just want to be honest about what happened.'

'I don't see wot could've 'appened tew yew that was so bad.'

I told him I was sexually abused by our mother when we were very young. He didn't betray the slightest flicker of a reaction. I found myself fielding his questions with a growing sense that whatever came out of my mouth was only adding to his conviction that his sister was insane. I was just one in a long line of crazy women, culminating in Great Aunt Amelia before me, who died in the asylum.

'I'm tryin' tew gauge your emotional and psychological state,' Charles let slip at last.

If I hadn't been so concerned to keep my cool, I might have laughed.

'Well, Charles, right now I feel sad that I've just told you, my only sibling, the worst thing that's ever happened to me and you're not showing any sign of concern.'

'Yew can't expect me tew be like your friends.'

'No. Perhaps I should just ask you directly, do you believe me?'

He mumbled his lips before responding. 'Er, well, I 'ear both sides. I'm in an 'alf an' 'alf 'ouse, aren't I?'

'Alright, but I want to assure you I'm not mentally ill. I'm just dealing with a huge amount of grief. And anger.'

My brother didn't even blink.

'Try tew get well,' he got in, just as we were ending the call.

Infuriated, I emailed him my parting shot. *If you can't find it in you to believe me, please don't contact me anymore.* And, since I knew he'd retaliate: *If you need to have the last word, take it.*

He took it: *You can believe what you like, but I have no agenda whatsoever and that is my right to tell the truth.*

I gave up. There was no hope to be had with him. Somewhere inside my brother, a little boy with a broken heart was hiding. Charles had banished this child to a dark corner, and even now I couldn't stand to know this. It hurt my own heart too much. I told myself I didn't understand the point of my brother, the vacant plutocrat. It was easier that way.

Visitation

I am on the train to Bradford, alone. As luck would have it, Dhal's mother has died and he has flown to Australia for the funeral. And now Peggy is dying, too. I am reading, again, the poem she wanted at her funeral.

'I have desired to go... to fields where flies no sharp and sided hail.

And a few lilies blow.'

My eyes stream for my poor, traumatised mother. What I fear the most is the tyrannical evidence of her ordinariness, her suburban life. She buys fish in the market, gives her neighbour a lift to the dentist, reads the fiction that gets the best reviews in her beloved *Times* newspaper. These things say: I am not dangerous; you would have to be mad to think so. I'm decent and unassuming. Benign.

I recall, too, the way she put a cool hand to my forehead when I vomited as a kid, to prevent me from straining so hard my face went down the toilet. I was never given the luxury of a bucket or a bowl, but this, surely, was a simple act of care. Perhaps some part of her knew I wasn't a shit after all. She put my tambourine by the bed and I would rattle it if I felt sick again, and she'd come running up the stairs.

In the past, these moments of ordinary solicitude were enough to make me doubt myself. Now I understand our multiplicity: a part of my mother wanted to love me if only she were able, and a part of her knew only how to exploit me and deny.

It seems right that I should have to return on my own. I'm curious to know if I can handle it, the familiar sense of being unseen, the unwavering denial. I am curious about Peggy and Chad, these two ancient people who coerced me all my life into being so unaware. How will they deal with me now? On the other hand, I'd rather not find out. There is still the option to change my mind. I could get out at Doncaster or Wakefield; I could walk between red brick buildings listening to the accents I've been away from for so long, until I find the kind of northern café that serves Whitby buns and orange tea in cracked mugs. When the train stops, I consider it. But I don't budge from my seat.

The train pulls into Bradford and already I'm a misfit. I have my hippy clothes on and seaside hair, sticky and unkempt from a quick dawn dip. I try to hold my ground.

I get a cab and watch the city roll past: Downwind Square, the children's hospital where Saville was a predator, Ash Grove where Sutcliffe killed, and then Holly Park in Meanward Valley, a place that seemed so magical in my teenage years I sometimes wonder if I've dreamt it. We cross the roundabout where Bournehill High School used to stand and I feel an ache for that brief time when I thought I was cool and in love with Anish.

The suburbs slide past and then a part of Bradford I'm unfamiliar with. A massive Sainsbury, a B&Q, a pet warehouse. We turn off the main road into a newly built estate. My parents' house is in a row of modern terraces with double glazed windows and railings round tiny gardens. The door opens and Chad appears. He has shrunk, even his semi-bald head looks smaller. He is unsteady on his feet. He looks scared as he tries to peer through the window of the cab. Haunted, even.

'Hi, Dad.'

'Helloo!' He says it too loudly. His mouth is crooked, his teeth are yellow.

'Shall I take that?' His hand is out, half-heartedly. My bag would topple him.

'No, it's okay. How are you?'

He doesn't hear me, he is already going back inside. The hallway smells of Peggy's perfume. My father pads to the modern kitchen with its slate-topped island. He is proud of this island; he understands the quality of it. The slate will endure longer than the house.

He is concerned with practicalities. He has his potatoes to boil, a piece of fish to fry. While he busies himself at the stove, I notice his paintings on the walls – ones I've never seen before. His style has changed. They seem starker, more urgent and once again I'm moved by his devotion. How does he manage it; how does he paint such skies and rivers with such love, when he has so much turmoil in him that never sees the light? I wonder if it has saved him, this unspoken yearning for a simpler life. When he dies, there will be a garage full of pictures to deal with. He doesn't try to sell them; it is one way he is too humble.

He puts two plates of food on the island, checks his watch. 'I've booked a taxi for two o'clock, so if we just eat this and get our shoes on, we should be ready for it by half past one.'

Hafpas wun. How my mother would say it. But the mad earliness is all Chad's and he has passed that onto me. Defensive pessimism, I have learned to call it. We plan for the worst, to keep our anxieties at bay.

His deafness, my deafness, is an excuse not to talk while we eat. Chad uses his thumb, pushing the fish onto his fork and chewing noisily. His eyes are watery, his forehead is red. I want to ask about his health. I wonder who has been the object of his neediness these past few years. Not Peggy. Not that he would tell me anyway.

When the taxi comes, he remembers I get car sick and lets me sit in front. It is easier than having to be by his side. At the hospital, he talks too loudly to the receptionist. I cringe away, embarrassed. He has no idea how needy he appears.

Peggy is on a different the ward this week. Chad doesn't quite remember where it is. We are told to follow the signs and, suddenly, we are companions in stupidity. We are as bad as each other at finding our way. Chad's lungs are working overtime. He pants, pausing to lean on the wall.

'This way, do you think? What was it she said?'

I shake my head, equally uncertain. 'I'll ask someone.'

He lets me do the asking while he catches his breath, then follows on behind. At the ward, he takes control again, accosts a nurse.

'I'm Peggotty Wilson's husband. I'm here with my daughter.'

He doesn't need to explain; she remembers him from yesterday. He told her I was coming.

'Oh, did I?' My father chuckles, content to play the endearing fool.

At the far end of the ward, furthest from the windows, Peggy is a tiny white head above a blanket. The pink of her scalp shows between the thinning strands of hair. I am moved, a little. And a little repulsed. The agony of our disconnection still whispers in me.

'Peg. Peg?'

I sense Chad's agitation; he is used to her being awake and ready. What if this time…? Perhaps it is good practice for him. My mother rouses, turns her face to where we stand at the side of the bed.

'Hello, love.' It's unclear whether she means me or Chad.

'How are you?' he asks, pleading for a good reply.

'I'm coping.' The old tone, half rebuttal, half wry acceptance of her fate.

Now, she is looking at me. Her eyes, the same colour as Chad's, are tiny and piercing. 'Hello, love.'

'Hello, Mam.' I feel tears coming. I sit, cautiously, on the side of her bed. Not touching her, too far away for her to touch me.

'Peg – I just need to pee,' my father says.

She nods, accustomed to his weak bladder.

'How was your journey?' she manages when he has gone.

Already I am disappointed. Is this what it will be, platitudes and politeness? I don't know what I expected. My Herculean, lifelong effort of separating from her has come to this. There ought to be more fanfare.

She is still looking at me, which is something. She sniffs and I don't flinch inside. I'm not frightened of her anymore. Water drips from her nose. Neither of us knows for sure whether she is crying. A hand escapes the blankets, creeps towards mine. I clutch it. The cool, dry hand, long-fingered, still with the well-kept fingernails. I know it of old.

But she doesn't want to hold my hand. She turns her wrist to disengage from me, points at the tissues. I pass them to her. She plucks one out and presses it to her nose, her eyes are closed.

'I'm sorry,' she says.

'It's okay.' I want to say, *I'm sorry, too.*

'No, it isn't.'

We are silent. Her face is sour. The crumpled tissue lies in her hand. Perhaps this is enough, sitting on her bed. Her last bed. I hope it goes easily for you, I say in my mind. I hope death is easy and that you will be free. No more guilt. This woman, this spectre in my mind. She is almost gone from me now. I look across the ward, wanting my father to come back.

He is coming, hobbling over the tiles in his soft shoes. He doesn't know what has passed between us. He pulls up a chair, close to Peggy's face, shielding me from her. He tells her about the garden, the bins, his broken car. She listens. I wonder if he

312

understands, in these moments, that she isn't coming home. She pretends the laundry he has done for her is worthwhile, that she is pleased he's ironed her blouse. I am in awe of their fruitless intimacy. They have held onto each other like lost children, hurting, and hurting each other, but holding on all the same, for over sixty years. I think of all the lovers I didn't even try to keep. I was too weak, too scared.

My parents are the heroes now.

Epilogue

Wolves

I wish that was what happened. I can imagine it that way; a final visit, the familiar narrative of confession, forgiveness and a reconciliation of sorts. That's what I expected.

In reality, I don't know if I'll ever see my mother again. Or any of them. Long ago, to save her own skin, my mother let me carry the pain she couldn't bear, and all the while she looked at me with feigned surprise – what the hell is wrong with you? My father stood by and let it happen, and my brother watched and waited, and eventually took their side.

Perpetrators don't want their victims to heal, because then they wouldn't be able to torment them anymore. This I learned from Richard Schwartz and, all the same, he has compassion beyond bounds.

In old age, Peggy has, perhaps, forgotten the past, just as I have forgotten swathes of my life because I was too dissociated, in too much pain. It is as though someone has scribbled across my years and trying to decipher all of it is hopeless. It would take forever. I make do with what I have. Besides, if I were to remember all the bleak and desolate times, I would have to include them here and they would be unreadable.

*

All my life, Peggy kept throwing me to the wolves. Now it's my turn. Except I can't do it; I've done enough. My mother is a traumatised woman; the causes of her trauma are lost in the past, exiled from her awareness and mine. I don't know her history, but I understand her only too well. I imagine at some point early in her life Peggy knew the energy of her own abuser. She endured that violation and her system did what any system would if it had the opportunity; what Jennifer Jane's system tried to do, what Mandy Skinner's did, what mine would have done if I hadn't been so wholly coerced into being good. My mother saw who had the power and copied them. Jay did that, too. These things are both calculated and deeply unconscious.

I was the child Peggy found pruriently shameful, the ignorant child, the child who forgot herself. My mother could put me to bed at night safe in the knowledge that by the morning only one of us would remember.

I stayed away from babies most of my adult life, not only because they triggered my woundedness and not only because I saw in them an appalling vulnerability, but because when Peggy violated my boundaries, her cruelty suffused my innocence. It's a well-kept secret that we survivors understand our abusers only too well. Many of us carry that abusive potential within ourselves; we know the precise flavour of the twisted pleasure it entails and we know we could use it to make others take our burden. And sometimes we do.

How can we have this known, and still be acceptable and understood? How can we end the scapegoating? Until we recognise what our minds and bodies are driven to do to survive intolerable pain, until we stop castigating each other, we don't have a hope in hell of healing.

*

Before I got a grip, my life see-sawed between people and places on the edge: the homeless hostel, Filchie, Oakham and the respectable company of people like Dan and Marianne and Philip. It took two years of trauma work before I realised I'd been living out a version of my childhood. Chad and Peggy were hard-working parents bringing up their children in a very ordinary neighbourhood; there was tea on the table each evening, football at the weekend for Charles, ballet for me.

No one came close to suspecting the level of wounding in our household, let alone attempting to address it. No wonder I wanted to achieve, to climb into the safety of the polite middle classes, and no wonder I failed. Before I'd found any true healing, I was compelled to live in pieces of myself.

*

When Marianne was doing her social work training, she told me that in cases where a child has been burnt at home, more often than not there's abuse going on. I didn't believe her at the time, but now I wonder how it would have been if some well-trained person had taken me in hand back then and encouraged me to draw or paint, to play with anatomical dolls, to role-play mummies and daddies. I imagine someone kind enough to coax me out of my silence, attentive enough to listen to my babble. I imagine the life I might have had once the discovery was made and I was whisked away from my mother.

But no, even then, they wouldn't have believed me.

We need to understand ourselves better before we can accept that such things happen in ordinary families, ordinary lives. Once we recognise our multiplicity, we will no longer speak in shocked tones about pillars of society who commit atrocities, nor will we be in awe of successful people from atrocious backgrounds. We will understand that when parts of us are compelled to act to keep us above the flames of pain at any cost, they can make us devastating. This is as true for survivors as it is for perpetrators.

The staff at Oakham encouraged us to employ self-discipline and willpower, if not self-criticism and shame, to manage the feelings and impulses that hurt us. But no amount of trauma can be healed by thinking; it's a mistake to try and end our suffering that way. Everything we feel and think and do has its own implacable logic, and yet it will not respond to reason, nor cease in its single-minded mission to fend off agony. Not until it is heard and honoured, loved and understood. To realise that mental illness is a protector from unendurable pain, not a pathology, is too radical for most, too countercultural. Yet this understanding holds the promise of healing.

*

Keep going. It was thirty years before I understood why that instruction, given to me with such authority by Mr Frame, was catastrophic. When the unspeakable happens before we have words or agency, our conscious self is obliterated, thrown out, to protect it from experiencing an atrocity that would otherwise be too much to bear. What's left is a mind in denial holding onto a thousand fractures – an insurmountable level of terror.

My mind wasn't ready for what Mr Frame tried to take me to. The potential for psychosis can be laid down at a tender age, alongside, if we're lucky, a steely will to survive that those who've had it easier will never need to know. An internal system that's found a delicate sort of stasis, a way to hold the unbearable at bay, becomes chaotic if it's pushed too quickly towards change. What began to surface through the layers of amnesia was a violation he would never have been able to countenance, let alone help me to contain.

My madness blew apart any possibility of re-experiencing my past. Anything would do to save me from myself, to avoid that annihilating hellfire. What Mr Frame ought to have said was, 'Slow down'.

*

Given how very young I was when I was violated, and who the perpetrator was, I've sometimes wondered why my life hasn't been even more disordered – why I haven't done more harm. It's not a sign of virtue. Some of us are 'lovely' because we were in fear for our lives.

I don't know how I knew I was so damaged while the rest of my family remained oblivious to their dysfunction. I don't know what drove me to heal, on my knees, at any cost, nor how it was that I had some vague intimation that other people were more comfortable in their skin, and to want that for myself. Perhaps it was those Christmases with Chad, his helpless recognition of my creativity, the stained drops of affection I got from him while my brother was neglected.

After two years of work with Clara, a hundred hours of sitting with my grief and rage and despair, I reached a tipping point. I found the part of me that had slipped sideways and brought it home. I experienced a sense of connection and aliveness I'd never known before. Three weeks later, I began to get hot flushes, and while the barrier against my vulnerability was so permeable, the sense of worthlessness I'd fought against all my life could no longer be denied. This time, I had the courage to listen. I'd been annihilated by my mother's disdain; she'd made me her object. I held that worthless part of me and began to love it better, and over time it was transformed.

I'm a different person these days, with a different mind and nervous system. I still live with a continuous two-frequency tinnitus that's like forever standing in a wind tunnel next to a whistling kettle, and at the time of writing this I'm waiting to go back to the hospital about my remaining breast. But the old shooting headaches don't torment me so much anymore. I've become more solid; I don't dissociate. I don't get scared by phantoms from the past. The anger that lives in me is like a furnace – it keeps me warm at night. Clara and I are still working to help the force of it move through me and, just recently, I've felt more self-respect. I've had moments close to joy.

All the same, there have been times when I've had a whisper of regret for ever having opened this can of worms. I imagine my mother would like to die feeling lovable. My act of saving myself won't quite let her; my estrangement must be a mystery to her friends. As she approaches the end of her life, what does she say to the neighbours, the well-wishers, about her absent daughter?

*

My connection with my family, forged in denial, is over. I live in a different reality. If we were to meet, if they were to see the colours of my mind these days, they wouldn't recognise me. Those of us who find some meaning and agency are fortunate, unlike those who fail spectacularly, as my mother failed. As I failed for so many years.

And I give this to my mother, this silent message. I am sorry it is this way. I don't know all the thousand causes and conditions that led you to do what you did, to be as you are. We do what we can, with what we are given. Peggy wouldn't have therapy or confess. She did her best; she made use of me to keep us both in denial. No doubt she got almost as much cruel pleasure from knowing I'd forgotten what she'd done as she did from the abuse itself.

Forgiveness is beside the point; I do better than that. I sit, day after day, with my broken heart, clearing the legacy my family forced me to carry. My mother will never know I've lived with an open wound these past several years, so it can be healed. She will never know the depth of the devastation she visited on me, nor will she ever recognise the dread I lived with all my life, until love and rage and Schwartzy's method healed me. And even so, a small part of me loves my mother. And will always love her, no matter what she did.

*

I want to write that down again. A small part of me will always love my mother. And I know that, after all, love cannot be broken.

May 2023

Acknowledgements

With immense gratitude to Richard Schwartz and the real Clara; without you, this story would never have been told. Thanks to the real Dan for permission to include Storm Eyes. Love to the patched-up people of Tastings for sticking around while I went down this particular rabbit hole, and to my Dhal, my best ever, for helping me find the way in.